RANDOM
HOUSE
LARGE
PRINT

BEAUTIFUL
COUNTRY

BEAUTIFUL COUNTRY

A MEMOIR

Qian Julie Wang

RANDOM HOUSE
LARGE PRINT

Cover photograph © Bud Glick
Cover design by Linda Huang

The Library of Congress has established a Cataloging-in-Publication record for this title.

ISBN: 978-0-593-46001-6

www.penguinrandomhouse.com/large-print-format-books

FIRST LARGE PRINT EDITION

Printed in the United States of America

10 9 8 7 6 5 4 3 2 1

This Large Print edition published in accord with the standards of the N.A.V.H.

For all those who remain in the shadows:

May you one day have no reason to fear the light.

Home is that youthful region where a child is the only real living inhabitant. Parents, siblings, and neighbors are mysterious apparitions who come, go, and do strange unfathomable things in and around the child, the region's only enfranchised citizen.

—MAYA ANGELOU, LETTER
TO MY DAUGHTER

CONTENTS

HOW IT BEGAN 1

Chapter 0   HOME 7

Chapter 1   ASCENT 9

Chapter 2   DANCES AND SHADOWS 17

Chapter 3   TYPE B 35

Chapter 4   THE BEAUTIFUL COUNTRY 48

Chapter 5   SILK 63

Chapter 6   NATIVE SPEAKER 83

Chapter 7   DUMPLINGS 109

Chapter 8   SUSHI 127

Chapter 9   LIGHTS 143

Chapter 10   CHATHAM SQUARE 160

Chapter 11   HAIR 165

Chapter 12   SHOPPING DAY 179

Chapter 13   MCDONALD'S 188

Chapter 14   SLEEPOVER 205

Chapter 15   TRAPDOORS   217

Chapter 16   SOLID GROUND   227

Chapter 17   AUNTIE LOVE   236

Chapter 18   NORMALCY   251

Chapter 19   MARILYN   265

Chapter 20   GRAFFITI   279

Chapter 21   JULIE   288

Chapter 22   HOSPITAL   306

Chapter 23   MOTHERS   319

Chapter 24   SURGERY   338

Chapter 25   GIFTED   351

Chapter 26   GRADUATION   367

Chapter 27   TAMAGOTCHI   376

Chapter 28   COMMUNITY   393

Chapter 29   GONE   409

Chapter 30   HOME   421

HOW IT BEGINS   426

BEAUTIFUL
COUNTRY

HOW IT BEGAN

....

My story starts decades before my birth. In my father's earliest memory, he is four years old, shooting a toy gun at nearby birds as he skips to the town square. There he halts, arrested by curious, swaying shapes that he is slow to recognize: two men dangling from a muscular tree.

He approaches slowly, pushing past the knees of adults encircling the tree. In the muggy late-summer air, mosquitoes and flies swarm the hanging corpses. The stench of decomposing flesh floods his nose.

He sees on the dirt ground a single character written in blood:

冤

Wrongly accused.

It is 1966 and China's Cultural Revolution has just begun. Even for a country marked by storied upheaval, the next decade would bring unparalleled turmoil. To this date, the actual death toll from the purges remains unspoken and, worse, unknown.

* * *

Three years later, my seven-year-old father watched as his eldest brother was placed under arrest. Weeks prior, my teenage uncle had criticized Mao Zedong in writing for manipulating the innocent people of China by pitting them against one another, just to centralize his power. My uncle had naïvely, heroically, stupidly distributed the essay to the public.

So there would be no high school graduation for him, only starvation and torture behind prison walls.

From then on, my father would spend his childhood bearing witness to his parents' public beatings, all while enduring his own humiliation at school, where he was forced to stand in the front of the classroom every morning as his teachers and classmates berated him and his "treasonous" family. Outside of school, adults and children alike pelted him with rocks, pebbles, shit. Gone was the honor of his grandfather, whose deft brokering had managed to shield their village from the rape and pillage of the Japanese occupation. Gone were the visitors to the Wang family courtyard who sought his father's calligraphy. From then on, it would just be his mother's bruised face. His father's silent, stoic tears. His four sisters' screams as the Red Guards ransacked their already shredded home.

It is against this backdrop that my parents' beginnings unfurled. My mother's pain was that of a daughter born to a family entangled in the government. None of her father's power was enough to insulate her from the unrest and sexism of her time. She grew up a hundred miles away from my father, and their hardships were at once the same and worlds apart.

Half a century and a migration across the world later, it would take therapy's slow and arduous unraveling for me to see that the thread of trauma was woven into every fiber of my family, my childhood.

* * *

On July 29, 1994, I arrived at JFK Airport on a visa that would expire much too quickly. Five days prior, I had turned seven years old, the same age at which my father had begun his daily wrestle with shame. My parents and I would spend the next five years in the furtive shadows of New York City, pushing past hunger pangs to labor at menial jobs, with no rights, no access to medical care, no hope of legality. The Chinese refer to being undocumented colloquially as "hei": being in the dark, being blacked out. And aptly so, because we spent those years shrouded in darkness while wrestling with hope and dignity.

Memory is a fickle thing, but other than names and certain identifying details—which I have changed out of respect for others' privacy—I have endeavored to document my family's undocumented years as authentically and intimately as possible. I regret that I can do no justice to my father's childhood, for it is pockmarked by more despair than I can ever know.

In some ways, this project has always been in me, but in a much larger way, I have the 2016 election to thank. I took my first laughable stab at this project during my college years, writing it as fiction, not understanding that it was impossible to find perspective on a still-festering wound.

After graduating from Yale Law School—where I could not have fit in less—I clerked for a federal appellate judge who instilled in me, even beyond my greatest, most idealistic hopes, an abiding faith in justice. During that clerkship year, I watched as the Obama administration talked out of both sides of its mouth, at once championing deferred action for Dreamers while issuing deportations at unprecedented rates. By the time the immigration cases got to our chambers on appeal, there was often very little my judge could do.

In May 2016, just shy of eight thousand days after I first landed in New York City—the only place my heart and spirit call home—I finally became a U.S. citizen. My journey to citizenship was difficult to the very end: torrential rain accompanied me on my walk through lower Manhattan to the federal courthouse where I was sworn in. I brought no guests, not even my parents.

The rain did not matter. I reveled in joyful solitude, my face soaked in rainwater and happy tears. At the end of the ceremony, a videotaped President Obama greeted me as a "fellow American," and it dawned on me that though I had become American decades ago, I had never before been recognized as one.

Six months later, I awoke to a somber and funereal New York, mourning for a nation that chose to elect a president on a platform of xenophobia and intolerance. It was then that I dug up my voice. Staring shame and self-doubt in the face, I tossed my first attempt at this project and put my fingers to the keyboard anew.

I document these stories for myself and my family, and not the least my uncle, our innominate hero. I write this also for Americans and immigrants everywhere. The heartbreak of one immigrant is never far from that of another.

Most of all, though, I put these stories to paper for this country's forgotten children, past and present, who grow up cloaked in fear, desolation, and the belief that their very existence is wrong, their very being illegal. I have been unfathomably lucky. But I dream of a day when being recognized as human requires no luck—when it is a right, not a privilege. And I dream of a day when each and every one of us will have no reason to fear stepping out of the shadows.

Whenever things got really bad during my family's dark years, I dreamed aloud that when I grew up, I would write our stories down so that others like us would know that they were not alone, that they could also survive. And my mother would then remind me that it was all temporary:

> **With your writing, Qian Qian, you can do anything.**
> **One day, you will have enough to eat.**
> **One day, you will have everything.**

May that resilient hope light the way.

Chapter 0
HOME

....

My oldest memories shine by incandescent light:

I bury my face deep in Lao Lao's chest, wrapped in red cotton. She smells sweet—like soap and warm milk all at once. I nuzzle deeper, digging closer, insatiable for the scent. She shakes with laughter.

"She keeps nuzzling, she keeps nuzzling!"

Joy is the song of my early childhood.

Next comes a scene that, for all I know, happens weeks, months, years later. Ma Ma and Ba Ba are each holding two corners of a thick, warm blanket. There I am, giggling, cocooned at the center of the blanket.

"Ready?" Ba Ba asks, eyes dancing.

I nod and off I go: with a flap of their arms, they send me soaring, flying, gliding, and I feel the air whooshing under, over, all around. I squeal, fearless, and soon I am back in the safety of the blanket. I laugh and nod some more, fingers grabbing toes, toes curling into fingers, lolling in my blanket nest.

"Look, she wants to go again!"

And it continues like this for eternity: I am by turns soaring through the air with boundless flight and returning to the blanket's embrace, my parents looking on with doting eyes, my heart pulsing with nothing but warmth, safety, love.

Chapter 1

ASCENT

....

I ascended to adulthood at cruising altitude. The takeoff was bumpy, and my braided pigtails, each with its own silk red ribbon, bobbed around the sides of my seven-year-old face. In my lap sat my favorite doll, ladylike in her frilly dress. Her eyes, with their long lashes, flicked open and closed with the turbulence. Her legs were snapped into my seat belt, so I knew she was safe.

Next to me, Ma Ma was slumped over into herself, her dress wrapped around her, her arms guarding her midsection, her face folded into her chest.

I had never seen her like that before. Minutes before, the flight attendant with the fake eyelashes and the drawn eyebrows and the tomato lips bent over me and asked if Ma Ma had her seat belt on.

"Ma Ma," I squeaked, poking her side.

Ma Ma made no response.

"Make sure her seat belt is on," said the red lips lined with a darker red.

"Ma Ma," I ventured again.

Nothing.

"I saw her buckle it earlier."

"Really?" The eyebrows went up. Sometimes da ren, the big people, the grown-ups, didn't believe little kids like me.

"Yeah."

She stared at me for the longest second of my short life. Finally, she moved down the aisle, the only witness to my first lie.

* * *

Ma Ma always suffered from horrible motion sickness. It didn't matter how we traveled. Once, when we took the bus to Bao Ding, she threw up the entire trip, making animal sounds. It smelled so bad that another lady on the bus started throwing up and making the same sounds, and soon the smell and sounds were all around me.

The only difference was that, that time, Lao Lao, Grandma, was with us and it wasn't just me and Ma Ma alone in a fei ji, a flying machine, going to a different country. And I didn't have to make sure Ma Ma was wearing a seat belt or lie about it because Lao Lao was the one who did it. The seat belt part, at least. I didn't know if Lao Lao ever had to lie for Ma Ma.

I was not happy about being in the flying machine.

I had turned seven just five days before, and a few weeks before that, Da Jiu Jiu, the older of Ma Ma's two younger brothers, had gotten me my very first bike. It was white with pink tassels on the handlebars and flowers on the basket. He said he would teach me to ride it but then he had to travel for work, so I spent my time walking the pretty bike around the courtyard of Lao Lao's building.

"What a pretty bike," a passing da ren said.

"Xie xie."

"The tassels match your dress," another remarked.

"Xie xie," I said again, resisting the urge to yank at the frilly lace dress Ma Ma had forced on me.

Now the bike was in Lao Lao's storage unit, waiting for my return.

"Ma Ma." I poked at her side again. "When will we go back?"

A grunt came but nothing else.

We had found out that we would be leaving just a few weeks before my birthday. Ba Ba had left for Mei Guo, America, two years earlier, and Ma Ma had been trying to get a visitor's visa for almost a year. Four times, Ma Ma left our home and traveled hours away to Beijing, where the embassy for Mei Guo, a name that translated literally into "Beautiful Country," kept telling her no.

Da Yi, Ma Ma's older sister, lived in Beijing, and every time Ma Ma went to get another no, she stayed overnight with her, leaving me with Lao Lao and Lao Ye, Grandpa. Each time, I had trouble sleeping, crying tsunamis into Lao Lao's arms.

"What if she doesn't come back, like Ba Ba?"

The last time, I threw such a fit that Ma Ma took me to Beijing with her. In the morning, as she was preparing to leave for the embassy from Da Yi's, I burst into tears again.

"Why not take her?" Da Yi was always on my side.

Ma Ma stared at my swollen red face and shook her head. "She'll cry."

"That might be good," brokered my ally. "She's cute."

Ma Ma looked at me again and I tried to look my cutest, dripping snot and all.

And so it was that I ended up in the cab with her and a handful of tissues.

"When we get there, Qian Qian, don't make a scene." Ma Ma used her serious voice, so I knew to look very serious and nod very seriously.

"You can say you miss Ba Ba, but don't go crazy, okay?"

I nodded, but I was never crazy. Da ren were the ones who were crazy.

When we got out of the cab, we waited in a

long line that wrapped around the block of the giant building. There were many flags around, flags of a design I'd never seen before, with red, white, and blue and stripes and stars.

Our flag had stars, too, but it was red and yellow, just like the colors on my face when I was crying.

When we finally got inside the building, I thought it meant we would get to go home soon, but instead we got a ticket that had a long number on it, and we sat and waited some more in slippery plastic white chairs in a room full of da ren. It was boring but at least I was with Ma Ma, and if she left to go somewhere, I would go with her. I wouldn't have to point at the flying machines in the sky and say, "That's where Ma Ma went," like I did with Ba Ba.

After what felt like days, a bald little man in a booth called a number and Ma Ma rushed up quickly. I ambled behind in the wake of her skirt. The man was behind a glass window. I realized that he looked little because he was sitting. There were holes in the glass and he talked to us through it. Did we have to pay him money? I had only ever seen those booths on the roads when we were in a taxi or bus and the driver had to give money to the man inside.

Ma Ma put her purse on the counter, which was very high, so I kept jumping up and down to see the bald man. Every time I jumped high enough, I waved at him. He didn't seem to see me, so I kept jumping.

"Qian Qian, bie nong."

Recognizing the tone in Ma Ma's voice, I stopped. But it grew boring so I pulled at her skirt until she had to pick me up and sit me on the counter. From my new perch, I could see that the little bald man had only a few stray hairs on his shiny head. He sat in front of a monitor and a pile of papers bearing the red markings of rubber stamps.

I wondered if his stamps made colorful animal shapes like mine did.

The glass connected to the counter at the bottom and there was a little slot of space between the two. I stuck my fingers under the glass and waved them at the man, who still did not see me.

"Qian Qian, bie nong."

I tried to sit still and look cute again.

"Please," Ma Ma was saying. "My husband hasn't seen his daughter in two years. She doesn't even remember what he looks like anymore."

This was true. I had only a general impression of Ba Ba. In my head, he was the man who played Emperor Qian Long on the show on TV. This meant I was supposed to be a ge ge, a princess, with a pretty headdress and servants who walked behind me with fans.

I turned toward the booth and saw that the little bald man was shaking his head now. Ma Ma's own head dropped and she began to collect her things.

"I miss Ba Ba!"

My face was our flag again, red and yellow, gushing tears. I didn't know where they came from. I just knew that it was the right time for them.

The little bald man looked up and looked away just as quickly. He sighed, then picked up a stamp and pounded it on the papers in front of him. He then stuck them through the slot and waved us away without another look.

I didn't know what it meant, but I knew Ma Ma's face. As we hurried out of the embassy, I reveled in the thought there was a good chance I would get to eat Beijing duck that night.

* * *

On the flying machine, the lady with the fake face was now pushing a skinny cart down the aisle. Clanking in the cart were cans of pretty colors. I wanted to drink them all. I wanted to ask her if she had the sweet yogurt drink Lao Lao got me from the market, but when I opened my mouth to speak it felt as if someone had shut the doors to my ears. So instead I just asked for a small cup of water, warm, as we always drank it at home.

"Ma Ma." I prodded. "My ears can't breathe, Ma Ma."

She looked at me but there was no life in her eyes. I jabbed my pinkie into my ear, trying to break through.

"Bie nong." She swatted my arm away and coiled back into her seat.

I sat on my hands and tried to ignore my ears, my mouth, and all my senses as the flying machine bumped and shook us all around, the rest of the world sounding as if it were several rooms away.

Chapter 2
DANCES AND SHADOWS

....

B a Ba loved to dance. Before he left for Mei Guo, he went to the dance hall every week. Ma Ma did not enjoy it as much, so she often had me go with him instead. There were too many women, she said, and it helped to have his daughter there to remind them he was married.

Ba Ba was a professor, like Ma Ma. But where Ma Ma taught math, Ba Ba taught English literature. He was tall, but not very tall. Still, that didn't keep his students from blushing when they saw Wang Lao Shi, Professor Wang. He liked to wear white gloves to teach. I thought they were funny and made him look like Mickey Mouse. He also had a pointer stick that extended and collapsed. He could never find it because I often took it to teach my dolls the ways of the world, and to launch stealth attacks on Ma Ma when she was cooking.

Before Ba Ba left, my childhood was simple in the way most childhoods are: joy was a way of being. My favorite things in the world were my train set and the building's sandbox. Da ren often told me that I didn't act like how little girls were supposed to act. I was dirty and smelly and I liked to run around with equally smelly and dirty boys who lived in our complex.

I acted like a girl, though, in one respect: I loved to dance. So going to the dance hall was double joy for me—I could dance and I had a duty to discharge: keep the ladies from Ba Ba. And boy, did I dance. I stood on Ba Ba's feet and he shuffled me about the room. Other times I hopped, skipped, and twirled in a big frilly dress—always a frilly dress; Ma Ma insisted— and acted like a wild, rhythmless banshee who fancied herself the most graceful of gazelles.

Dancing, too, was a way of life. I danced every- where. On summer nights, the lao ren, elderly, sat on stools in the courtyard eating sunflower seeds, chatting, and playing go. I loved to jump in front of them and command: "Watch me!" before dancing to no music other than that playing in my head. They clapped their hands and I wouldn't stop until hours later, when Ma Ma dragged me away because the lao ren had to sleep.

Dancing was breathing. I shook around and con- vulsed even as Ma Ma cooked to radio music. Ma Ma said that I danced before I walked. Whenever music came on while she was pregnant, I shook my as-yet-undeveloped legs in her belly. And she liked to tell me that when I was born, I didn't cry but instead kicked my legs and yanked my already-long hair before letting out a big, satisfying sneeze.

Ba Ba and I shared a special dance. When I was just a few months old, he made up a song for us, all in gibberish:

Xi mou hou
Li da so
Li wa li ga li sa sa
Ah-ah, Ah-ah, Ah-ah-ah

We sang it always twice in a row, always while dancing, my little feet on his big feet. It was a ritual we played at every day, as soon as Ba Ba got home from work. It became such a fixture that Ba Ba started calling me "Xi Mou Hou."

For a long time, I thought the lyrics were actual words that I had not yet learned. But even then, I didn't need to understand the words to know that they meant that Ba Ba loved me very, very much.

* * *

Ma Ma taught me about duty. She showed me that when your daughter got chickenpox and woke up every night scratching herself, you did whatever it took to help her, even if it meant kneeling for hours in your neighbor's aloe vera garden, picking through the plants as they pricked your already-bloody fingers. Later, between cooking dinner, preparing for the next day's lecture, and washing our clothes, Ma Ma peeled and boiled the plant until it became a gooey balm, which she then layered on my reddened body, all as I screamed in her ear.

But it was Ba Ba who taught me that when I couldn't fall asleep in the big bed the three of us shared, when I couldn't keep my nails off the red, puckered, oozing skin, I could distract myself from the itch that crawled all through me and into the center of my brain by holding my hands up in the space between the wall and the little bent-over lamp with the long neck—the one that reminded me of Ma Ma, hunched over at the sink—and move my hands this way and that to make different animals: a duck here, a bird there. And in the moment that Ba Ba's bird came swooping over my quacking duck and I shrieked with laughter, the itch and the red spots disappeared. All I could see was a pond and a happy duck playing with her flying bird.

It was also during those shadow puppet plays that I learned that while Ma Ma's job was to always be there, Ba Ba was allowed to go away, even if his body stayed. Occasionally, I turned away from the wall and caught that, though Ba Ba's bird continued to fly about this way and that, his eyes had been taken over by a shadow. The bird was still there with me, flying and swaying, but Ba Ba, he had gone to another place. Sometimes he returned quickly, in only the time it took me to beckon him, and other times, he seemed so deaf to my ventures that I wondered if he would stay like that, a zombie whose mind went away while his hands continued to flap like a shadow bird for eternity.

Ba Ba taught me that fun was to be relished, in part because I never knew when it would end. When I was five, just before he left, Ba Ba made a kite in the shape of a diamond, split into four triangles, each a different color, and we flew it around the cliff near our complex. The cliff looked over a stinky ditch into which people threw trash. It must have smelled terrible, but I never noticed because I was too busy running around with the kite trailing behind me. The last time we went to fly our kite—weeks before Ba Ba left—it got caught on a tree branch and when I yanked it, the kite disentangled from the tree before coming loose from the string. Ba Ba and I watched, mouths helplessly open, as the colorful diamond careened down the rocky hill and into the trash pile.

"How will we get it back, Ba Ba?"

"Don't worry, Xi Mou Hou. I'll make you another one."

We didn't know then that he would never have the chance.

* * *

Ba Ba was popular. He could make a whole room burst into laughter with just a few sentences. He tended to be quiet when we were alone, but the more people there were, the more he came alive. He had a deep, booming voice that demanded attention. And he had a way of weaving little words into one giant poetic blanket. The whole world admired him as much as I did.

Ba Ba also read a lot, and had many thoughts that he couldn't say in public. He said them at home but I wasn't allowed to repeat them: he hated the government, and he hated being told what to think.

"They won't let us question them, but that is what we must do."

I had no idea who "they" were, but I was afraid to ask.

Ba Ba did not notice the confusion that had colonized my face. He continued, "But don't let them know it. The smartest people always appear to be the dumbest. Mian li cang zhen."

Hide the needle in the silk floss.

* * *

Ba Ba's parents, Ye Ye and Nai Nai, lived in the Chunchang village of Handan, which was somehow in the same province where we lived while feeling like a universe away. We had to sit on a crowded train for several hours—such that the uniformed men with the little food cart would roll past us at least twice—before we arrived. Then we had to get into a car that took us close enough to the village, which was still called that even though it now had many tall buildings that were younger than Ba Ba.

We didn't make the trip very often because, instead of Mandarin, Ba Ba's family spoke only their local dialect, which Ma Ma and I could not speak. And Ma Ma did not like it there because the family was very poor. The home was in an old-fashioned courtyard. It had no showers or bathrooms. We had to walk down several hu tong, the alleys between courtyards, to get to the public bathroom. But there were no showers or faucets there. There was just one long ditch with no running water, piles of dung on other dung, flies swarming all about, the stink invading our nostrils.

I loved it there anyway. Lao Ye and Lao Lao called me their "wai" granddaughter, or outside granddaughter, because I was born to their daughter. But to Ye Ye and Nai Nai, I was a full, unconditional granddaughter. In fact, I was the only full granddaughter, my dad being the only son to have had a daughter. Ba Ba told me that this meant I was the "pearl" of the family. But I don't know if this was why Chunchang, for all of its discomforts, felt like my true home. All I know is that my memories of those rare visits are coded into my senses:

Running down the hu tong. Little feet tripping on uneven ground, kicking up yellow dirt, impatient to reach the Wang courtyard, beckoning Ma Ma and Ba Ba to walk faster. The smell of burning coal growing as we get closer. The fragrance of home.

I step through the familiar gate adorned with tattered strips of red paper and black calligraphy characters. In my earlier memories, Nai Nai is always in the courtyard, no matter the season, moving between the basin of cold water and the tiny, dark little kitchen, cooking, cleaning, placing before me big steaming bowls of this and that, homemade noodles and dumplings and congee. In later memories, the courtyard is sadder; Nai Nai is in bed, always in bed, paralyzed from stroke, taking care of me now only by voice, reminding me to eat.

There are other members of the family, cousins and uncles and aunts, milling all around, impossible to tell apart because they all look so alike, so much like me and Ba Ba. The generations are always difficult—there are people I call cousins, the children of Ba Ba's eldest siblings, who look like they should be aunts and uncles; and people I call aunts and uncles, several degrees removed, who look like they should be cousins. But no matter: they are always happy to see us, rushing to us in a clamoring wave, a big, draping quilt all knit from the same thread.

And then there is Ye Ye, his face fanning open into light at the very sight of me. He is reading the paper, fingers stained black, or riding his bike laden with groceries, or reaching out to take me by the hand on a walk. Always, he has a cigarette dangling from his mouth.

Ma Ma tells me that I took my very first steps toward Ye Ye, in the nearby town square where Ba Ba once saw some awful, terrible things. But I don't remember any of that. I remember only that Chunchang sits at the core of everything I know as home, belonging.

* * *

I was not made for Zhong Guo—China, the self-named Central Country, the Middle Kingdom. In prekindergarten, as everywhere, we were required to take a wu jiao, nap, in the middle of the day. I hated it. I would either stay awake the whole time or fall into resistant sleep, only to awake with a headache. I would have much rather spent the time dancing, drawing, or playing in the dirt outside.

But in Zhong Guo, everyone had to do the same thing at the very same time, and for an hour every day, I lay in my criblike bed, amid my classmates in their own beds, and stared at the ceiling, counting numbers and singing songs in my head. On other days, I stewed, growing angrier that I was the only one awake until I decided to poke at the kids on either side of me.

"Hey, hey," and after a few vigorous jabbings my friend would finally awaken.

"What?" The face that uttered this word was unfailingly drowsy, irritated.

"What are you doing?"

"Sleeping!"

"Oh." Desperate to prolong the conversation, I inquired further: "Do you like it?"

At this she usually groaned and turn her back to me, but there was almost always another kid on the other side for me to try again.

This exercise reliably consumed ten minutes of nap time.

I was also bad in Zhong Guo because I asked questions that my teachers said were unnecessary. Once, I made the mistake of asking why two plus two equaled four. As punishment, the teacher forced me to write "Wo dui bu qi," I'm sorry, in characters one hundred times. Despite that it cost me an extra character per sentence, I proudly wrote instead: "Wo **bu** dui bu qi." I am **not** sorry.

The teacher never noticed because it was not what we wrote that mattered. It was the ability to control us.

* * *

One day, Ba Ba came home and told Ma Ma that he said the wrong thing again in class. He often came home mad. He did not like that they were told what to say, and that they could not answer when students asked about something called the Cultural Revolution.

"They are always listening to us, watching us. Don't talk about this, don't acknowledge that. Ta ma de." As he said this, he emptied his small glass of strong-smelling rice wine in one gulp.

Ba Ba looked forlorn so I snuck onto his lap. At this, he smiled, but it lasted for only a minute.

"It's too much." And he shook his head.

A little while later, Ma Ma and Ba Ba decided that Ba Ba would go to Mei Guo. Everyone in our family had something to say about it.

"It is beautiful there, but they don't treat the Chinese very well," declared Lao Ye.

"Aiya," cried Lao Lao. "They shoot people on the street."

"I heard everyone starves and they have no food for anyone," came from Da Jiu Jiu.

"How great," celebrated Xiao Jiu Jiu, Ma Ma's youngest brother, "I heard the roads are covered with money and gold."

Once, I saw Mei Guo on TV. There were rows and rows of dirty da ren and children in rags sitting on the street, holding rusted bowls. At one point, someone found a hamburger, and everyone dove for it. Before I knew it, I couldn't tell one person's head from another's hands as they became a giant blob that ripped at itself. It reminded me of another scary movie Ma Ma had let me see, where birds attacked until one person's head became just a skull.

I didn't want to go to Mei Guo. I had had a hamburger only once and I did not like it. The hamburger had been from a restaurant in Beijing. The restaurant had the scariest thing: a white clown with red hair, a giant red mouth, and big red shoes.

What would I eat when I lived on the street in Mei Guo? I didn't like the frilly dresses Ma Ma made me wear in Zhong Guo, but the rags I saw in the Mei Guo on TV barely covered anything and they looked smelly. But Ba Ba had to go to Mei Guo, for some reason. And although I was sad, I wasn't sure that I wanted to go with him.

———

Ma Ma and Ba Ba took me to the airport with them on the day he left. I had never been to an airport before. It looked like a giant mall except it didn't have places that sold dolls. We waited with Ba Ba in a long line with other da ren. Everyone in line had suitcases so big I could have fit inside them with all of my toys. As I looked around, my eyes landed on three figures dressed all in black with strips of white. I pointed and screamed and soon the black blurred in my eyes because I was crying.

One of the figures said something to me in passing. I didn't speak English at the time and wouldn't know that the figure was a nun and that she was blessing me until Ba Ba explained. In the moment, I knew only that the figure spoke in an incomprehensible tongue and had blue eyes, which I didn't even know existed.

By the time my tears had dried and my throat was too hoarse to let out a single decibel, Ba Ba had dropped off his me-size suitcase on a moving belt. We then took escalators and walked down one hall after another before being directed to a doorway with ropes around it and da ren who were all dressed alike. Ba Ba stooped down to my level, and I knew then that what he was about to say was Very Serious, and for me only. It was important for me to listen closely, I knew, and I dared not breathe or blink.

"Guai, Xi Mou Hou, ting Ma Ma de hua, unh?"

I nodded. I would be a good girl and listen to Ma Ma.

"Try your best to nap at lunchtime, even if it's just pretend, and even if you are just asking questions with your eyes closed."

I nodded some more. I was still moving my head when Ba Ba bent over and pressed his lips to my left cheek.

Out of nowhere, there was a frog in my throat and a rock in my heart.

I watched Ba Ba unfold to his full height. He and Ma Ma exchanged words I was too short to hear, and then, for the only time in my life, I saw them exchange a kiss. He then waved and took big strides toward the ropes and the da ren with the same clothes. As Ba Ba was about to walk into the world behind the ropes, I saw my arms unfurl before me and a cry escape from my mouth: "Ba Ba!"

Ba Ba would later tell me that he saw my outstretched arms whenever he closed his eyes, every single day for years to come.

And in the millisecond that he turned to me, I saw that his face was like mine, yellow and red like our flag, wrinkled like a used napkin.

Then just like that, he was gone.

* * *

Now Ma Ma and I were also on the flying machine to Mei Guo. It was finally time for us to get off, but Ma Ma was still collapsed into her chest.

"Ma Ma," I said, prodding her. "We're in Mei Guo now!"

The lady with the fake face was walking past us.

"No, dear," she said, bending over and putting her now-melted face much too close to mine. I pulled my face back. I had never seen anything like it before.

"We are in Ri Ben," Japan.

I didn't know what Ri Ben was so I figured that we must have gotten on the wrong flying machine. This one had not taken us to Ba Ba. But I didn't want to frighten Ma Ma, so I stayed silent.

"Looks like your mother needs a wheelchair. Someone will meet you at the gate—he will take you to your connection."

I nodded in the way that I did when I needed to pretend that I was not confused or scared. Ma Ma was still asleep and I would have to figure out what a connection was and whether it would take us to Ba Ba or home. Maybe we would get home in time to eat Lao Lao's chive-and-pork dumplings. Maybe the sun would still be out and I could go to the little shed where I had had to lock up all my things and pull out my bike and dolls and say, "Surprise! I didn't disappear like Ba Ba."

When the lights in the flying machine came on, Ma Ma could barely stand up. She leaned on me, and I became her legs. It was the most weight I had ever carried. I pretended I was just carrying a book bag or a giant teddy bear. I stowed my doll away in my backpack, telling that her that it would be only a moment— I needed both hands to hold on to Ma Ma.

Ma Ma had put one full vomit bag on the floor but was carrying another. I don't remember how we got our suitcases out or who carried them, only that it wasn't me. It couldn't have been me; supporting Ma Ma was all I could handle.

It was a long trek down the narrow aisle out of the flying machine, and once we were out, I saw that we were in a hallway that was not really a hallway. I knew because there were some tiny windows just a little higher than I was tall and when I looked out on tiptoes, I saw that we were very high off the ground. I choked on my breath and Ma Ma roused.

"What?"

"Don't look, Ma Ma," I said and slunk my way down the fake hallway with her in tow, wondering if Ri Ben was some weird place high up in the sky.

At the end of the journey, we met a da ren who looked just like the other da ren at home, except he was smaller and shorter. He had a big wheelchair with him.

"Ni hao," I said.

"Ni hao," he responded, but his tones were strange, making him sound mechanical.

"Has your mother had water?"

I nodded, feeling important like a da ren.

Ma Ma gave a weak smile to the confusing man and settled into the wheelchair.

We walked down one corridor and then another, past many strong-smelling restaurants that made Ma Ma gag into the remaining bag, until finally we turned to an area where many paler, wider, taller da ren spoke the same scary tongue as had the blue-eyed figure in black. Most of them wore similar outfits: shorts, T-shirts, sneakers, and little black bags strapped around their balloon waists. Their clothes were in all different colors yet they all looked the same.

The Chinese-but-not-Chinese da ren parked Ma Ma in front of a seat in the waiting area and she slid into it while keeping her eyes closed. He folded the chair up and looked at her, then me, for a while. I looked back and smiled, doing what I did when any da ren looked at me, clueless to the fact that he was awaiting his tip. He looked away and then looked back expectantly at Ma Ma, who stayed curled into her chest, desperate, she said, to keep the room from spinning. A few more seconds passed before his shoulders slumped ever so slightly and he walked away.

Then it was just me and a sleepy Ma Ma again, waiting in front of the big door to a second floating hallway and a second flying machine, which the Chinese-but-not-Chinese da ren had told me about. I sat next to Ma Ma, on the lookout for any predators that might come. It was my mission to get us to the safety of Ba Ba's arms.

Chapter 3
TYPE B

·········

After Ba Ba left Zhong Guo, Ma Ma and I moved in with Lao Lao and Lao Ye. Da Jiu Jiu lived there, too, so every day should have been a party. But I became very unlucky.

The first time Ma Ma and I went grocery shopping after Ba Ba left, it suddenly became important to me to show how much of a big girl I had become. After we had returned from the store, as Ma Ma was locking her bike outside our building, I grabbed from the bike basket a carton of eggs and a glass bottle of vinegar—things that Ba Ba would have carried to our top-floor apartment. I darted into the building and up the stairs before Ma Ma took notice. By the time she screamed, "Qian Qian, be careful! Don't fall!" I was already running up the second of five tall flights.

Ma Ma's steps approached soon after, but by then it was too late. When she finally came into view on the fourth-floor landing, I was already on the ground, having tripped on loose laces, my white frilly dress covered with the yellow-brown of raw eggs and vinegar, broken glass and cracked shells framing my bloody right arm.

From then on, I started falling more and more. It was almost as if the shards of glass from the vinegar bottle had stayed in my right side, tipping me off balance. Going down escalators became particularly treacherous. I took to committing to the first step gingerly, my heart thumping in my throat, but it rarely worked. Over and over, I fell. I kept thinking that I would get used to having the spiked teeth chew into my sides as I rolled down each metal step—then, at least, I would act like a big girl and not cry. But each time, the pain surprised me and brought big baby drops to my eyes. Once, just after it happened in a store, as my tears were still drying and my face was not yet puffy, Ma Ma pointed to a big wheel a few steps away from the landing.

"Look, Qian Qian," she said. "You can spin it to win a toy. You love those things!"

But I saw that there was already a crowd around the wheel, with girls and boys of various ages, each of them holding the hands of their ba bas on one side, their ma mas on the other.

I shook my head and declared, "No, I'm bad

luck now." I then pulled Ma Ma by one hand, away from the wheel and toward the next down escalator, to which my other hand reached.

* * *

Ma Ma talked less and smiled less. I figured this was because I had disappointed her by not being a big girl. We used to have a game where I pointed out characters on street signs and asked her what they meant. We would pass hours doing this, She answering heartily and I throwing myself into pointing and asking. But after Ba Ba left, she often didn't respond at all. Although her outer shell stayed the same, she no longer lived inside.

Ma Ma was meaner, too. I was the kid who stuffed her face and always ate what she was given. But just as I had to ask what every character was, I had to ask what I was eating. Ma Ma knew the question was a pre-meal ritual, but when I engaged in it one day after Ba Ba left, Ma Ma attacked me with barks that I had never heard from her. Lao Lao was also at the table and opened her mouth to object, but that only caused Ma Ma to bark some more.

"Don't tell her," she commanded. "She's only pretending not to know for attention. She's spoiled rotten."

We passed the rest of the meal in silence, Lao

Lao speechless, I questioning what I had done wrong.

At night I heard Ma Ma sniffle into her pillow in the bed we shared, and I wondered whether someone had come one night to take away my dear Ma Ma and replace her with an imposter.

Another thing that changed after Ba Ba left was our Sunday nights. We started walking through the night market, but we never stopped at the stalls to taste the source of their yummy aromas. Instead, we kept going until we got to the giant brown building where Lao Ye worked. The building's windows watched us like the government's eyes. Ma Ma always looked around before opening the main door and having us climb the stairs in darkness.

"Where are the lights, Ma Ma?"

No answer. But I knew she was there because I was holding her hand.

After thirty-four steps—I made sure to count each time, and each time I worried that the number ended in four, which was bad luck because the character was pronounced **si**, like death—we fumbled in the dark and opened another door and walked down the hallway. After several steps, Ma Ma unlocked a door and we went into a room and sat down, Ma Ma always on the desk chair and I always on the couch, my feet dangling off the ground. The room did not seem to have lights, either, so I could make out only the shape of Ma Ma's silhouette against the slices of streetlamp light sneaking in through the window blinds. The phone had a big wheel in the middle with numbers on it, making a **clack-clack-clack** sound to which I kicked my legs. Sometimes it was so dark that Ma Ma made mistakes and would have to start over, and it would be many clacks and leg kicks before I heard Ba Ba's voice from the handle.

Ma Ma always talked to him first. From the couch, I heard that Ba Ba sounded sick, with a hoarser, deeper voice that was sometimes interrupted by sniffles. Most of the calls were uneventful, filled by Ma Ma's voice assuring him that everything was okay at home.

Every now and then, though, Ma Ma would say, "You're never coming back, are you? It's a new number every month. You'll never make enough. It'll never be enough."

I had no idea what she was talking about, but I shuffled to Ma Ma to comfort her, sliding into her lap and giving her a tight hug. Sometimes she sobbed into my hair, her breath sending a tingling warmth onto my scalp. Other times she did not seem to notice me at all, patting me on the back in the absent way that I hated, until I couldn't bear to comfort her any longer and crawled back to my couch in the corner.

My conversations with Ba Ba were always the same. I told him about the game I played at school, including the mother hen game in which I was invariably the hen who had the job of protecting all of her chicks. Every now and then, Ba Ba offered "Unh, unh" in acknowledgment, but he never had anything to say or ask. I had never known him to be like that before, so it was all I could do to continue talking until Ba Ba or Ma Ma said, "Hao, Qian Qian, give the phone back to Ma Ma."

As the months ticked on, this happened more and more often until Ba Ba spoke only one sentence to me before asking me to give the phone back to Ma Ma: "Guai, Qian Qian, Ba Ba xiang ni." He always made sure to tell me how much he missed me. And then, with a "good night" to Ma Ma, Ba Ba's voice disappeared.

* * *

Just before Ba Ba left for Mei Guo, I went with him to the doctor to get his exam and shots. We walked to the clinic that smelled like chemicals and that was white for the most part, except where the walls had started to yellow. Ma Ma was working, and it was up to me to make sure that Ba Ba went through with everything. This was because I was the only one who was more afraid than Ba Ba of the yi sheng, the scary old men in white jackets, and he had to be a good example and show me how to be brave. I learned all of this by listening to Ma Ma whisper it to Ba Ba at night when they thought I was asleep.

I'd always been sneaky.

When it was Ba Ba's turn to get shots, he had to take his pants off and get the shot on his butt. He had been very busy for the weeks before, wrapping up his job and packing his things, so he was a smaller Ba Ba than I had ever known. The image of his gaunt butt cheeks on that day carved itself into my skull. I did not know until then just how bony butts could be. I had only ever seen my friends' butts, which were very round and sometimes dirty, on the playground. I was chewing on this discovery when the yi sheng stuck a shiny metal needle into Ba Ba's butt and automatically, uncontrollably, I wailed. I heard myself wailing but couldn't stop, and I continued until Ba Ba ran over while pulling on his pants. He stopped short and looked down at the ground, and only then did I realize I had dropped the bottle of pills I had been holding for him. The little capsules splayed all over the floor, like freckles on a butt. The hu shi, nurse, and yi sheng looked at me and laughed, but I didn't care because I could not stop wailing.

Ba Ba scooped me up and ran me out of the room. I began to recover a bit, licking up the tears that had dripped down my cheeks and onto my chin. "Mei shi, mei shi," he lulled, but only later, over ice pops on the sidewalk, was he able to convince me that the yi sheng had not wrecked him and his bony butt, and that everything was okay.

* * *

Two years later, it was my turn to endure the same indignity. By psychological designs beyond my grasp, I remember no part of the process during which the needle was inserted into my not-so-bony butt cheek. All I remember is getting the blood test results and finding out that my blood was not Type A, but rather what I knew, from the order of the English alphabet, to be the inferior Type B. My face drooped and I shared my dismay with Ma Ma, who laughed and laughed and said not to worry—she was Type B, too. This did not reassure me at all. It told me only that my inferiority was coded into my blood and my genes.

The next stop was the dentist, whom I hated even more than the yi sheng because he wielded loud and metallic tools that I knew were designed to crack his victims' skulls open. The dentist was mean. I couldn't see his mouth because he wore a white cloth over the lower part of his face but his eyes were dark. I had a hole in my tooth that needed to be filled, he declared as he cranked a lever to lower the long chair I was on. He placed a small metal thing on my tongue and I froze. Next, he took a drill and aimed it at a poor tooth in the back, causing stars and light to fly across my eyes.

"Aughhh." Out burst a scream as saliva pooled in my mouth.

"You stupid child. You swallowed the filling!" He ripped his mask off and I saw that his mouth was as downturned and dark as his eyes.

"Dui bu qi," I squeaked out in a garbled apology while balancing the tools that were still dangling from my mouth.

He produced another gray metal chunk, which he again placed on my tongue.

"Let's try this again," he said. "Do. Not. Swallow."

I nodded and then kept my tongue perfectly still as a memory from the first week of school floated to my brain. The boy sitting next to me had stapled the flesh of his thumb in the little space between his nail and the skin. I looked on while he watched without expression as his nail popped off the top of his thumb and blood squirted onto his shirt and my desk. A few weeks later, I saw the same boy run down the hallway as a teacher chased him with a broomstick. He refused to listen in class and kept sticking things in his body.

If the boy could survive that, I could survive

this. I kept my muscles so rapt at this memory that I moved not an inch. The rest of the procedure must have gone on, but I remember none of it.

* * *

The second part of our long trip to Mei Guo was uneventful. I was exhausted from my sentry post and felt all of my muscles unclench the minute I strapped myself and Ma Ma into our seats. Ma Ma, I assumed, was empty and spent from throwing up what seemed to be all of her organs. The two of us collapsed into each other. Ma Ma fell asleep while I only pretended to sleep, keeping my eyes closed but my ears on guard. I did not open my eyes again until the cabin's overhead lights flickered on and we had no choice but to gather ourselves up from the sunken, worn-out seats.

I do not remember much of customs. I do recall Ma Ma being wheeled off the plane again as a man appeared—he was actually Chinese this time—and helped us answer questions from a uniformed man with white skin and eyes that were green instead of blue. Before we approached, Ma Ma turned to me and instructed, "Bie shuo hua." She would say this more and more to me during our time to come in Mei Guo.

Be silent. Say nothing.

My voice no longer had a place.

After the questions, the Chinese man told us to walk through a large set of doors before taking Ma Ma's empty wheelchair and saying goodbye. The doors opened to a large room with flat circular belts, each with suitcases on them. We found our two giant suitcases, which we had packed tightly with ribbons tied around them. The ribbons were gone now, and the black cloth of our new luggage greeted us, naked and exposed. A feeble Ma Ma shook as she dragged each suitcase off the flat escalators and onto the cart she got for them. I helped her push the cart, but the handlebars went over my head. The cart, along with the suitcases, all but obscured my vision of where we were walking.

After some more lines before uniformed people in booths, of which I have but a vague memory, another pair of doors opened up to a bustling room holding people of all different shades. I had never seen anything like it before. Some were like us; others darker, brown; still others like the nun I'd seen two years ago, with eyes that were not just blue or green but blue-green, green-brown! Humans were a moving kaleidoscope of colors I did not know were possible.

Seeing Ba Ba again in that crowd was like

looking at my own knee right after a fall—
he looked new yet familiar, mine yet not mine.
Like a joint newly reddened, blood seeping out
from cracks in the skin, Ba Ba looked like
himself, but skinnier, gaunter, more tired. A
caved-in sallowness had taken over his face, over
all of him. He wore a plain white shirt that was
starting to fray at the edges, and wrinkled pants.

"Ba Ba?" Somehow, it emerged as a squeaky
question, not an excited greeting.

"Qian Qian, ni zhe me da le!"

How big I had gotten.

Ba Ba, how short you've gotten. How skinny
and old you've gotten. But I bit my tongue and
he and Ma Ma greeted each other with a long
embrace. We then wheeled our suitcases out and
placed them in a yellow car with a man sitting
in front, on the other side of a screen.

In Zhong Guo, I had sat in similar cars with
Ma Ma, except the car was not yellow and the
driver was Chinese. I would learn later that Ba
Ba had saved up for months just to be able to
welcome us to Mei Guo with a yellow car.

Ba Ba said something to the man in English,
who brought the car into motion. Then Ba Ba
turned to us, patting my head with one hand
and rubbing Ma Ma's shoulders with the other.

"Zen me yang? E bu e? Lei bu lei?"

Were we hungry? Were we tired? Yes and yes.

But most of all, we were happy to have our little family reunited.

It was then, with my head on Ba Ba's shoulder, the new city's wild lights flashing outside the window, and my doll forgotten on the floor, that I finally fell into a deep and safe sleep.

Chapter 4

THE BEAUTIFUL COUNTRY

....

Mei Guo was nothing like what everyone promised. Everything smelled strange and looked different. We lived in a place that Ba Ba called Brooklyn. Most of the people around us had brown skin and dark hair. Other than our Cantonese landlady, we rarely ever saw anybody who looked like us, and when we did, they never talked to us in Chinese. I wondered if we had left behind the only place in the world that had our people.

Our new home was a single room on the second floor of a three-story wooden house that was always groaning under our weight. The other bedroom on our floor was occupied by a revolving carousel of new immigrants like us who could just barely put together enough money to pay for it. The door next to that was a bathroom that everyone shared. One of the first things Ma Ma said to me in Mei Guo was that I had to always lock the door when I was in there. We were not in Zhong Guo anymore. I could not leave the door unlocked. And I'd better not ever leave it open.

On the first floor were two bedrooms. Another family lived in one of the rooms. Ba Ba said they were Puerto Rican. Even in Chinese, those were words I had never heard before. The communal kitchen was also on the first floor. Though it was the worst house I had ever been in, it had the largest kitchen I had ever seen. Chinese kitchens were female spaces, so they shared with out-houses the lowest status in the home. Kitchens were often relegated to the smallest, dirtiest, and least ventilated areas. And even though we had to share our new kitchen with everyone else in the house and all the cockroaches, it had an island and a walk-in closet.

For some reason, our landlady liked to hide in the closet while everyone ate. She was a little old woman with a kindly face, white hair, and a hunchback that reminded me of a steamed bun. Every time I said anything while we were in the kitchen, Ba Ba shushed me and pointed to the closet, reminding me that the little hunch-back lady was in there. I didn't believe him for the first month, until one day I turned the light off after dinner and hid behind the island. After just a few minutes, I heard the closet door creak and the house grunt under new movement and shifting weight. Peering out from the corner of the island, I spotted our landlady's stooped back making its way toward the door.

She left the closet door open behind her. I had never seen it open before, so I took the chance to run in. I pressed the door closed behind me, the click of the knob echoing through the wooden chamber. There was a vent by the door, along the bottom of one of the walls. I slid down, placing my eyes against the slats. Sure enough, I could see out perfectly. Lying on my side with my eyes looking through the vent, I stayed on the hard ground, waiting for someone to spy on. It must not have been too uncomfortable because I slipped off into sleep.

The next thing I remember is waking up to the old lady's eyes, lined with wrinkles and cloudy with cataracts. She was yelling in incomprehensible Cantonese, leaning her weight on her scratched cane. As all of the blood rushed to my face, I squeaked out an apology—"Dui bu qi!"—and slid through the opening of the door before bounding up the stairs to our room.

I don't remember where Ma Ma and Ba Ba were during this time, only that in Mei Guo, they left me on my own more than I had ever been before. They never found out about the incident, even though I held my breath in the days after, awaiting my punishment. The next time I saw the closet door open again, the little room was no longer empty but full of bags of rice and cans of cat food.

* * *

At night in our new home, Ma Ma and I sat draped in darkness, far from the window. Each time I inched closer to the window or the light, Ma Ma shouted, "Wei xian!" Dangerous. According to Ma Ma, everything in our new country was dangerous. It was dangerous even to step close to the windows or turn the lights on. The popping sounds outside were gunshots, she said, and if they saw that we were home, they might shoot us, too.

I never questioned what she told me. And I was too scared to ask why people would want to shoot us.

So every night we sat in darkness, I in my little bed inches away from Ma Ma in her somewhat bigger bed, both of us sitting up and leaning on the wall opposite the window, until we heard Ba Ba's tired steps climb the stairs to our room. He always flicked on the lights as soon as he entered.

"Wei shen me guan zhe?"

Why were the lights off, Ba Ba invariably demanded of Ma Ma. There was no need, he insisted. But Ma Ma, she became unsure of everything in Mei Guo when Ba Ba was not there.

"Qian Qian, ni kan," Ba Ba said, gesturing to

me with a brown paper bag. He held the bag oddly, on its side, laid across both hands.

"Shen me?"

"Ni kai ya!" Open it, he commanded.

So I snatched the bag from his hands and twirled it upright, as it should have been, I thought.

"Xiao xin!" Ba Ba said.

I had always wondered why "little heart" meant "be careful" in Chinese.

Opening the bag reminded me of that one time I looked into the mouth of a bulldog. Ma Ma's friend had brought him over and he had come right up to me. Steam swallowed my face and crept into my pores, and I reeled from a strong smell.

"Gou!" I shouted in disgust, drawing peals of laughter from my parents. Ba Ba explained that there was no dog meat, that it was just what the Americans called "pizza."

My handling of the bag had caused the pizza to roll into itself, giving it a wraplike quality. The cheese stretched and pulled in strings as I bit a piece off. They were tenacious, sticking to my fingers, the paper bag, my chin, propelling me into a fit of giggles. What was this terrifying, amazing, delicious substance, and why was this the first I had ever tasted of it?

It took me a second to discover the sliced

brown mushrooms, also unlike anything I had ever had before: a little rubbery, a little less flavorful. After a second chomping of the "pizza," I passed it along to Ma Ma, content to savor the leftovers stuck on my fingers.

The brown bag contained one slice, dinner for all three of us. I had already learned that meals were much smaller in Mei Guo. The food we ate filled us up quickly, cheese and dairy being things we had rarely eaten before. Yet I always got hungry again within the hour. Eating American food was like gulping down giant and instantly gratifying bubbles of air.

* * *

The stray cats were my favorite part of our new home. The house had an enclosed backyard full of them. Throughout the yard, the old landlady set out trays of cheap cat food mixed with rice and bowls of water that had once been fresh, but that were soon muddied with leaves, dirt, and rainwater. There were cats of all colors: white with black spots; tabby; striped. There were rarely ever stray animals in Zhong Guo, and when Da Jiu Jiu told me I'd see things in Mei Guo I'd never seen, I never imagined that I would be so lucky as to live among cats. But if the cats were any indication, Mei Guo was to be full of unreliable friends. Every day I went out in hopes of finding them, and some days they were there, friendly and cajoling. Other days, they were aloof, hiding in cracks and corners, making me pursue them. Their eyes seemed to change with the weather, one second admiring, the next dismissive. It seemed that their moods changed as quickly as life had for us.

I found a far more steadfast friend in the yard. The back wall of the yard had a narrow platform affixed to it, with a slight protruding roof. On that platform was a Buddhist shrine, which contained framed photos of people who looked like the landlady but who were by turns older and younger, along with incense and plates of fruit. On the end of the platform was the smallest television I had ever seen, spanning maybe twelve inches in width.

The first time I came upon the platform, the only source of noise came from **The Simpsons** airing on the small TV. None of the words made sense to me, but I could not look away from the bright colors and the odd-looking characters. The white characters had darker yellow skin and the Chinese characters had lighter yellow skin. I knew they were supposed to be Chinese because they had eyes that were thinner, elongated, and slanted. I had no idea before then that Chinese eyes were supposed to look like that, but it quickly became how

I saw myself, teaching me then that there was something wrong with my eyes.

Seeing my race through the white gaze brought to my mind a story that Ba Ba had shared with me in China. One of his fellow English professors had come to Mei Guo before he did. Unlike him, she returned to China to recount her experiences. She told Ba Ba that she had never before realized how flat our faces were, and how three-dimensional and mountainous white people's faces were, with protrusions in the brows, cheeks, and noses that we so envied. All of this was drilled into her spirit when she heard a white colleague referring to her as a "pancake face." Ba Ba and I shared a laugh because we thought this was the most ridiculous thing we had ever heard. But the colleague, she had not found it so funny. She had told Ba Ba, in English for emphasis: "I cried for days and nights."

For the first time, I felt her sadness. But I tried to console myself with the fact that everyone was odd-looking in **The Simpsons**. For example, the mother's head was impossible: tall, long, and blue. I started going to the shrine every day at the same time, and after a few days, I came to recognize most of the characters, with their bulgy eyes, jagged spikes and all.

The next week, Ba Ba came home with a

little TV that he had found by trash bags on the sidewalk. It was even smaller than the one at the shrine and had a crack along the back of its plastic casing. I loved it. It introduced me to PBS Kids, a new world of friends. Ba Ba had to go to work and Ma Ma had to find a job, but it was still summer and school had not started yet. So for a few days, I stayed in our room alone under strict instructions not to leave, except to use the bathroom and to go to the kitchen for food, which I was to bring back and eat in the room. Over the course of those long hours, the TV and I became kindred spirits. Like me, it was sad and lonely, having been abandoned on the curb by its bigger and less cracked Ma Ma.

The TV was always on in our room, even when I was reading or napping. The free channels— FOX 5, PBS 13, and the later-named UPN 9, and WB 11 —made my life feel less empty. Before leaving Zhong Guo, I had never been alone. So it was nice to be embraced again by the sounds of people, even if they were in a little screen, even if they spoke in a language I did not yet speak. PBS Kids, in particular, supplied me with my surrogate family members, from shows I would later recognize to be **Reading Rainbow** and **Mister Rogers' Neighborhood**. And new shows joined my family soon after, such as **The Puzzle Place** and **Wishbone**. Though my parents were gone, Mr. Rogers was there, telling me that there was only one me, and that he liked me just as I was, even if I did not yet have the English to understand it.

The Puzzle Place was my absolute favorite. I watched it with relish whenever it was on, even if they were repeats of episodes I had already seen. I loved that all of the puppets seemed to be friends even though they were different. There was one puppet of each race, and something about this felt right to me. Even though the puppets' faces hinted at their race, they all looked similar, human and happy.

Of the puppets, my favorite was Julie. She was Chinese and every now and then, she shared things from our culture that I was able to recognize through the thick fog of English. And in those slivers of time, it was almost as if I were home again.

* * *

In real life, the rare Chinese people we saw acted nothing like Julie. I was so excited the first time I saw another Chinese person on the street that I opened my mouth to exclaim, "Ni hao." The only thing that stopped me was Ma Ma's warning about talking to random people.

Don't talk to anyone, she said. **We can't trust anyone.**

No one? What about police officers, Ma Ma?

No one. Especially police officers. If you see a uniform, turn around and walk the opposite way.

Why, Ma Ma?

It's dangerous. We're not allowed here. Don't trust anyone.

I didn't understand what that meant, but every time we walked past other Chinese people, I could tell that they didn't trust us, either. They wore a look that I had never before seen in Zhong Guo. Their eyes did not greet mine when I looked at them; their mouths did not smile; and the pall of exhaustion shaded their faces. Mei Guo had done something to them to change them forever. It was the same look I had seen for the first time on Ba Ba at the airport, and it was a look that was permanent for the Ba Ba I knew in Mei Guo. I started to wonder if that was how I looked, too. Every night in the shared bathroom, I stared at my own reflection, poking at my cheeks and tugging at my eyelids. I was confused each time. I didn't look any different. But why did everything feel so, so different?

Ma Ma and Ba Ba were overtaken by shadows. They were still attentive and doting at times, but more often they were distracted, elsewhere, sighing and saying big words to each other that held no meaning for me. Many of the words they used I had never heard before, nor had I heard them all jumbled together like that, rolling out through tired tongues.

Whenever I had a question, I had to repeat myself at least twice before Ma Ma and Ba Ba noticed. "Ma Ma, zhe shi shen me?" I'd ask about the endless new things all around us. But Ma Ma and Ba Ba were by now both replaced by shells. They always seemed to be looking around, scanning our environment for something. I wished that I could help them find whatever they were looking for so they could focus on me again. Even when we sang and danced to **Xi Mou Hou**, which we did now on only rare occasions, Ba Ba had a faraway look in his eyes that told me that he was not really there. **Xi Mou Hou** had once been the highlight of his day, and now it was a burden.

As for strangers, I began to fear the humiliation they brought. I was no longer a normal kid, and everything I did was wrong even though I didn't understand why. I quickly learned that it was not okay, even in Chinese, to ask Ba Ba on the subway why a Black man had hair like that, because it would cause Ba Ba to laugh and the man to get upset. I also learned not to go into the kitchen whenever our roommates were there because they would pull at the corners of their

eyes and make faces at me. And I learned not
to make too much noise eating, because even
though we were supposed to do that to show Ma
Ma that we enjoyed the food she made, doing it
in Mei Guo just made others laugh at us.

Most of all, I learned that we were "chinks"
now, even though I wasn't allowed to use the
word. Almost every day, someone said it to us
as they walked by on the street. The first time I
heard the word, a big boy leaned over from his
passing bike and shouted it deep into my ear.
Everything sounded a little farther away through
that ear for a while after. Ma Ma had startled
and screamed, but I only knew that because I
heard it with my other ear.

That day, we went home to ask Ba Ba what it
meant, but he refused to tell us. Then I said that
it was probably Mei Guo's word for Chinese
people, that that's what we were called: "We are
chinks now, Ba Ba!" This brought Ba Ba back
from his faraway dream, and he looked right
into my eyes before speaking: "That is a very bad
word, Qian Qian. Don't you ever use it." Then,
just as quickly, he looked away and drifted off
again.

I wanted his attention back, badly. I considered using the word again, because that seemed
to work. But instead I just sat there, worrying
that I might do something wrong again, biting

the inside of my mouth as I listened to the ringing in my damaged ear.

* * *

I learned quickly that people were dangerous.
But I also learned that there were certain expressions, of anger and coldness, that I could wear
to keep people a little farther away. I started to
put on a mask of those expressions every time I
left home.

The mask did not work all the time. Ma Ma
and I were walking in our neighborhood one
day when we passed a sad old house, set back
from the sidewalk with a fence that had holes in
the chain links and patches of rust everywhere.
The gate had only one hinge that was attached
to the fence; the other hinge was loose. Ma Ma
and I were almost entirely past the fence when
we saw a white thing burst out from the house.
The gate and the fence did little to block it, and
the thing came to us first only as a blur. I saw
only a jaw, full of teeth, open and snatching in
the air as the thing lunged toward us.

I ducked and shielded my face. My arm suffered the brunt, but when I looked up, I found
no blood. The skin on my arm had managed to
survive untouched, though my right sleeve was
in shreds. By then, the owner of the dog had
emerged from the house. He was white like his

dog, who was now gnawing on the ripped cloth of my sleeve. We could tell that the man had seen what happened, but he said nothing and wore a smirk on his face. Ma Ma mirrored his silence and dragged me down the block by my other arm, my feet stumbling to keep pace, my tattered right sleeve flapping in the wind as it chased after us.

Chapter 5

SILK

....

The summer days in Mei Guo were long, much longer than they had been in Zhong Guo. I was to start second grade in September. But just before that, I started another form of school. That school's lessons stayed with me for far longer than anything I learned off a chalkboard.

Before leaving for work one day, Ba Ba told Ma Ma that she could try to find work on East Broadway in Chinatown, and that bosses in the area would be more understanding of her bringing me because they were all Chinese. While Ma Ma and I wandered down that street, I timed myself to see how long I could go without breathing in the tempting, delicious smells that made my stomach growl.

Halfway down one block full of restaurants we could not afford, we were stopped by a squat lady with a meat pie for a face. "Eh, eh," she said. "Na zhe!" She stuffed a slip of paper into Ma Ma's hand and tottered away.

I had by then learned enough characters to

read chapter books, but could not make out everything that was on the slip of paper: **No something papers**, it said, **no problem**.

"Ma Ma, what's it say?"

Ma Ma did not respond. Instead, she directed us down this street and the next, finding our way to a one-room squalor. We met with peeling walls and crowds of Chinese people, none of them like the ones in Zhong Guo.

"I need a job." Ma Ma was from the north, blunt and to the point.

"What can you do?" a fat man responded. The shape of his face reminded me of a steaming pork bun. Saliva formed in my mouth.

"I was a math and computers professor in Hebei Province."

"Mei yong," he shook his head. Useless.

"Ever wash dishes?"

"Ma Ma is good at everything," I interjected after swallowing my drool.

No one heard me. This was my new reality. There was a lot of noise in Mei Guo, and my voice was no longer loud enough.

"I'm really good at sewing."

"Unh. Na zhe." And another slip of paper was stuffed into her hand.

Wading through the viscous August heat, Ma Ma and I made our way to a warehouse-like building on Division Street, across from a red-brick building that Ma Ma told me was an elementary school. We climbed three flights of stairs and were rewarded with a gym-size room. Red and black cloth covered the two windows—the only source of natural light—recalling to me the calligraphy strips on the threshold of the Wang courtyard.

In that room, there was no day or night; there was only work. The air was infused with steamed rice and salty sweat. Overhead, fans whirred, their blackened, rusted blades playing tag with swarms of flies.

Visible from the door were rows upon rows of sewing machines, each with its own hunchback guarding the post. The hunchbacks moved minimally, as if each movement caused blood to drain from their wrists. Most of the hunchbacks were women, though a scattered few were men. And here and there, there was a little girl around my age. The curved backs of the people reminded me of freshly steamed mantou in different flavors. Here one clothed in white, plain flavor; there a purple one, taro, maybe.

"You, sit here," I barely made out from the Cantonese emerging from a lady whose skin reminded me of a dumpling wrapper pulled taut against too much filling.

She planted me in front of a stool at the edge of a planked wooden table.

"You, sit there," she commanded Ma Ma, directing her to a sewing machine to my left.

Before us stood mountains of cloth in two large canvas carts. In a basket on the table, a molehill of small white labels.

Ma Ma grabbed a handful of cloth—they were shirts, I saw up close—and set them on her left. And then I watched as Ma Ma turned into a hunchback, taking a label and placing it on the seam of a shirt by the neck. She pressed down on the pedal under the machine, which whirred awake and spat out black thread.

Once, back in Zhong Guo, I sat with Lao Lao in her bedroom as she was rounded over, knitting in front of the TV. Like I had taken to doing since leaving Zhong Guo, Lao Lao only listened to the TV; she never looked up. She was too entranced by the blur of wooden needles and red acrylic yarn in her hands. On that particular day, a documentary had been on. A chubby silkworm stared at me with beady black eyes as its fuzzy face spat white strings.

The silkworm is an honorable creature, the TV informed us, **that we have bred for thousands of years.**

Ma Ma's machine did not have a fuzzy face or beady eyes, but it spat out string just the same.

———

After Ma Ma finished attaching a label onto an article of clothing, she tossed it into an empty cart behind us. I had my own mountain and my own empty cart. I had my own job, too: to cut all the loose strings dangling off the seams. I had my own pair of scissors with a black handle and long metal blades. My right hand and wrist could barely support their weight. I had to put the scissors down after every other piece and shake my hand out. I tried to use it with my left hand once, but found that it was too heavy for that hand to use at all.

In Zhong Guo, I had a pair of bright-orange plastic scissors. They were blunt with rounded tips, designed to pretend-cut things that were already cut. I wished for real scissors like the ones Ba Ba often used to cut his papers into strips, which he would then rip into even smaller pieces. So I was happy when I got to Mei Guo and received my very own pair at the sweatshop.

Before he left Zhong Guo, Ba Ba warned me never to run with scissors, which of course prompted me to grab the pair from his desk and run circles around our apartment. I had made only three laps when I tripped on my train set, causing the scissors to bite a long angry gash in my left palm.

"Ni kan kan," Ba Ba chided. But his voice was gauze, not mad at all.

After Ba Ba left Zhong Guo, there was no one to tell me not to run with scissors. So I stopped doing it because it was no longer fun.

On the anniversary of the day Ba Ba left, I took his scissors—rusty from abandonment—and snip, snip, snipped at our leather couch. The cuts made two wings with a dip in the middle, like a TV show had taught me. (The TV show also taught me to snip only paper.) When Ma Ma walked into the living room, she yelled at me, not about running with scissors but about using them.

"Qian Qian, what is this?"

I thought it was obvious. But sometimes you had to explain things to da ren. They were too big to see the important things.

"They are swallows, Ma Ma. The TV taught me." She blinked at me and this told me I had to be patient and explain some more. Sometimes da ren were a little slow.

"They will fly to see Ba Ba in Mei Guo to make sure he's not lonely."

Ma Ma walked out of the room, but I heard her sob in the kitchen.

* * *

I played hide-and-seek every day at the sweatshop. The game was to find as many loose strings as quickly as possible, and it was easier to do this when I forced myself to blink less. On some pieces, there weren't as many loose threads as I would have liked. When that happened, I yanked a thread loose just so I could trim it.

I had always been an overachiever.

The silkworm brings great pride to our country and we must uphold the honor it brings.

The hours crawled along, Ma Ma attaching the labels, my finding (or creating) and trimming the loose threads. It was important for us to put all finished items in the empty carts. Ma Ma made three cents for each piece. I made one cent. Every piece mattered.

The only sounds in the room came from the sewing machines, the fans, the flies, and every now and then, a coughing hunchback. No one budged other than to move pieces of clothing. I don't even remember going to the bathroom—was there a bathroom? There had been one, surely?—or drinking water.

Around hour six, a buzzer vibrated across the room. As if emerging from hypnosis, we all unhunched and straightened at the smell of steamed rice. Until I stood up straight, I did not feel the pain that rested at the base of my neck and trickled down my back. It wasn't until

I uncurled my spine that I realized how round I had become.

We all got up and walked to the back of the room, lining up in front of the rice cooker.

My mouth watered.

I swallowed.

Some of the workers had packed their own dishes, once warm but long cold in containers, which they brought with them in line at the ready to receive the fresh steamed rice.

I rubbernecked to survey what my fellow hunchbacks packed.

Stir-fried potatoes, edges browned just so with soy sauce.

Tomatoes and egg.

Bean curd with string beans.

From my tummy came the rumbling of a boiling pot.

To harvest the silk and keep it perfect, we must boil the cocoon before the silk moth emerges.

Ma Ma and I did not have containers of our own. When we were in front of the rice cooker, the scented steam danced in my face and tickled my nostrils. Here was the dumpling-faced woman again, dropping one scoop of rice each onto two paper plates. I held mine in my right hand but the plate buckled, straining to support the weight of the rice that almost fell to the floor. I joined my left hand with my right.

"Mei you kuai zi, Ma Ma."

"That's okay. It'll be a fun game. How many grains of rice can you pick up at once with your left hand?"

So it didn't matter that we didn't have chopsticks—that was the point of the game we began the minute we returned to our posts. Ma Ma rested her plate under the sewing machine, the needle with its single eye staring, ravenous for the rice.

"Ready? Go!"

At this I clawed at my plate with my left hand, moving it like an escalator to my mouth. I kept my right hand behind my back. Rules were rules.

Ma Ma moved slowly. She grabbed just a few grains at once, and gnawed on each of them, as if searching for a hidden message inside each grain.

My hand was smaller but I won easily. I showed her my empty plate, as a few grains stuck to my cheeks and the corners of my mouth.

"Wow, you are so fast!"

I didn't let Ma Ma in on my strategy. What if there was another race?

My left hand was sticky with starch. I wiped it on the stiff yellow smiley face on my shirt. I put one grain on the crimson tongue. Everyone needed something to eat.

The buzzer had not gone off yet. This meant I had some time to roam the room.

I crept up row by row. I wanted to see what the room looked like from the very front. The farther up I got, the fewer paper plates there were. In the first row, everyone was still eating. They hovered over their containers of stir-fry. But the stir-fry looked different for some reason. It took me a few seconds to realize why: these people had stewed meat! Salted fish, even. And chicken legs.

Down the row, I spotted a single round egg, gleaming proudly under the naked light bulbs dangling from the ceiling. The owner of that egg was a girl around my age. She showed it no respect. She poked it around the container with her chopsticks, not even eating it.

I hated her.

I slinked to our row in the back. Ma Ma was still chewing on single kernels. She was never going to beat me at our game.

"Ma Ma, can we sit in the front row?"

"No."

"Why not?"

"It's for people who sew buttons."

I grabbed a grain of rice from her plate and chewed on this.

"Can I sew buttons?"

"Yes. But not yet."

I rolled my empty plate up into a tube.

"How many cents do the Button People make?"

"Ten."

I started using the tube to beat on the planked table and our piles of clothes.

Half of Ma Ma's scoop still sat on her plate. She pushed it at me, bartering it for my make-shift stick.

I pretended it was the race again. I grabbed the entire remaining mound with my left hand and shoved it into my face.

And then the buzzer rang, sending us back into our trance.

* * *

Each stump had its own hunchback with its own stories. Ma Ma heard them over time, though I would not hear about them until years later, and then only secondhand. Her favorite was from a woman who was always rooted at her station, working without pause from the beginning of her twelve-hour shift through the very end. Not once do I remember her getting up for rice, for water, for the bathroom. Ma Ma, ever generous, offered to grab her a plate as she continued to push the reams of fabric into the mouth of her hungry machine. When Ma Ma returned, the woman nodded up at her in appreciation, but almost immediately, she looked back down at her machine and returned to her concentrated labor.

It was not until after a month or so of such interaction—Ma Ma leaving the plate at the woman's elbow, wondering when she would ever stop long enough to scoop the rice into her mouth—that the woman apologized for her focus. She had to make a certain amount of money, she explained, within a certain amount of time. There had been an accident. She had come to Mei Guo over a year ago with the hope that her son would soon follow, just as soon as she paid the snakehead for her fee, and then his. But bad news found her within months of her arrival. Her son had stayed behind in her ancestral home in the country-side, with her parents and her brother, who loved motorcycles. One afternoon, the brother parked his motorcycle in the family shed and neglected to fully turn it off. Gas leaked every-where and fire caught, burning over half of her young son's body.

He needs surgery, but we can't afford it, I imagine her recounting through quiet tears, Ma Ma's and hers.

Not yet, anyway. As soon as I pay off the snake-head, I can get the rest to him. I tried to use the

money to go back, and then I tried to send it home, but each time the snakehead found out and said he would kill us.

What good am I to him if I'm dead? Even more useless than I am now. What kind of mother leaves her son behind, across the world, to be burned?

I see Ma Ma shaking her head and patting the woman on her back, injecting a current of compassion into the dark room. **It was not your fault**, she would say, her heart in torsion over the thought of it being me who burned instead of that poor little boy.

What purpose do I have now, but to make American dollars through these ugly clothes? I can picture the woman choking on her words just before turning back to her task.

I came here for him, Ma Ma recalled the woman repeating through sobs, **I only came here for him.**

* * *

Ma Ma was not meant to work at a sweatshop.

She was the most beautiful person in the world. In Zhong Guo, she and Lao Lao often talked about how her eyes were too small, her lips too thin, and how she carried too much weight around her chest and hips. But I didn't know what any of that meant. To me, she was the sun, a mug of steamed milk on a cold winter's night, everything warm.

Ma Ma was taller than most women in Zhong Guo, and, I later learned, most women in Mei Guo. She wore her hair in cascading waves, born from plastic green and pink rollers with foam cylinders in the middle. When we packed for Mei Guo, she jammed the rollers along the inner edges of our suitcase. The foam would slowly lose shape, but every night, in anticipation of her day at the sweatshop, she went to bed with a head full of them.

Ma Ma liked to say that a woman could be beautiful without being pretty, but that a woman could not be beautiful without having dignity. It would take me decades to unravel what that meant.

In Zhong Guo, Ma Ma wore giant glasses with frames the same shape as the large computer she sat in front of every day. The machine had a blank black face. On it was a dancing white bar that appeared and disappeared at the top left corner. So many times, I watched Ma Ma type in "CC:\DOS" while speaking it out loud, pronouncing it "say say daws." The machine spoke along with her, beeping like the roadrunner that the cartoon coyote could never catch.

A year before we moved to Mei Guo, when I was six, which meant she must have been thirty-one, Ma Ma published two textbooks on mathematics and computer science. By then Ba Ba had already left, so she showed the books to me. "Look, Qian Qian," she said with the same pride I bestowed upon my favorite pet rock, pointing to the bottom of the covers. "That's my name!"

I took in her name—indeed, there it was—and thumbed through the books. They mostly contained symbols and Chinese characters that I'd never seen before.

"Wow, Ma Ma." I did my duty by smiling my biggest wide-eyed smile. Then I walked away to play with my Ninja Turtles.

Sometimes when we walked around our hometown, Shijiazhuang, we ran into people who called Ma Ma "Lao Shi," Professor. But until I left Zhong Guo, I didn't register that it was possible for women to be anything other than a mother. To me, that was all Ma Ma was, and it was exactly what she was born to do.

Once, a da ren asked me what I wanted to be when I grew up, and I beamed and declared, "I want to be Ma Ma."

Misunderstanding that I wanted to be just any mother, Ma Ma scolded me.

"Qian Qian, how shameful! You should dream of becoming something more than a mother."

But to me there was nothing nobler, nothing greater, than being Ma Ma.

———

Ma Ma was good at everything. She cooked the best meals. In Zhong Guo, I had a little stool by the sink that I stood on, sometimes to help her wash dishes, sometimes just to watch her. She peeled apples magically, keeping the detached skin all connected in one long coil. I played with the coil and made it dance in the air, until I inevitably broke it in half and then laid it to rest in the trash can.

Ma Ma made everything a game. The tomatoes talked and the cucumbers laughed, and washing them was not a chore but the joyous task of giving them a bath.

Ma Ma didn't know it, but she was the reason my imagination burned alive everywhere I went, the reason I saw love in all beings and things.

Once, Ma Ma brought home two crabs and left them on the living room floor, handing me a pair of chopsticks so I could play with them. It was the best hour of my young life. The crabs followed me this way and that, waving their claws about as I hooted with glee.

Later, I put them in the sink so they could have a drink. As they blew bubbles in the water, Ma Ma filled up a pot.

"Why don't you go out to the sandbox and play for a while? Let the crabs take a nap."

She didn't have to tell me twice. I bounded out.

I returned to the dinner table to see my two

hard-shelled playmates—now red, no longer
blue—on a plate.

"Are they still sleeping, Ma Ma?"

"No, Qian Qian. Come on, let's eat." She
handed me my small pink chopsticks.

And so we ate, my meal seasoned with tears.

* * *

Ma Ma was particularly good at design and sewing. We didn't need to make our own clothes in
Zhong Guo, but she had a talent for it, and she
could never sit still. Ma Ma was always working, even when she was not teaching or writing.
Every week she came up with a new design,
always a dress, always with lace. She spent much
of each weekend bent over our sewing machine,
humming to herself while alternating between
pressing the pedal and marking up reams of
cloth with chalk.

I protested every Sunday when she put her
new creation on me, always complete with a
matching ribbon for my hair. "It's itchy!"

"But look how pretty you are. Stop tugging,
please. No squirming, either."

She sometimes made matching outfits for
the two of us. My favorite was red with white
polka dots, in silk. Both of our dresses had fitted
bodices and full, A-line skirts. When we walked
down the street, I felt as pretty as Minnie Mouse.

The polka-dot dress was different from Ma Ma's other designs. That one was so comfortable I could even be myself in it. I wore it regularly to the sandbox with my best friend, a boy just as smelly as me, but who didn't have to wear itchy, frilly socks with lace edging his dirt-covered ankles.

I don't remember what happened to that dress, or any of Ma Ma's designs. When we boarded the plane in Beijing airport, I never saw them again.

* * *

The cocoon is boiled with the silkworm inside. The heat kills the silkworm but the water makes the cocoon easy to unravel.

At hour twelve in the sweatshop, we were processed and released. I don't remember how much I made that day. I don't remember how much I made on any given day. But I do remember asking, as usual, to be paid in pennies instead of bills.

That way, it felt like more.

Ma Ma usually agreed, but only for one dollar.

My pennies fit in a box the size of a deck of cards. I jangled it. It was my tambourine all the way to the East Broadway subway station.

As we descended the stairs of the station, pain

burned at the back of my neck, uncoiling and worming its way down my spine, inch by inch.

* * *

We harvest the silk and eat the silkworm.

Once, before Mei Guo was ever part of our thoughts, I ate a fried silkworm. Ma Ma bought it off the street from the dark, hairy man with the greasy cart. Ma Ma biked past him every day after she picked me up from preschool. Those rides were my favorite. From my bucket seat, I pointed at the signs we passed and asked her what each character said and how it was pronounced and what it meant. She answered unfailingly through her white cloth mask—a biking necessity in the pollution—even though I asked her about the same characters for days on end.

I panted when I saw the shiny, greasy cart, beckoning its hello under the sleepy sun. Adorning the cart were various brown-yellow creatures and body parts on sticks: scorpions, frog legs, silkworms, crickets. I poked at Ma Ma's back and begged her to stop. She always pretended to consider it for a second before agreeing. The seasoned whole quails were my absolute favorite. I felt like a da ren because the vendor would smile at me, say xie xie, and hand me—not Ma Ma, but **me**—the stick that ran up the middle of the prostrate bird. Ma Ma would get going again and the rest of the ride would blur by. I always started with the beak. First, I poked Ma Ma in the back with it, then I stuffed it in my mouth, crunching on it and working my way past the eyeballs, the brains, and down the spine.

But one day, the quails were sold out.

The vendor gave me a silkworm instead, free, he said, for his favorite little customer. I stared at its ridges, disappointed that there was no beak. I could not even make out eyeballs, which were the best part. I chewed on one end, but did not know whether I was eating the face or the butt. It didn't seem to be a thing that had once been alive. Yet it was savory, just like the crab.

Chapter 6

NATIVE SPEAKER

....

I had many first days of school, and I never liked any of them. On the eve of my first-ever day of school in Zhong Guo, when Ma Ma told me I would be starting school the next morning, I dissolved into a puddle of sadness. This had Ma Ma and Ba Ba laughing, something da ren liked to do when kids cried.

"Ni ku shen me?"

Da ren were always asking me to justify my emotions.

School was scary, I sputtered. I didn't know what it was and I wanted to stay home, where I could play with my dolls and train set.

You'll like it, they promised.

But the more they insisted, the more I resisted, and the next morning found my face bloated from tears. I refused to get dressed until finally Ma Ma had to rush out of the door for her class.

Ba Ba stayed. He sat across from me, staring me into submission.

It won't work, I thought. I was his child and

if there ever was someone more stubborn than him, it was me.

There was a Chinese idiom I came to know later because Ma Ma and Ba Ba would repeat it to me in those moments: "Purple comes from blue but is superior to blue." It was inevitable, they seemed to believe, that I would one day outshine them in the best and worst ways.

After untold minutes of staring at the half-genuine misery painted on my crumpled face, Ba Ba relented.

"Hao, hao."

He walked to the kitchen and returned with my favorite kind of ice pop, as much for the taste as for the fact that it turned my tongue blue. "I know what it's like. I never wanted to go to school, either."

"Really?" I asked, eyes still wet but wide open.

He gave a quiet, sad nod. I saw him go away for a while, like he did sometimes when we played with the shadow birds at night. Then he offered, "How about we put off school for another day and instead go to the zoo?"

I nodded my head as vigorously as I could while still holding on to the quickly disappearing pop.

And so I donned my jacket and my new backpack—why not carry it, Ba Ba said, since it went well with my polka-dot dress—and skipped downstairs, climbing victoriously into the seat at the back of Ba Ba's bicycle. How smart was I, I thought as we passed through town, that I had tricked Ba Ba out of a full day of school. I could keep this up forever, and every day we'd just go to the zoo.

When we turned the last corner, though, it was not the smell of grass, monkeys, and manure that greeted us. Instead, it was the sight of red gates, of a hundred little kids just like me, running around with their pigtails and their backpacks. Worst of all, they did not even seem upset that they'd been conned into being there. By the time Ba Ba got off his seat and kicked down the stand of his bike, I was crying again. In disbelief, I watched him lead me by the hand to the gate and place my hand in that of a woman with big square glasses. Through the betrayal, I saw him give me a kiss on each cheek and tell me that Ma Ma would come get me in a few hours. That I should be good for Lao Shi. That I should have fun. I watched as he kicked up the stand of his bike, mounted it, and rode away. And in that moment, I swore that I would not forget the joy-turned-bitterness of betrayal, that I would never believe Ba Ba again.

But I did believe him again. The next morning, in fact, when I pleaded to skip school that day—I couldn't go back there again—not today, not so soon, and again Ba Ba seemed to relent and again I climbed aboard the bike happily, thrilled to actually go to the zoo this time. I forgot all about my resolve from the previous morning until we turned the corner and I saw the red gates yet again.

The next morning, I cried again, but I did not ask to stay home. And I never again believed Ba Ba—not in the same way; not when he told me we were going somewhere fun; not when he told me he'd come back from Mei Guo in a month, then another month, then the month after that; and certainly not when he told me that everything would be okay.

* * *

The first day of school in Mei Guo was also full of false promises, but in the worst way, because they were of a new kind. For weeks, when we had walked past the neighborhood school, gated with a barbed-wire fence, Ma Ma and Ba Ba had told me that it was the school I would be starting at in September, and each time, Ba Ba reminded me that on that day in September, I was to tell everyone that I had been born in Mei Guo, that I had always lived here. Each time he said it, I wondered why it mattered, and how anyone could believe me.

We only ever saw brown children funnel into the graffitied building. I wondered why Ba Ba wanted me there, given the rules that he had prescribed me for our new life, the ones that I had memorized without question: None of the other races were our friends. The white people had the most money, but the others were dangerous, too. To all of them, we were weak, easy targets who wouldn't fight back.

Just remember this, Qian Qian: we are safe only with our own kind.

On the actual day in September when Ba Ba brought me to the school, my face again stained with sadness, he seemed to see for the first time how very different we were from everyone else, how unwelcome we were, how poorly we fit in.

Staring down the pipeline of my future as playground roadkill, Ba Ba stopped short of approaching the school and turned to me. He asked whether I wanted to start school a different day. Sure from our past that he would only lead me to an even scarier school, I nodded anyway, and followed him with bated breath as we walked away from the school, down the blocks, into the subway, onto the train, then after many, many stops, out of the station, and several blocks down. I did not resume my natural breathing until I saw that he had brought me to the door of the sweatshop. I ran upstairs, eager to find Ma Ma and get to work before Ba Ba changed his mind. I spent the rest of the day wondering why Ba Ba had told the truth this time, and whether I would be spending the rest of my days in that dark room, yanking threads loose and then cutting them.

The next morning, I thought Ba Ba would bring me to the sweatshop again, but just as we approached the grimy street entrance, its steps lined with abandoned bottles of yellow and brown liquids, Ba Ba crossed the street and I chased along. He stopped there for a second and knelt down to my level to utter the sentence that I already knew by heart: "Gao su ta men ni zai zhe li sheng de, ni yi zhi jiu zai Mei Guo." **Tell them I was born here, that I have always lived in America.** I nodded while repeating the sentence back.

Ba Ba then climbed up the few small steps of the red building I'd admired for weeks, as much for its clean façade as for its windows, which were not only many in number but wide and papered with beautiful colors and fun drawings. It was the kind of building where, when you looked at it, you knew life abounded within. It was beautiful for the same reason that the sweatshop was not.

Ba Ba led me into the lobby and down

the halls, which matched the windows in its colorful papering—of cats, dogs, babies, and rainbows—of real and surreal drawings of childhood that I hadn't seen since entering Mei Guo's gray world. During that walk, my new world grew many shades brighter, and I passed by one drawing after another to both the palpitation of excitement and the chorus of fear and dread.

Having found the room of da ren he seemed to be looking for, Ba Ba guided us in and led me to a tall and skinny man with a handsome but very rectangular face. The lines of his face were so severe and angular that he reminded me of a robot. He didn't seem to speak Chinese, though, choosing instead to talk to me in the sharp, brusque tones that I had begun to recognize as English. I did what I could, smiling and staring back blankly, while Ba Ba exchanged the same tones with the man.

Ba Ba then knelt down and told me to be good, guai, and to remember what he had told me time and again. He said that Ma Ma would meet me outside, on the steps, when the day was over. And then he was gone, leaving me with the tall robot, who steered me up the stairs and down another hall, full of more colors that were already losing their effect on me.

Robot Man brought me into a large, sunny classroom—the sunniest room I'd been in since boarding the plane. The room was full of kids grouped into fours, with each of their desks pushed together into rectangular clusters. At each rectangle, two kids on one side faced two kids on the other side. Facing the front of the room on each desk was a white placard with letters on them. The cards all stood at attention facing a woman in a long dress who was writing on the chalkboard. She was Chinese and wore a big smile. She reminded me of an ah yi, an auntie, one of Ma Ma's friends back home.

All eyes turned to me as I entered the room with Robot Man. I felt the warmth of embarrassment take over my face and neck. Without even realizing it, I resorted to the mantra Ba Ba had bestowed upon me: "Wo zai zhe li sheng de, wo yi zhi jiu zai Mei Guo." But each time I assured myself under my breath that I belonged there, that I was born there, I believed it that much less.

There was a pause, too long for comfort, before anyone did anything. No one smiled at me but Ah Yi. Relieved to have something to distract me from the mantra and the sharp pangs in my stomach it stirred up, I smiled back at her as the Robot Man shared a few incomprehensible tones with her, and then turned to me with a quick, efficient grin, before clicking out of the room.

Ah yi, who told me her name was Tang Lao Shi, spoke Mandarin with a tongue that seemed to have been stung by a bee. None of the words sounded quite right, but with some careful deliberation—which, I realized only in hindsight, must have convinced her that I was not too bright—I pieced together what she was trying to say.

After some whispering by Tang Lao Shi and reshuffling of my classmates, including a girl in a pink dress who was not happy to be separated from her friend in a ponytail, Tang Lao Shi sat me at the cluster of four closest to the chalkboard. I turned to examine the girl with the ponytail, who was now next to me.

"Wo jiao Janie." She wore a scowl as she said this. Her Mandarin was better than Tang Lao Shi's, but it was caked with an accent I had never heard before.

"Wo jiao Wang Qian."

"Wang Qian," Tang Lao Shi assured me in Mandarin, "Janie will translate everything for you, because everyone only speaks English or Cantonese. But if you have a question, just raise your hand, okay?"

I nodded.

"Can you write your name on this card here for everybody?"

I wrote the two Chinese characters that had

taken me months to perfect. The second character in my name was particularly hard and I
could never get it quite right without sticking
my tongue slightly. As I finished it, I looked up
and saw Tang Lao Shi grin, and all too conscious
of my face, I retracted my tongue.

"No, in English. Can you write it in English?"

"I don't know English."

"Pinyin?"

That I knew. And with an uneven hand I drew
out in even more uneven letters my pinyin
name: WANG QIAN.

"Can you write it . . . can you write it small-
case? Smaller?"

Why, I thought, would she want it smaller? I
had written it as large as I could so she could see
it from the front. Shrugging, I duplicated what I
had written on the other side of the placard, this
time writing as small as I could: WANG QIAN.

Tang Lao Shi's forehead bunched up. "Not like
that . . . small . . . lowercase. . . . Do you know
the difference?"

I had no idea what she was trying to say and
figured it must be that beesting on her tongue
that made her speak funny. Picking up on my
blank look, Tang Lao Shi gave up.

"It's okay, Qian. You will learn."

I had never had anyone call me "Qian" without a "Wang" before it or another "Qian" after

it, but for the rest of the day, it was all Tang
Lao Shi and Janie called me. Just like that, I had
been reborn as a girl divorced from her family
name, orphaned from her Chinese past.

I spent the morning in a thick fog. It felt as
if I were back on the plane again, with the doors
shut to my ears. Janie said very little to me and
bothered to translate a few spare words here
and there only when Tang Lao Shi admonished
her. After what felt like weeks, Tang Lao Shi told
us it was lunchtime and all the kids got up. Not
knowing what else to do, I followed Janie, who
ran to the girl in the pink dress and locked arms
with her. The two turned back to look at me
before turning around to whisper and giggle.

You don't have to whisper, I thought. **I don't
speak English anyway.**

After I followed the laughing pair down
the stairs and through two sets of halls, Janie
unlinked her arm and turned to me again.

Maybe, I thought, she was ready to be
friends now.

"Qian," she declared in a self-serious tone, "I am
Tang Lao Shi's favorite. That's why she chose me
to help you. But I will help you only during class,
and then, only when I feel like it. Got that?"

I stared back into her large brown eyes, nar-
rowed into a glare.

"During lunch, you are on your own. And don't you ever think of complaining about me to Tang Lao Shi. No one understands you and your loser language but me."

Neither of us moved, and I continued staring, locked in stalemate.

"It's lunch now. Get lost."

And with that, she went back to her giggly friend.

I had to use the bathroom—I had had to use the restroom for hours, in fact; I waited because I had not wanted to annoy Janie by asking— but I didn't know where it was, so I fell in with the current of kids who flowed into a large room with long benches and tables like at the sweat- shop, except it was brighter and smelled better. Across the hall from the large room were two doors. I stepped away from the large room and approached them just as a boy came out of one of them, the sounds of water running and toilets flushing emanating from within. As soon as the door swung shut after him, I pushed my way in.

I was so eager to relieve myself that I did not realize something was wrong until I got to the stall doors. And then I had to blink to see that, in fact, many things were wrong. It took me too long to see there were only boys in the room. By then, they had already started laughing and pointing. My cheeks flushing with heat, I ran out of the boys' bathroom through the swinging door, only to bump into two more boys. After a moment, they also pointed their fingers at me, chortling. Their faces were still scrunched up in laughter and their fingers still raised at me as they pushed through the swinging door of the bathroom.

I placed my hands on either side of my burning red face and avoided the eyes of my classmates, many of whom had already seen me and were still laughing. I walked into the adjacent door, after a girl who gave me a sad smile, and ran into a stall, slamming the door shut. After I relieved myself, I stayed seated without flushing. I sat there thinking about how in Zhong Guo, my class had a single bathroom that boys and girls took turns using. I sat there thinking about what Ba Ba and Ma Ma had told me: that Mandarin was not the loser language but the language of the educated, and anyone who didn't speak it well was likely a farmer. I sat there and puzzled over all the ways in which my simple life had changed, all the while listening to the rumbling of my tummy as the large, white-faced clock with black numbers ticked the seconds and minutes away, until I guessed it would soon be time to return to class. Then I slowly stood up, flushed, and left my only sanctuary.

The rest of the day passed in the same way the morning had. A handful of times, I dared to ask Janie what was going on, but she acted like I did not exist. At one point, Tang Lao Shi came over to see if I was understanding everything, and Janie started talking before I could respond, answering for me by explaining something in English, which caused Tang Lao Shi to look at me with her forehead scrunched up again. I said nothing, not wanting to alienate the closest thing I had to a friend, but something at the bottom of my stomach ached and I contented myself with resting my face on my forearms, one stacked upon the other, until the end of the day.

At the end of the day, I followed the stream of classmates as I had at lunch. I felt Tang Lao Shi's steady eyes on me but told myself to ignore the ache in my stomach, the ache in my head, the ache everywhere. It would all be better, I thought, once I met Ma Ma on the steps outside, and had some rice at the sweatshop to settle my empty tummy.

* * *

In Zhong Guo, I had adjusted quickly to school. After the second day, Ba Ba no longer needed to pretend to take me to the zoo. After the second week, I no longer awoke with tears; instead, I was excited, and often rushed Ma Ma and Ba Ba out the door so I could see my friends sooner.

I had collected friends easily. I was precociously vain, often wearing a brand-new dress, top, or ribbon Ma Ma had designed and sewn for me. And beyond that, I was bossy. At that age, it was all I needed to be a leader. During recess, before our parents picked us up, I led my gaggle of friends—all but one or two of the girls in my class, all of us clad in dresses of bright, clashing colors—in a game of my choice. Often it was an old favorite, like duck, duck, goose or musical chairs, but at times I even had the power to make up a new game altogether. Those rarely worked out, since I never thought the rules out far enough. But my friends played anyway. They never went against me.

One of our old standbys was mother hen. All but one of us lined up in a row, each with her hands on the shoulders of the girl in front. It was the duty of the mother hen (the one at the very front of the line, usually me) to protect her baby chicks (those behind her in line). It was the task of the odd girl out—the eagle, the vulture, or some other hungry predator—to "catch" a chick by tapping her anywhere. The "caught" chick would then become the vulture, and the game would start anew, with the mother hen forever at her protective post.

It didn't take long for the game to seep into my friendships. I became the mother hen in matters big and small. My friends asked me everything: What should Tang Yuan wear to school tomorrow? What should Xiao Hong ask her mother to cook for dinner? Should Fei Fei poop at school or wait until she was picked up? So it came to be that I barked out orders left and right, my authority feeding upon itself.

One day, just after we had resumed school after the New Year break, Ma Ma met me at the school gates with her eyes aglow.

"Qian Qian!" she exclaimed. "You've made me a celebrity!"

I responded with a wet peck on her cheek. "What did I do?"

Ma Ma explained to me that she had just met Xiao Hong's mother, who was so excited to be meeting the famous Wang Qian's mother.

"She really was! She even said, 'Oh, so **you** are Wang Qian's mother! It's wonderful to meet you!'

"Then she said Hong Hong couldn't do anything over break without lamenting, 'Oh I should ask Wang Qian what to do—she would know!' And, 'If only I had school today, I could ask Wang Qian.'

"She even thanked me for making her daughter so excited to go back to school! Can you believe it?"

It was true, Xiao Hong had been particularly excited to see me that morning, but so had many others. She pestered me all day through class and recess with questions, so much so that Lao Shi made her sit in a corner in silence for ten minutes. It had been hard to focus on the lesson. For the first time, I saw that there was a downside to being a bossy know-it-all.

I was happy, though, that I had brought pride to my sweet Ma Ma, so I said nothing and smiled as she boasted on.

"How did you do it, Qian Qian?"

"Oh, I don't know, mei shen me. I just answer their questions."

Ma Ma beamed back at me, and for the following weeks she retold the story of the famous Wang Qian to family, friends, strangers.

* * *

On the morning of my second day of school in Mei Guo, Ba Ba dropped me off at the school lobby. From there, I went up the stairs and found the classroom. I was sitting obediently by Janie's side, feeling the growing knots in my stomach and anticipating the slow day of incomprehension to come, when Tang Lao Shi gestured me to her desk at the front of the classroom.

"Qian," she said so warmly that I knew bad news had to follow, "ni gen wo lai."

I was to follow her.

My mind raced. I had been found out. I should have said more of the phrase Ba Ba had given me! Was it too late?

"Lai, na zhe." It seemed to be a permanent change, because Tang Lao Shi grabbed my backpack. Yet another permanent change. Didn't Tang Lao Shi know that my backpack was already exhausted from flying all the way from Zhong Guo to Brooklyn and then Brooklyn to here? But of course how could she know? **Wo zai zhe li sheng de. Wo yi zhi jiu zai Mei Guo.**

After issuing a quick, stern sentence to the class, Tang Lao Shi took my hand and walked me down to the end of the hall, to a room with large windows—one window looked into the hallway but another divided the interior of the room in half. I saw one child playing in a life-size fort while another around my age sat at a small desk, coloring with a blue crayon inside and outside an outline of a rabbit. There were still others milling about the room, but they have faded into the recesses of my memory.

Through her swollen-tongue Mandarin, Tang Lao Shi explained to me that this was the classroom for students who did not speak English. The room was also for, as I could barely make out, children with "special needs." I had no idea what "special needs" were, but I asked who else in the classroom did not speak English. She told me I was the only one.

There was one teacher—much younger than any of the others I had seen in the school—for the many students in that classroom. Tang Lao Shi introduced me to her quickly before leaving, but I had so little interaction with that teacher that I don't even remember her name. The teacher had kind, soft eyes, but they were red and had bags under them. She led me to a tiny table across the room from the coloring boy and handed me a picture book with a few Chinese words on each page.

I explained to her in Mandarin that I had read that book years ago and that I was far beyond picture books in Chinese. If she understood Mandarin, she chose not to respond. She spent most of the time with the coloring boy, who had by then moved beyond the blue bunny and was drawing on the desk.

The rest of the day passed in solitude. No one talked to me, and I was left with just the picture book for company. Lunch was less painful, though. There was a bathroom just across the hall from the classroom and I hid there in peace and quiet for the hour. The teacher did not seem to notice me at all, and I wondered whether I should just go to the sweatshop instead.

In the end, I decided to return to the classroom—I had lived in Zhong Guo for seven years, after all, and had some obedience drilled into me—but in an act of defiance, I grabbed a few English picture books on the way back in and spent my afternoon with those instead. One in particular featured a giant red dog, which over the course of the afternoon, I came to understand as being named Clifford, because that was the word on the cover and on every page where he showed up. I felt fortunate that Ba Ba had taught me many of the English letters and sounds before leaving Zhong Guo. The rest of the day passed in much more joy as I shared in the company of Clifford, his happy owner— a little white girl with yellow hair whom I came to envy—and their friends.

* * *

Trusting that I had learned to cross the street and get to the sweatshop on my own on the first day, Ma Ma did not pick me up on the school steps on the second day. When I got to the stool by her side, I stayed silent about the change in my schooling during our shift and on the walk home. As I had come to expect, Ma Ma was quiet after our shift—silent but for the sniffles she tried to hide, and which I pretended not to notice. I didn't know why pretending was necessary, only that she wanted me to do it and I, badly as ever, wanted to make Ma Ma happy.

Ba Ba didn't come home from his shift at the laundromat until I was already tucked into bed, eyes and ears muggy with sleep. Ba Ba's work was hard, but not as hard as the job he told us he had had before we had arrived. Back then, he had worked long hours in a place for people who he said were crazy and had to be locked up. He was the only Chinese person who worked there. He told us that the other workers had called him names and banded together so that he was always the one stuck with the worst tasks, like cleaning the toilets and showering the patients, chasing them down the hall when they ran out of the bathroom, water dripping from their bare butts and legs as they slid on the floors. Ba Ba explained that in our new world, we were thought of as just Asian—like the Koreans, the Japanese, the Filipinos, and the Thai—and together we were all considered the weakest race, small and fragile. He told me that he had been considered a full man in Zhong Guo, but that he was no longer one in Mei Guo. Maybe that wasn't how it was among the rich—he said he had no way of knowing, that maybe one day I could find out—but it was how it went among the poor. Until I was rich, I had to be careful, he said. We all had to be very careful.

Ma Ma and Ba Ba's bed was no more than an arm's length away from mine, and usually when Ba Ba returned, I half awakened—amid warm dreams of being back home with Lao Lao and Lao Ye—to whispers, grunts, and moans.

Ba Ba liked to brag about how many dollars he had collected from random pants pockets, by turns gloating about his finds and warning me to never be as careless as lao wai, the white people, were. I assumed that that was what those late-night whispers were about, but I could not explain the other sounds. I intuited only that I was not supposed to hear them, so as those nights piled up on top of one another, I developed a habit of ducking my face under the comforters. I also covered my ears with my hands and made quiet grumbling noises until the moaning faded into soft breaths and snores. It was hard to be sure when they were over, and I dreaded uncovering my ears, so I stayed grumbling under the covers for as long as I could. Sometimes I fell back asleep that way, waking to the morning light like a beetle, curled up into myself.

* * *

On our way to school the next morning, I finally told Ba Ba about the change, and he said that Tang Lao Shi must have insisted on sending me to the other class, and why hadn't I claimed to be an American, as he had told me to?

"If you had said you were born here, Qian Qian, they wouldn't have treated us like this."

Years later, Ba Ba told me that on my second day of school, the Robot Man, the vice principal, had confronted him about the fake address Ba Ba had used to get me into the school. Yes, it was in Manhattan, the Robot Man had said, but it was not a residential address; it was a warehouse, and an abandoned one at that. Ba Ba did not dare push back, for fear of further questioning. In my mind's eye, I picture him keeling over with apologies, explaining that I could not go to our local school, where no one spoke Chinese, and that I was a good, easy child who would make no trouble. Whatever he did or said that day, they had decided to let him go and let me stay.

Only later, after living many years in fear, would I understand that the risks were much lower than we believed at the time. But in the vacuum of anxiety that was undocumented life, fear was gaseous: it expanded to fill our entire world until it was all we could breathe.

In the weeks that followed, as the leaves changed colors and the air grew sharp, I spent my school days much as I had spent my second day of school: in the company of the Cat in the Hat, the Very Hungry Caterpillar, the Berenstain Bears, Amelia Bedelia, and Shel Silverstein. I made my way through the classroom bookcase as the coloring boy made his way through the crayon box: every day he went through a different color, and every day I learned a few new words. I read until my loneliness dulled, and I felt myself to be in the good company of all my vibrantly colored, two-dimensional friends. I read until excitement replaced hopelessness. I marveled that I was teaching myself to read English—slowly, of course, but without an adult next to me. I was excited to meet the whole new worlds waiting for me on the bookshelves and tables. Each book had a place and a role. Even the ones meant for the boy who colored were among the most helpful guides in my journey through basic English, because I could press the large buttons that spoke words to me loudly. So it was that I felt my way around colors, shapes, and animals in our new country.

By October, I developed a habit of pleading with Ba Ba to get me back in Ms. Tang's classroom, showing off the English I had taught myself. I must have been somewhat convincing, or at least annoying, because when we got to the red-brick building one day, Ba Ba went into the school with me, and asked me to wait outside the office on the first floor.

When he came out, I was sitting on the floor and leaning against the wall, my knees weary with impatience. He looked as frazzled as he had when he went in, but in his eyes was a foreign glint of victory.

"Okay, Qian Qian, you can go back to Ms. Tang's class. But they are going to treat you like any other student."

"Good!"

"Are you sure? You're going to have to take tests like everyone else, and follow along somehow. Can you do that?"

I didn't know that I could for sure. But as Sister Bear had felt at the end of her first day of school, I had the sense that I would be able to figure it out as I went. That had been enough for her, so that was enough for me.

"Yes, Ba Ba." I barely took the time to reach for a hug before running up the stairway and toward Ms. Tang's classroom.

* * *

There was a spelling test during my first week back in Ms. Tang's class. By spelling out words that were on the signs hung around the room— A for Apple, D for Dog—writing gibberish, and copying not so covertly from a handwritten list of words I had in my pocket (Ms. Tang caught me twice, though she said nothing), I scored a proud 33 percent. So began my path to graduating from college with an English degree fifteen years later.

By Halloween, when Ms. Tang gave each of us a tiny pumpkin and a knife with the smallest and dullest of blades, I was able to generally muddle through class without incurring Janie's wrath. In fact, when Ms. Tang told us to empty out the pumpkin's belly innards before carving three triangles—two facing down at the top for eyes, one facing up at the middle for a mouth—I understood instantly and went to work. And by November, I was even able to tell when Janie took credit for my answers, which I occasionally offered by raising my hand and then whispering to her. So proud was I to have figured out what was going on that I didn't even bother to rat on her. I knew that soon I wouldn't need her at all. Soon, I would make Ma Ma and Ba Ba proud, and it would be just as if I had always been here, as if I had been born here, a native English speaker at last.

Chapter 7

DUMPLINGS

·········

America was a living lesson in hunger. Our kitchen contained more cockroaches than food. I learned quickly and out of necessity that I could get away with tiny, nimble thefts from our roommates' shelves, but because they were small enough to go unnoticed, they fed me only in spirit.

I also learned to be vindictive. In payback for the jeers and faces, I developed a habit of dipping the other family's toothbrushes into the toilet whenever I was in the bathroom. But over time, this didn't seem like enough. So one day, while pondering another act of minimal thievery, I studied the contents of the fridge and noticed a container of vanilla ice cream. The paper carton was cheaply made: instead of a lid, the carton simply closed shut with four extended flaps. I peeled each flap open to find the ice cream, untouched, white, and marked only by brown specks and the flaps' indentations. I knew that a missing spoonful would be too risky. So instead, I contented myself with running my tongue, flat, across the entire surface. I tasted only a few small bits of sugar and cream. It left me wanting more, but I knew I could not get away with it. If discovered by the roommate—the one who put on the squinting, bucktoothed face every time I saw him—he would just scream "chink" louder in Ma Ma's face next time.

This left me only one choice. On his family's shelf in the pantry, I recovered four white-and-blue packets of salt, next to two brazen cockroaches who looked back at me before sauntering away. I opened the packets all at once, ripping them across the top, turning their open mouths upside down over the ice cream, and distributing them with a smooth motion across the surface. Someone watching me might have thought that I had done it before, that I was a professional ice cream salter.

I put the lid back and returned it to the freezer, its label facing in as it had been when I found it. I closed the door and took a step away before something dawned on me. I stepped back and removed the carton from the freezer again. This time, I placed it upside down, with its top lid on the island. I grabbed two more white-and-blue packets from the same shelf before unfolding the bottom of the paper carton, gently ripping apart the flaps congealed on top of each other. I then salted the bottom surface before placing the flaps back into place and orienting the container as I had found it in its frozen home.

*   *   *

We didn't eat much in the kitchen, but I spent a lot of time there anyway. At night, long after all of the tenants had eaten their last meals and had returned to their one-room apartments, I snuck back. I liked to cower under the light switch and listen to the **tap-tap-tap**s against the wood-like walls across the entire kitchen. Counting to an arbitrary number in silence—sometimes ten, sometimes two—I stayed crouched but reached up and flicked the light switch as quickly as I could. I then watched the walls as they receded in color from dark brown to tan as the cockroaches that papered them in darkness retreated to their lairs. As soon as the walls regained their full tan color, I flicked the switch back down again, waiting and listening as a single tap emerged, then another, and then another, a new chorus crescendoing. And then, as with mother hen, the game would start anew.

*   *   *

In daylight, time passed in a molasses of hunger. That I might be far hungrier in the Beautiful Country than I had ever been in my short, lucky life in Zhong Guo occurred to me just a few days after we got off that plane. When we walked past bakeries and stores now, there was no pausing, no pushing our noses up against the window, no lingering before we decided to go in because we deserved to treat ourselves. It was almost as if Ma Ma no longer saw my hunger.

Hunger was a constant, reliable friend in Mei Guo. She came second only to loneliness. Hunger slept only when I did, and sometimes not even then. In China, all I needed to do was say that she was there, and Ma Ma would find food for me. In Mei Guo, I quickly learned that I could not voice her presence. It only hurt Ma Ma. Her face reflected the pangs in my stomach, and the few times when I ventured to ask for food, Ma Ma did something she had never done before: she told me that hunger was good, that it was fine to feel shaky and distracted, and that I should see if I could hold on until the cold sweat came, because that would mean that I was really growing and really getting stronger. If that was true, I must have grown extraordinarily strong that first year in Mei Guo, because I felt the cold sweat come on every time I walked past a grocery store or restaurant, and every time I saw someone my age slurping a melting ice-cream cone.

* * *

In time, I found ways to help Ma Ma without her knowing. As my English grew, I learned that there were some things that Ma Ma didn't know how to do, but that I did. Over time, she came to see that, too. As I stopped asking her questions, she started asking more of me.

"Qian Qian," she would say in a quiet, biding tone, and I would know a Big Question was coming.

Then she would launch into questions, like should she ask Ba Ba for more cash for groceries? No, I'd say, we don't want to deal with his temper tonight. We had twenty dollars every week, and that would have to be enough.

Should we go back to Zhong Guo? Yes, of course, always. China was home and America smelled like pee.

As these questions came and she listened to my answers, not always in her actions but always at least in the moment, I learned that life for adults was much harder than I had previously realized.

One night, on our walk home from the sweatshop after a full day of school and a fuller day of snipping threads, I turned to Ma Ma and told her that I no longer needed breakfast.

"Wei shen me?"

Because like lunch, breakfast was free at school.

"Ah! Wei shen me bu zao shuo? Ke yi sheng bu

shao." Why didn't I tell her sooner? We stood to save a lot of money.

Actually, because we lived a long commute away and I never got enough sleep after our sweatshop evenings, I hadn't mentioned it earlier because I never got to school early enough to eat the mythical free breakfasts I had only ever heard about.

I didn't say this, though. Instead, I apologized to Ma Ma for being greedy, and said that she would no longer need to feed me two meals at home.

From then on, her face glowed a little bit brighter, and whenever she phoned home to Lao Lao, telling her of the beautiful home we did not live in, the overflowing, steaming bowls we only dreamed about, she also told her about how wonderful and generous Mei Guo was. Here, they fed kids for free twice a day!

* * *

My reality was far darker than the vision in Lao Lao's and Ma Ma's minds. In the long hours ticking toward noon, I spent my time in the classroom going through my memory's catalog of delicious meals I'd had in Zhong Guo: roasted duck covered with oily, crispy skin; stir-fried tofu with onions and peppers; stewed beef dripping with soy sauce. Over the course of the morning, my hunger fed on itself and cast shadows over everything, its heart beating with the ticking of the classroom clock, its cavernous mouth swallowing the classroom whole.

By twenty minutes past noon, the chalk on the board was powdered sugar, my number-two pencils were breadsticks, and my teacher's coiled hair was a taro bun. And the instant lunchtime arrived, all the energy in my body drained to my legs, which carried me to the school's auditorium-cafeteria, where I lined up with my back stiff and straight against the wall, holding my place in line among the other poor, unfed, unwashed kids. It would be several minutes more before the rich kids trickled in slothily, towing multicolored lunch bags full of homemade food. And though we poor kids were the first to arrive, we were the last to eat. As the richer, cleaner, less hungry kids opened up their containers of yummy meats, sandwiches, and cheese sticks, ate half of their bounty and discarded the rest, we stood on the sidelines, stomachs grumbling and mouths drooling, leaning on the walls. We were the rich's Atlases, charged with holding up their lunchroom ceiling as they ate.

The poor kids, we never looked one another in the eyes. We exchanged a few words whenever one cut another in line—no one wanted to be later to receive the congealed brown sludge that the lunch ladies, with their gray hair trapped under nets, slopped onto our disposable trays. But beyond that, acknowledging one another would bring into too much focus the fact that we each were just like the hungry, stinky kid standing next to us, with an itchy, flaky scalp and an itchier dry throat.

Usually, by the time the line started moving, most of the rich kids were already finished eating and out at recess. The beginning of our lunch was the end of theirs. By then, I was often light-headed and dizzy, and I trudged through the line listlessly until I plopped down at one of the table-benches to swallow my entire lunch whole. It took just a few minutes for my stomach to bounce from the ache of emptiness to the ache of eating too much, too quickly. It took much longer before I registered with any satisfaction the new, temporary fullness. But by then, I was already downing the free carton of milk, eager to fill my stomach with something, anything.

Out in the playground, rarely was I able to run or play. My stomach and bowels spent the afternoons in a civil war, wrestling with each other as the pockets of air that formed in the morning did a painful dance with the clumps of food and milk. I spent most afternoons with one hand on careful guard in front of my tummy, in case it betrayed gassy gurgles to my less tortured classmates. I trained my mind on controlling the sounds of my belly, and on the rice that awaited after school, at the sweatshop.

* * *

As bad as normal days were, half days were worse. Most often, I forgot they were happening and instead spent the morning luxuriating in the happy delusion that soon I would have lunch. The realization always came in a jolt. My shoes filled with lead as my classmates skipped to the lobby. I cheered and celebrated along with everyone else, if only to mask the rumbles from my stomach. It seemed like everyone else always had fun plans and big lunches for those abbreviated days, though I'm sure some were, like me, quietly dreading the early end of the school day. But for the most part, my classmates talked so much of their great plans that I was often relieved by the time I got to the door. From there, they went bounding down the street toward their embracing homes and piping-hot meals, leaving me alone to walk toward the Confucius statue on the corner of Division and Bowery.

Confucius was more noble on some days than others. Some days, Confucius had large clumps of pigeon poop on his shoulders, and sometimes he even had a pigeon standing proudly atop his head. The statue threw my life into relief. It was a shitty day even for Confucius. Who was I to complain?

Bread crumbs often lay scattered before the Confucius statue, a feast for the birds of Chinatown. The sight of the bread crumbs, browned with dirt, was especially painful on half days, when drool pooled in my mouth and my stomach gnawed on itself with particular ferocity.

On half days, I tried to walk past the statue with rare focus, determined to avoid the crumbs. On most of those afternoons, I was torn between the free rice that awaited me in that dank, dark sweatshop room and the hungry freedom that abounded outside. I usually lasted only an hour before succumbing to the pull of the cavernous food.

I had a typical route that I took before reporting to the sweatshop. I turned onto Catherine Street and then East Broadway, making my way past the shops. I loved browsing in my favorite store, one that sold stationery, touching a Hello Kitty pen here and a Keroppi sticker there, dreaming of the day when I might get to take one home. But my stomach was easier to ignore when my arms and legs were also complaining, so I continued down East Broadway, hoping to chance upon free samples or newly abandoned food.

Chinatown bakeries rarely helped because they did not have the bowls of free bread that I had been lucky to find a few times in white stores. Instead, Chinatown bakeries just taunted my senses, causing me to drool more. The fish smells from the markets were a handy antidote to this, and I was grateful for the nauseating scents by the time I got to the Manhattan Bridge overpass. I was luckiest when I came upon a restaurant just as a busboy dumped pails of brown-gray water off the edge of the sidewalk. Staring at that muddy river helped stave off the angry hunger roiling my stomach.

Sometimes, though, it backfired: sometimes the sludge and water reminded me only of black sesame and chocolate milk. Sometimes even the fish smell—which the white tourists unfailingly wrinkled their large noses at—lulled me back to a warmer, safer place in Zhong Guo, where it was once possible to eat too much and be too full.

I typically pushed on until Pike Street, which found me standing in front of Hong Kong Supermarket. On lucky days, there were free samples, and I savored each chew of those morsels. But on occasion the samples only made the hunger angrier, and it was all I could do to run to the open mouth of the sweatshop's rice cooker, succumbing to the cold sweat oozing out of my pores.

On one specific half day, there had been no samples at Hong Kong Supermarket, and I had pushed onward along East Broadway. I soon came upon Seward Park, by the F station. There, a mirage greeted me: a truck of people handing containers to a line of old and not-so-old Chinese people. My nose knew the containers' contents long before my eyes did. The scent of fried rice was so vivid that I had to pinch myself with shaky fingers.

I joined the queue without thought. Only while waiting, while the tremors in my arms and legs came on full display, did I start thinking. As the processional moved, from the twenty-some people before me to fifteen, then ten, I began squinting my eyes toward the window of the truck, attempting to make out who was handing out the food.

They were uniformed, I saw.

Were they asking for IDs?

I didn't think so, but I couldn't tell for sure.

Should I risk it?

What would I give them if they did ask?

I needed certainty, so I squinted some more. I squinted until my eyes became slits and I became a caricature of my race. I squinted with all of the remaining force of my being. But I still couldn't be sure enough.

I would never be sure enough.

Still, I stayed in line, my body fighting my brain in a living deadlock.

Then there were seven people in front of me and I still couldn't be sure that I wouldn't be caught.

Always walk the other way when you see the police, Qian Qian. Ba Ba's voice guided me wherever I went. **If anyone asks you for documents, say you don't know, say that your ba ba has them. Say that you were born here, that you've always lived in America.**

This was not China, and I could no longer get by on the color of my skin and my gap-toothed smile. I was no longer normal: I was never to forget that.

Six people.

My entire body joined my hands in their shaking, but it had nothing to do with hunger.

Five.

I can't get caught, I thought. I can't get caught, was all I could think. Illegal. Deported. I don't know. Ba Ba has them. I was born here, I've always lived in America. I can't get caught.

Four people.

How would Ma Ma and Ba Ba find me if I got caught? No, I couldn't get caught.

Three people.

I was so close that I could see the uniformed people's white hats, their shirts and skin in matching color. They were smiling big, wide, open smiles. They were holding only containers. I looked into one of the women's eyes and she looked back with a smile that hugged me from head to toe.

I could trust her. It wasn't a trap. No, I couldn't. Yes, it was.

At this point I was dizzy from arguing with myself, spent from fighting every urge.

I didn't know at what point the stalemate broke. I didn't even register it. But it happened. My body gave in and, as it has all my life, my mind triumphed. Before my legs could protest, I broke into a full-on sprint, speeding down the street toward the safety of the sweatshop.

It was pleasant for a while. I stopped being hungry. I no longer smelled food. I couldn't hear my stomach rumble. My mind and body knew nothing but to run. By the time I realized what had happened, I was many blocks down the wrong direction, by Grand Street, but I didn't stop. Tears clouded my already-eroded vision, but I didn't dare stop. I kept going until salt was all I tasted. I kept going until the only shaking I felt came from my aching feet as they pounded against the concrete to the rhythm of my palpitating heart. Still, I kept going. Forever would I keep going. **Keep going, Qian Qian. Keep going until the hunger is gone.**

On that run, only one thing kept pace with me, and it was not hunger. It was fear. Fear was all I tasted; fear was all I contained; fear was all I was.

* * *

Not everything was bad. Hardship is dimly lit, and its darkness shielded us. It was all we knew in America so it was simply something we accepted and took for granted, as much as the air flowing through our nostrils and the sunlight shining onto our heads. And then there were things that we no longer took for granted—that we could never again take for granted—simply because of how they now contrasted with our every day.

Once in a while, we got to enjoy a truly delicious meal. Whether it was delicious only because my hunger had grown to a certain peak, or whether it was objectively, inherently delicious, I will never know. But to this day, stored in my senses are the filling, delectable feasts that Ma Ma somehow conjured out of our weekly twenty dollars. Ma Ma made use out of every sliver of food. I don't know if it was her culinary alchemy, my hunger, the rosy distance of time, or most probably, a combination of all three, but there are still moments when I find myself craving the taste of her salted watermelon rinds and her vinegared carrot peels.

And on an even rarer occasion—a handful of days, really—Ma Ma returned from the store with a box of Entenmann's baked goods. I liked the small dusted donuts the best. I stuffed them in my mouth so fast that they made me cough and coat the air with a blizzard of powdered sugar.

And then there were Sundays. Sunday was the only day that stayed somewhat similar in Mei Guo and Zhong Guo. For, in both places, Sunday was for dumplings. Every Sunday, Ma Ma and I scraped together the ingredients in our communal kitchen, cobbling together leftover meat, Chinese lettuce, and garlic from meals long past. Occasionally, one of our roommates popped his head in.

"Sunday dumplings again?"

We never took the bait. Where in Zhong Guo we welcomed guests and gave away extras, we now had no food to spare.

On the Sundays when Ba Ba was also home, he made the wrappers, rolled vigorously from all-purpose flour. He was more forceful than Ma Ma was with the rolling pin we got from the 99-cent store, the one that always seemed seconds away from dissolving into wooden dust. We dreamed of one day buying the premade wrappers on display at Hong Kong Supermarket, but Ma Ma said they were too expensive, and she was sure they didn't taste all that great anyway.

Dumplings were a four-hour event on the only day Ma Ma stayed home from the sweatshop. Some days, depending on how tired she was from the week, we sat in meditative silence, our breaths punctuated by the rocking of the rolling pin and the clacking of chopsticks against the rusting, metallic bowl that held the dumpling filling.

Other days, when the week had not drained all light from her face, Ma Ma reminded me how fun Sundays had been at Lao Lao's.

"Remember, Qian Qian? Da Jiu Jiu would make the wrappers, and it would be a race to see if we could finish making the previous dumpling before his new wrapper hit the board!"

At this, I heard the laughter that rollicked as the competition got under way.

"Remember, Qian Qian, when you had a competition with Lao Ye to see who could eat the most dumplings and you ate twenty all at once and couldn't even move?"

For a second, I was no longer hungry. I was full. Stuffed, even. I could fit no more into a single crevice of my stomach. I was so full I almost burped, and for a moment I believed that the rumblings from my belly were actually sounds of digestion.

"And we would sit together at the kitchen table, and we would dip the dumplings in that sweet-sour vinegar—remember that vinegar? And the meal would last hours; remember that, Qian Qian?"

I did not remember how long the meals took, but I tasted the sweetness of the vinegar, its darkness marking the corners of my lips. I remembered the taste of the chives and pork as they mushed and blended under my teeth and slid down my throat.

But most of all, I felt the warmth of Lao Lao's dining table, the love of family wrapping me in its embrace, crossing borders and living on through time.

Chapter 8

SUSHI

....

Thanks to the one-room employment agency, Ma Ma had many jobs: some all at once, others swiftly, one after another. Ma Ma cried more now, regularly, and depending on the job, she cried more some days than others.

"I quit," she announced with triumph, surprising me after school one day on the steps of PS 124. She was supposed to be at her shift bussing tables at a Cantonese restaurant on East Broadway.

"I spat in a dish—so what?" she huffed as we walked down Division Street. "They can serve one customer leftovers from another's plate, but I can't spit in some bastard's food. Did they ask me why I did it? They don't give one shit about me."

By then, Ma Ma had taken to telling me absolutely everything, and, as on the playground in China, I slipped easily, naturally, into the role of the mother hen. In fact, I was very happy to be, as she called me, her "xiao yi sheng," her little doctor, her on-call therapist.

"It's okay, Ma Ma," I soothed. "There are other jobs you can do."

"But what do you think, Qian Qian—should I try another restaurant?"

She went on without giving me a chance to respond. And it didn't matter what I had to say, because I knew there was much more she needed to get out first.

"Everyone says a restaurant gig is the job to get, once you make your way up to waitress and get those tips! Especially the lao wai, they give so much. But I don't know if I can make it that long, Qian Qian. You should see how they treat me.

"I was a professor. I was published. And now it all means nothing."

I intuited that there was more yet and that if I kept listening, she would be able to spew it all out and then I could lull her into peace.

"Mandarin is the language of the Chinese intellectuals. Of the Beijingers. But no, here, all these Cantonese assume that if you speak Mandarin you're a farmer from Fuzhou."

At this, I thought back to the jab I had felt in my gut when Janie called Mandarin my "loser language." But still I said nothing.

"Me, a farmer! Really. Our world has really turned upside down, hasn't it, Qian Qian?"

I nodded in support, projecting the content-ment I wished for Ma Ma. I steered us toward the other side of the street, to the door of the sweatshop, which she had quit in a fury earlier that week.

She refused to follow. "I told them I'd die before stepping foot back in that place again, and I meant it. Let's go see what shit they have for us today at the agency."

Ma Ma had a flair for melodrama.

As it turned out, the job on offer that day was at a sushi-processing plant. It would win the competitive title of Ma Ma's worst job during those dark years, but we did not know it then. That day, we only saw the number after the dollar sign, wooed by the—relatively, it was always relative—lucrative pay and our dreams of a better life. And really, Ma Ma said, how bad could it be?

I would not know how bad it was until a few days later. The next morning, Ma Ma went off to the address the fat man had scribbled on the slip of paper. It was somewhere by the Holland Tunnel, she told me, in an undeveloped part of Manhattan. It was too far for me to walk on my own after school, so Ma Ma told me it was better to go to Ba Ba after school, and then go home with him.

It seemed indulgent to me, lazy even, to not work after class but instead to just focus on my homework. But I was selfish and lazy, so I agreed.

* * *

Ba Ba had, meanwhile, quit his laundromat job. A friend of his from Zhong Guo, Lao Bai, had started working as an interpreter and clerk for a white immigration lawyer with an office on East Broadway. The lao wai had only Chinese clients, and most of them spoke no English. He felt no compunction, though, about taking any client who walked in the door, legitimate immigration claim or not. Those unique ethics had made him more money than he knew what to do with, and he was looking to hire another clerk. It was good pay, Lao Bai had promised, and the lawyer was never there. The clerks were the ones who ran the office and did the legal work.

"What kind of a lawyer is that? Ta ma de." (Ba Ba's favorite curse literally translated to "His mom's.") "Mei Guo really is almost as fucked up as Zhong Guo." Ba Ba took another puff of his cigarette as we walked down East Broadway with Lao Bai.

"Who cares? He hasn't made many citizens but he's made lots of money." Lao Bai chuckled. "We may as well take some of it." Even more so than the lao wai lawyer, Lao Bai had a moral flexibility unique to those determined to survive at all costs. Ba Ba told me that years ago, Lao Bai had joined the Communist Party in Zhong

Guo, pledging his allegiance to it, even though he had zero faith in the party or the government, and no intention of staying in the country. Ba Ba had refused to do the same, even though the pressure grew over time as each of his friends joined. When I asked why, Ba Ba's face darkened and he said he would never forget what they did to him. He would happily eat America's shit before feasting on China's fruits.

Ba Ba joined Lao Bai one morning in the thin brown building, climbing the smoke-filled flights up to the one-room office. It was the kind of office where, to use the bathroom, you had to get a key with a long wooden bar attached to it by a paper clip, and if you were gone too long, someone banged on the rattling door. (I knew this because it was there that I strained after school, poop-shy, until a lady from down the hall slammed on the door and shouted in Mandarin, deliberately for my benefit, "That little kid is shitting again!") In the summer, the office was cooled by one rusty floor fan, and in the winter it was heated by cigarette smoke and the hot air flowing out of too many mouths. Four desks were strewn about the room, one facing this way, another facing that way. Three were for the clerks, and one, with an ever-vacant leather chair, was for the absent lawyer.

The third clerk was a younger woman with an

impressively round and always-made-up face. Her skin was alabaster, pale like the skin on Clifford's owner and on the white children I had already learned to envy. Everyone called her Zhu Xiao Jie, or Ms. Zhu, a homonym in Chinese for both Miss Piggy (how Ba Ba referred to her) and Ms. Pearl (how I thought of her until I learned of Ba Ba's disdain for her strong will). To this day, I remember Ms. Zhu by her most distinctive attributes: her large eyes, round like her face; her penchant for stir-fried fish cakes, which she ate every day at her desk, filling the entire room with the smell of yummy grease; her burgundy lipstick, which she reapplied after eating; and her acerbic tongue, something I admired more than I realized at the time, and a model for my future self.

Ms. Zhu was the most glamorous woman I met during those years, and she was the only woman who could have held her own in that room, against Lao Bai, Ba Ba, and the droves of immigrant men who sought out her desk, forming a line that sometimes led out of the room and down the hall.

When I went to the office with Ba Ba after school, I got to sit on the steps just outside of the office, at the end of the hallway. Sometimes Ms. Zhu's clients waited there with me. They were a smoky, creepy, amusing bunch. So even setting aside the reprieve from work, I was happy to go to the office, and eagerly anticipated finishing my homework early to relish the people watching.

On one particular day, I sat on the steps and found myself distracted by the stories that the immigrants were telling each other and to Ms. Zhu, Lao Bai, and Ba Ba. One man had arrived almost six years ago and had never met his son. By the time he finally paid off his snakehead, his son was five and it was all he could do to send money and toys home every month, hoping they got there soundly, and that they would be some comfort to his motherless child. His wife had died from cancer. And the last lawyer had taken all his money and closed up the makeshift law office. Wasn't there anything they could do?

Another man had an aging mother with no one in Zhong Guo to care for her. He had paid an orphan from the deeper countryside to be her nanny, but the nanny had robbed his mom and run off with the neighbor's son. It was his mom's dying wish to see him again. How could he get to her? Wasn't there anything they could do?

I could have answered the questions before Ba Ba and Ms. Zhu did. The answer was always the same: "Oh, no, I am so sorry. That is awful. We can try, but it will be difficult and expensive."

The clients, almost always men, brought me candies, pastries, and leftovers from their restaurant shifts. I must have reminded them of a daughter they had in recent years seen only through photos. They, too, were a salve for not just my belly but also for the aching in my heart for Ye Ye, Jiu Jiu, and Lao Ye.

So I was not entirely without family in Mei Guo. They simply came to me in short, sporadic moments. Over time, I fashioned a little office scrapbook, in which I hung on to these treasured moments with sketches of my adoptive family and their souvenirs—a candy wrapper glued to one page, a greasy pastry bag, crumbs and all, taped to another.

Even the lawyer, the one time I met him, reminded me of family. He was white, and not at all Chinese, but he had fair skin with some pink peeking through, just like Lao Ye, who, when he traveled abroad for the government, was always mistaken for a lao wai and greeted with English. The lawyer was tall like Lao Ye, too, with thinning silver hair. There the similarities ended, but for a child who had left her home without a photo of her beloved grandfather, he might as well have been Lao Ye himself.

Donning a full gray suit under a tan trench coat and carrying a peeling black leather briefcase, he strode down the hall toward me one afternoon, slowing down by the office door, then walking past it and coming up to the steps.

"Why, you've got to be Chan," his tongue stumbling over my name as all white tongues did. "You look just like a little Vincent!"

I recognized Ba Ba's English name, bestowed upon him by the Italian landlord he had lived with on Staten Island before Ma Ma and I arrived, but resented the comparison. I looked nothing like a boy.

"I was hoping to run into you today, in fact!" he continued, clueless in the way that da ren tended to be, and reached into his trench coat pocket.

"Here it is! For you." His palm was wrinkly but white like his face, with purple and pink veins running through it. In its center was a wooden, rectangular pillbox, its corners rounded and smooth. It was the color of his coat.

"Open it."

I obeyed, flicking the top up at the hinge. Greeting me from within was a wooden lady-bug, painted red, with five black dots on her back—an odd number of dots was good luck; evens were bad, Ma Ma had told me once while my knees were still in the dirt of our building's sandbox. Or was it the other way around? I could never keep it straight, and, after all, this was a lifetime ago, back in China, when I still played and Ma Ma still had time for me.

The bug had googly eyes that moved. A skinny wooden stick poked out of her belly, making her look like she was standing in midair. Her four toothpick legs, also painted black, had a slight bend to them and were hinged but not fixed to her torso. I shook the box and the legs danced, sending me into giggles.

"Thank you!" I looked at the lawyer in time to catch his smile as he walked toward the office door, disappearing into the room. Not wanting to miss the dance, I returned to the googly eyes, which were now crossed toward one another.

Ba Ba would tell me later that the lawyer was a rich man who had gone to Harvard Law School. But he had a tendency to get married and divorced, and he had some lazy children to support, which Ba Ba said was common among lao wai. Each time the lawyer got married and had a lazy child, he had that much less money for himself, so Ba Ba reminded me that I should be very grateful for the gift.

Ba Ba's caution was unnecessary. I treasured that ladybug. It was the first gift I ever got in America.

* * *

On the first Saturday after she had gotten the new slip from the fat man, Ma Ma woke me early. Drunk with sleep, I followed her to the subway station, napping on the train and then sleepwalking out of the station, down several blocks, up and down a pedestrian bridge or two, before waking up to find us on a deserted block, the streets lined with cobblestone and buildings all in drab gray and brown. There must have been water nearby because the smell in the air reminded me of the one time I had been to the ocean and a crab had grabbed my big toe. It was only a version of that smell, though. The smell in my nose now was thicker, putrid, more viscous than what that scent had been. There was no lightness. It was heavy, as if the crab on my toe had stayed there and died.

As it happened, this was not too far from the address Ba Ba had given to my school. But it was clear even to me that no one had lived there for a long, long time.

Ma Ma led me up the chipped steps in front of one brown building with dark-brown liquid pooling out of one of the open side doors and all the way onto the road. When she opened the other door, I smelled what was inside before I could see any of it: it was the scent of the sea, mixed with the scent of what I somehow knew to be death. My nose saw a thousand squids as they lay dying, a hundred eels making their final squirms through a sewage pipe.

As I peered in, I saw that the humans within

were like those in the sweatshop. All cloaked in light-blue plastic, they did not notice us entering and instead stayed focused on their work with deadened determination. They stood hunched over a long, steel, tubular trough that snaked its way, mazelike, through the room.

Ma Ma gestured for me to enter and I pinched my nose shut before stepping into an anteroom with hooks from which plastic onesies dangled, each of them looking like a blue man who had given up on life—one hollow, three-dimensional hangman after another. It was only when the door shut with a smelly whoosh that I realized that though it was early winter outside, it was even colder inside. Ma Ma rescued a hanging blue man from his hook and handed him to me.

"Put this on, quickly. It will warm you up."

It was too long in the arms, the legs, the everywhere, but I obliged. The hood fell down past the bridge of my nose and I shoved it up, once, twice, three times before it obeyed. I scrunched the sleeves up, crinkling with every movement as if I were made of foil. Ma Ma had her blue man over her too now, and we were twins, one short and shriveled up, one tall and fully grown.

She was putting boots on now, boots made of rubber and smellier than even the room, with the same sludge tracked on each bottom. She handed me a pair large enough to hold three of my feet, but I bent down to put them on anyway. As I reached to pull the boot up, my sleeves fell down again, and then my hood did, too. I could see nothing, touch nothing, move nowhere. Laughter convulsed through me as I became a large blue plastic bag, shaking in the sea-stink wind. I nudged the hood up again and, just before it fell, I caught the sight of Ma Ma smiling despite herself.

We trudged into the main room, me much slower than Ma Ma, and I followed her to a post by the basin. We were at the corner of the room, where the trough changed directions.

I stood with my torso pressed against the steel wall of the tub. I was just tall enough to look over the boards that lined the edge of the basin and see the water slushing out of the faucets fixed above. Beyond that there was a moving belt of fish, whole, silver, and still. Water flowed across the trough, over and through the crevices between ice cubes crowded together and stacked upon each other. To Ma Ma's left, a small bucket sat suspended over the flowing water, fixed onto the edges of the basin.

The cold supplants many of my memories from that room. I can no longer tell whether the images come to me from my firsthand experience or whether they have since been diluted by scenes filtered in from movies and documentaries. But in my mind's eye, I see Ma Ma whisking a dead fish out of the cold water and placing it on the chopping board, slicing its belly open and then beheading it, exposing the orange flesh inside. With a few flicks of the knife she removes bloody innards, which she dumps into the bucket. She then puts the fish on the belt, which carries it around the room to the next station, where the fish loses its fins, and then another station, where it surely would have been sliced and cut, and so on and so forth, until it becomes just a bunch of flattened orange pieces that I would not taste for the first time until many, many years later. I see blue-draped women and men slicing with flicks of their bony wrists, removing large white bones, and then smaller white bones with pliers. Some of the bones are so small that I can barely see them, even as I creep up the stations and to the men and women holding pliers in their hands, purple from the cold.

When the fish complete the journey around the room, they end up with a pudgy woman in a gray plastic suit. She places them in a bin and every now and then, she takes that bin behind a set of steel doors.

This I do remember just as if I am right back in the room: at the bottom of the basins where Ma Ma worked, there were small cracks that set free drops of water that fell onto the ground, our boots, and occasionally our socks as they glided down across the surface of our plastic blue garb. Over the course of the day, ice water gathered on the floor and inside our boots, chilling us just like the salmon.

Shaking and numbness spread by the hour. I watched as Ma Ma's hands pruned while our shivers expanded from our fingertips to our palms and then to our arms, until our whole bodies convulsed all over. There were rubber gloves, Ma Ma said, but they made the knives hard to grab.

To stay warm, I took many walks around the room, looking at each person at her station. Only one person has stayed with me over the years. She was an old woman around Lao Lao's age. Even through the blue plastic, hers and mine, I could tell that her skin was purple all over. Her lips came in a matching color, protruding and swollen. There was wetness on her cheeks. At first, I thought she was sweating, but no, of course not. The source of the drops was not her pores but her eyes, cloudy and gray. She was too old to be so cold. Too old to be there.

When I returned to Ma Ma's side, her eyes turned to me for a second before returning their focus, and there I stood on a stool, just as I had in our kitchen in China, grabbing the fish for her to slice. We worked until, in the world outside, the sun set. Farther uptown, sushi restaurants opened and then closed, their waitstaff placing chairs and barstools on top of the tables, locking the doors and rolling down the gates. In the time it took the city to wake up, get dressed, go out, and crawl to bed, we in that room stayed frozen: frozen with our fish, frozen in our boots, frozen at our stations. And all that time, my mind never strayed far from the lao lao just a few rows over, a cold wind and a bin of fish away from giving up.

The fish plant hovered over us long after Ma Ma and I unveiled ourselves of the blue plastic, unshelled our frozen feet of their rubber casings. We continued shaking on our walk to the subway, braving the cold outdoors, which mixed with the cold of the room, the cold that flooded our veins. The fish smell stayed on our skin and in our hair until our next washing, and we did not stop shaking until long after we wrapped ourselves deep in our comforters, our purple arms with their goose bumps and dark-blue veins crossed against our chests.

I drifted off to sleep that night with thoughts of my luck. The day after tomorrow, which was our off day, our lucky day, I would have school. I would not have to return to the plant until a full week later. My skin would have time to chase away the goose bumps, to regain its pink smoothness. Ma Ma's would never look the same.

Chapter 9

LIGHTS

....

We spent our first winter in Mei Guo by turns cloaked in darkness and emboldened by light. Before we knew it, all the trees were naked, their crunchy orange clothing shed to the ground and then covered with the sheen of frost. Lao Lao started mailing us the itchy sweaters that she made at her post in front of the TV. Her packages smelled like mothballs, a scent I came to associate with Lao Lao's home, and I loved to bring the sweaters to my nose and feel their scratchy tendrils, the smells of family climbing up my airways and stepping into my lungs. Sometimes Lao Lao's packages came preopened, ripped and then taped back together, the letters—with characters blacked out—wrinkled. The outsides of the packages were covered with rubberstamp markings, indicating that they had passed censor board approval and were allowed to leave Zhong Guo and fly here.

The heater was not on very often in our room, and we could see our breath when we exhaled.

When we got home, I crawled into bed long before I was ready for sleep. While we were awake, we piled the comforters from both beds onto one for warmth. Under them, I wore layers of sweaters on top of one another and all of my socks on my feet. When the heat did come on, there was a telltale metallic smell, followed by a hissing from the radiator. At that sound, which never came until late in the evening, I hurried to the radiator with my hands out, fingers dancing as I hopped from one foot to the other. As soon as I felt the heat spread through my fingertips and up my arms, I ran downstairs to the kitchen to retrieve Ma Ma; so desperate was she to thaw from the sushi plant that she spent hours sitting by the stove, boiling and reboiling tap water.

"Ma Ma, Ma Ma, lai ya!"

She could tell from the rosiness in my cheeks and the fire in my eyes that warmth had finally found our cold little room, so we bounded up the stairs like two squirrels on a carefree chase. Once inside, I pulled Ma Ma's still-shaking purple hands to the radiator and beamed.

It was in moments like this that Ma Ma's eyes filled with an inscrutable gaze, one of joy and sadness, love and despair all at once. Only looking back at the scene through an adult lens do I see in the cracks of her face the sweet pain Ma

Ma must have felt in those moments. Gratitude for the little she had. Heartbreak in needing it. Confusion over what our lives had become.

* * *

In the middle of one freezing winter night, we awoke to a thud, a squeak, and several thunks just outside our room. It was not the light tapping of cockroach feet that we had grown used to. No, it was made by a much larger, commanding subject, in the hallway outside.

"Shh. I'll go." Ba Ba was up with a leap, already by the window and then the door. In the light that streaked in, I could see that he had the face he put on to look brave when he was really terrified. I had seen it when he had gone on a Ferris wheel with me in Beijing, his eyes not daring to look down, around, or at me, but his face the mask of courage.

I sat up in my bed as Ma Ma crept to the door behind Ba Ba. He opened the door with a creak and stuck his head out. The flood of light through the cracks told me that he had dared to flick on the hallway light. With it came a squeak.

"Eh! Wang sheng!"

It was the tired voice of our little old landlady. I hopped up and joined my parents at the door, sticking my head out in between their bodies.

She, a lady of eighty-some years, was at the top of a six-step ladder that leaned against the wall dividing our room from the hall. Those wrinkly hands with tubular, bulbous veins were on the heater control panel at the very top, where the wall met the ceiling.

"What are you doing? Do you need help?" Ba Ba ventured a few steps forward, voice low in observance of our many roommates.

"Lou shang kai da chuang ya. Baby hao xin ku ya!"

Her Mandarin-Cantonese-English-jammered speech—which I realize now must have been impeded by dentures—had always been somewhat incomprehensible, but grew all the more so in the dead of night.

"Oh." Feigned courage dropped off Ba Ba's face. Pretend comprehension took its place.

"Mei shi le, mei shi le." She descended the ladder, step by meager step, socked foot slipping in frilly slippers, frilly slippers sliding on wooden rungs. Ba Ba ran over to hold the ladder steady against the wall. As soon as the landlady got to the ground, she started sliding the ladder against the wall and toward the bathroom, next to which I saw an always-locked closet door open for the very first time. With determination, she brushed Ba Ba aside and took just a few seconds too long to stow the ladder into the closet.

"Mei shi le, mei shi le," she continued her mantra as she creaked and lowered her weight down the staircase.

With a wave of the hand, Ba Ba ushered us back into our room and shut the door. As soon as the lock clicked shut, he burst into laughter.

I started giggling, too, excited to see Ba Ba happier than I could remember seeing him in Mei Guo. Here he was again: Ba Ba of the past, the younger man who had never left China, the man who was worlds lighter because he had yet to experience day-to-day bullying, yet to chase down a naked man in the halls of a psychiatric institution.

Ma Ma looked at the two of us, confused, and asked, "Ni xiao shen me?"—why are you laughing?—before catching the bug herself.

"She said—she said she had to turn the heater off because—it's too hot!" Ba Ba could barely get the sentence out between his laughs. "She said the baby upstairs has had such a hard life because it's too hot. The parents even have to open the windows!"

The family upstairs was the richest in the house, which really did not mean much, but to me, they were glamorous. They were also Puerto Rican, like many of our other roommates, but out of everyone in the house, they had the lightest skin by far. To me, they may as well have been white and wealthy: they rented the entire top floor with two bedrooms, a living room, and their **very own bathroom**. When I passed the mother in the hallway or kitchen, I couldn't help but stare at her wrists and neck, wondering whether it was the private bathroom that caused her skin to look so much whiter, so much better than mine.

"Can you imagine that! Can you imagine"— at this, Ba Ba, blessed with the art of drama, held his hand below his mouth and blew into the air. His hot breath condensed into misty fog before our eyes—"this being too hot!"

I don't know if it was the night's cold, which had already started to sink to a graver depth, or our hunger for joy, but the three of us returned to the warmth of our comforters and laughed until our tummies ached and tears flowed out of our eyes. I was too cold to reach my hands out to wipe the wetness away from my face, so I fell asleep with it still drying.

The next morning, when I awakened with the skin around my eyes taut from evaporated tears, I heard the pale father from upstairs lumbering around in the hall, by the heater control panel, muttering, "Stupid old communist bitch. Fucking twenty degrees outside and she turns the heater off."

We spent the rest of that winter shivering

under our two comforters, listening to the nightly thuds and creaks. And every time it happened, we shared a little chuckle.

* * *

Christmas quickly became my favorite time in Mei Guo. On Thanksgiving I had only gotten to watch on our tiny TV how lao wai celebrated— eating dead turkeys fatter than Chinese babies, innards stuffed with bread crumbs and vegetables. We did not dream of being able to afford any of these things.

With Christmas, though, I got to participate. One day in early December, I walked into the classroom to find Ms. Tang in a red dress, with a small, spiky, plastic green tree standing on her desk.

"Today," she declared, "Christmas begins!"

She pressed a button on the class boom box and cheerful music blared out. She then passed two boxes around the room. I watched as my classmates rummaged through the boxes as they made their way closer to me. I could not see, though, what each child pulled out. When one of the boxes got to me, I realized that it was full of tiny delights, all with stringed loops coming out of them: shiny balls, dancing ballerinas, fat, bearded white men in red suits. I took so much time to make my selection that just as I had settled on a fuzzy cat playing with a ball of yarn, Janie tugged the box out of my hands.

Next, we went up, table by table, to hang our items on the tree. Its pines were coarse, bearing uneven, protruding rims of translucent green plastic. The branches were so loosely slatted into the trunk that several fell out as we hung our items. I placed my ornament with particular care, keeping my touch light so as to avoid disturbing the cat, the tree, and my very first Christmas experience.

As the little tree took on a heavier and heavier load, Ms. Tang talked to us about the holiday. She told us that on Christmas, Americans everywhere showed people their love by giving gifts, like Santa Claus did, and by doing acts of service. That meant that we, too, would learn to do that—by organizing a Secret Santa in class. Because the idea was not really about gifts but about love, Ms. Tang said we were not to spend more than ten dollars. At this, I was both elated and nervous. I could not believe that I would get a gift that would be worth ten whole dollars. At the same time, though, I wondered how I would be able to afford to buy such a gift for someone else.

When another box came around—this time to pick names, not ornaments—I happened to draw Jennifer Tan, the richest girl in our class. She lived in the residential building attached to the school, which made her royalty in my eyes. I had rolled my eyes just a few days ago when she had told her friend, the beautiful Julia Huang, that she was going to Disney World for Christmas. When Jennifer noticed me listening in, she gave me a friendly smile. This prompted me to turn to Janie and say, "Disney World, what a baby." Instead of looking at me, though, Janie turned to Jennifer and said, "I'm jealous— you are so lucky!"

There was no loyalty in Mei Guo.

The next week, I emptied into my school backpack the box of coins Ba Ba and Ma Ma had let me keep from my sweatshop shifts. Then, after school, with the coins jingling in my bag, I walked down East Broadway and into that stationery store. By then, I knew the store well—I was a frequent visitor, though never a customer. I went to the aisle that displayed the mechanical pencils I had ogled for months. There, I chose the pencil I had so coveted: a pink one with a round, white eraser at its head and Hello Kitty all over. It came out to just under three dollars, and I relished getting to spend a whole twelve hours with it before the gift exchange. The man at the counter with the gentle face placed the pencil in a little brown paper bag, and with a smile, I left the coins on the counter, ran out of the store, down the street, and up the flights of Ba Ba's office building. I did not stop until I hit the little sitting steps, where I held my breath as I pulled out the pencil and clicked it with relish until the gray lead showed its face through the small pink mouth. Delicately, with the slightest pressure, I pushed the tip onto the brown paper bag, writing out my name. The lead felt harder, more durable, than the lead that came out of the sharpened yellow pencils I took from Ba Ba's office. With this lead, I knew from having observed my classmates, there was no need to stop what I was doing just to stick it into the sharpener and grind it against the blade. No, this lead was reliable, not so needy.

I luxuriated in writing out my last name before stowing the treasure back in its paper pocket, and placing it deep in my backpack, hidden from temptation. But alas, it would reemerge several times that afternoon and evening, so much that I had to stop outside the school the next morning and rub the pink eraser tip of one of my yellow pencils against the brown paper bag, which was now full of markings.

* * *

The gift exchange was mortifying. Everyone else, it turned out, had placed their gifts in wrapping paper and gift bags of all colors—red and green and gold—and though I had no way of knowing how much each person spent, the gifts were much bigger than my tiny little brown package, still covered with eraser smudges, enclosing the tinier-still pencil. My face melted into embarrassment as my classmates opened their gifts—Lewis with his water gun; Julia and her beautiful hair clip covered with rhinestones; me, even, with my very first American teddy bear. Finally, it was Jennifer's turn: in front of a silent class, she unrolled the crinkled, smudged paper bag and produced the pencil.

I could not afford a card or gift tag, so I had simply written on the bag itself, "Merry Christmas, Jennifer! Love, Qian." Until then, I had thought that "Love," was how we signed everything in America, but judging by the giggles that rippled through the room after Jennifer read out the note, I was wrong. My face burned bright, matching the baby pink pencil I had gifted in foolishness. Every word that the gracious Jennifer shared to conceal her disappointment only made it worse.

Shame ensnared me, taking home in my body until I was tucked into bed that night, my arms wrapped around my new teddy bear, who still had tags on him. He was mine, all mine, just like the day's humiliation.

* * *

Fifth Avenue was my favorite thing about Christmas. One Sunday, Ma Ma wrapped me in two of Lao Lao's thickest sweaters and then piled my only coat on top, before covering my neck and mouth with her own itchy scarf.

"I can't breathe, Ma Ma," I muttered into the knit, feeling my warm, wet breath bouncing back at my chin and lips and all around.

"We can't afford for you to get sick! Now, come on."

Ma Ma led me to our regular subway station, but from there we transferred from one train to the next, each one marked by letters, numbers, and colors I'd never before seen on trains.

When we emerged from underground, I was shocked to see that the sun had set. But it took me a second to notice under the lights all around us. We walked a few blocks in throngs of people so thick it felt like we were back in Beijing. Then, Ma Ma led me to the base of the largest, brightest tree I had ever seen. The tree was surrounded by buildings, perfectly framed as I looked up at it against the night sky. Like the one in class, this tree wore decorations, balls, and figures of all kinds. Some were lit from within like Halloween decorations while others had glitter, and still others shone with their bright colors alone. I went up to one, a gold ball that was so shiny and large that I saw my own face in it. In the reflection, my eyes shone back at me a sparkle that I would carry in my body for the rest of the night.

Ma Ma had still more to show me, so she walked me onto the wide streets that had signs telling us that we were on Fifth Avenue. It was the cleanest and fanciest street I'd ever seen in Mei Guo. The storefronts were huge and tall, with men dressed in suits at the doors—some of them were white, some Black, but none Chinese. We stopped in the middle of a crowd of passersby admiring the front of a store that had strings of lights adorning its face. With a twinkle here and a flash there, the lights announced that a show was about to begin. I held my breath and waited, gripping Ma Ma's hand. Out of the corner of my eyes, I caught her smiling as the music began and filled the street. Slowly at first and then all of a sudden, more lights appeared, one light bulb giving birth to another, then another, before spreading across the entire building, each bulb dancing to the beat of the music. And though we'd never heard the melody before, soon Ma Ma and I began moving with the swaying crowd, shaking gently to the beat, joy vibrating through us. The whole world was dancing and so were we. We exchanged another smile and I marveled how, in all the stories of the gold-paved Mei Guo and the dangerous Mei Guo, no one in China knew about the lights of America, about how they were so delightful that they could stop us in the middle of the street, in the middle of our lives and our worries, in the middle of strangers living stranger lives, all just to fill us with music and hope.

Tracing it all back, I know now that it was the moment I first became enamored with the idea of America. It was the first time I saw the beauty and glamour of the country, and really, of New York City—though at that point the two were one and the same to me. The lights and the joy among the crowd that night showed me all that the city was and had to offer: a completely different face of America than the one we had come to know. Finally, the Beautiful Country's name made sense.

Amid the crowd of people, with eyes reflecting the lights on the buildings all around us, we kept walking as lit-up figures and animals in storefront windows danced and laughed. Ma Ma and I came upon a street that opened up to a fountain on the left. On the right, there was a building with many flags on its forehead. We walked through an area full of trees and greenery that I didn't know existed in America. Lining the edges of the tree area were horses, white, black, spotted, all wearing red headdresses that matched the harnesses on their backs and the plush lining of the seats in the carriages they pulled. I kept my eyes on the horses until Ma Ma pulled me into a large building with another serious man in a suit standing by the door.

The store was large and bright. Greeting us at the center was a fat old Santa Claus on his throne, a little white boy sitting on his lap. The boy had cowlicked hair and eyes spotted with excitement and fear. A line of people began a short distance from Santa and wound around the store, full of happy children and exhausted adults.

I pulled Ma Ma away from the line, too shy to approach the large white man. Her hand in mine, I walked down aisle after aisle with my other hand out, touching the soft and the fluffy, pressing down the plastic and the noisy, rattling this and grabbing that. It was the most I'd seen of toys since boarding that plane in Beijing. I was a wanderer who, upon stumbling on the desert's edge, could finally afford to recognize my monthslong thirst.

When the colorful aisles gave way to a stairway, I climbed them without hesitation. Ma Ma followed closely behind. At the landing, what came into view stopped my breath, already shallow with excitement. Before me was a giant keyboard that took up an entire section of the room. I had seen it on TV just weeks ago, when a white man had danced on it, making his own music. The scene had caused me to stand up and move closer to our tiny TV, so close that I had fogged up the screen with my hot breath in our cold room.

But there was no fog between me and the giant piano now. It was right there, for me to play with and dance on, and all for free. I could hardly believe it. There were already several children stomping on it when I approached, most of them white. I hung back, afraid of intruding. I looked to Ma Ma, who stood by the landing.

"Ni qu ya," she urged me on.

I walked forward, each step a little more sure than the last, and by the time I was on the keys, I had settled on my route: I hopped from one white plank to a black one and then back, the art of play coming back to me with the banging tones. It was a melody all my own, and when I closed my eyes, I traveled back to a time and place where it never occurred to me to question whether I belonged. I saw myself back in that courtyard, singing and dancing to a semicircle of captive audience, without worry or fear that I was singing out of tune, dancing out of step, or performing out of turn. That little stage had been mine, and now so was this one.

When we left the store later that night, I did not ask Ma Ma if I could buy a toy. I had recovered a little piece of my previous life, my former self. My heart glowed as Ma Ma and I walked hand in hand, past the lights and back into the shadows.

Chapter 10
CHATHAM SQUARE

....

I discovered Chatham Square early. A few weeks after I went back into her class, Ms. Tang guided me and my classmates out of the school, turning off of Division Street and onto East Broadway, before ushering us into the red door of a white building just a few steps away from Ba Ba's office.

The building, it turned out, was a branch of the public library, and its name was Chatham Square. Once inside, Ms. Tang led us up a flight of steps before telling us to sit on the floor in front of a lady in a chair. She had wild, curly hair and long chains made of beads of different colors that dangled from the legs of her gold-rimmed glasses. Once we were all seated, she pulled out **The Very Hungry Caterpillar,** a book I had read, reread, and read again during my time in the special-needs classroom. As the lady made her way through my hairy friend's journey to unfurling his beautiful butterfly wings, I realized that it was the first time I had heard the words spoken out loud. I knew them well, of course, having first stumbled over them, only to later fly past them, but it had all happened over the course of days spent in solitary silence. There was something reassuring, I realized, in hearing the words spoken by a grown adult, just for us.

After the lady finished the book and then another, Ms. Tang funneled us back down the stairs. From the top, I saw the children's section in a corner of the first floor, full of colorful books and bright posters encouraging us to READ. There were also clumsy computer stations scattered throughout, with an unwashed man sitting at one and a bespectacled lao lao at another. As Ms. Tang directed us out of the red door and back to school, I was sad, but I knew that it was just the beginning.

I returned hours later. Instead of going to Ba Ba's office after school, I walked past his building and in through the red door. I went straight to the children's section, where my mind had lingered all day. It was the brightest part of the library, and I could barely believe that I would get to read all of the books in it for free. Here and there, a few picture books were propped up for display. Old friends greeted me: Amelia Bedelia, the Berenstain Bears, and Clifford. For the first time since leaving Zhong Guo, I was home.

Every day after school, I passed countless hours in that little corner. I dove into one book after another, forgetting for stretches at a time where I was and what I had to worry about. Between each set of covers, I was just another American kid. This was especially true of The Baby-Sitters Club and Sweet Valley Twins, my two favorite series. In Stoneybrook and Sweet Valley, I was a normal girl cradled by supportive family and a stable circle of friends. I saw myself in Kristy Thomas and Elizabeth Wakefield, and in them my worries were no bigger than being grounded or doing poorly on tests.

I felt so at home at the library that I took it upon myself to keep it organized. I didn't like that the spines of all the picture books were lined up along the edges of the shelves. It was too precarious; their faces jutted out instead of sitting in safety toward the back. I also didn't like that they were not organized by height—they looked messy and sloppy, tall ones next to short ones, the tops of some books sticking out over the tops of others next to them. So I developed a daily habit of organizing the shelves, placing the larger, hardbound version of **Goodnight Moon** before the smaller, paperbacked Berenstain Bears books.

One day in the spring, I had engaged in this organization for the better part of an hour—small, dirty fingers working nimbly, tongue peeking out of dried lips, eyes dancing with excitement— when I was approached by a birdlike librarian with a nest for a bun at the top of her head.

"Can you stop that, please?"

"What?"

"Please stop moving the books around."

"But I'm helping you organize." Indignation was my only response.

"The titles are harder to read when the spines are farther from the edge. They can't be pushed all the way to the back."

"But they look better this way."

"Please stop."

She walked away but she must have known that I was sneaky. She looked back over at me every now and then, so I retreated back into my Stoneybrook corner, sad that I could not bring order even to this home.

* * *

From then on, there was no saving me. I lived and breathed books. Where else could I find such a steady supply of friends, comforts, and worlds, all free for the taking? And so portable, too—everywhere I went, there they were: on the subway, at recess, on the steps just outside of Ba Ba's office. Unlike my teachers and classmates, they were reliable.

But even though libraries were homes, bookstores were dangerous. I rarely let myself go in. I was afraid that they would show me that there were worlds beyond what was already freely available to me, and make me want more than I could afford. I resented even school book sales, when Ms. Tang made us stay in the school library for thirty minutes, locking us up among shelves whose free books were replaced with shiny bright volumes that cost as much as ten dollars apiece. Even then, I refused to contemplate what was just out of reach. Instead, I fixed my focus on the table of free bookmarks, which sometimes had characters from The Baby-Sitters Club on them, though most of the time they just showed addresses and photos of stores. Still, I willed myself not to look away from the free table, praying that none of my classmates would notice that the girl who brought the cheapest Secret Santa gift was also the one who only took free things from book sales.

Chapter 11

HAIR

....

Our first full summer in Mei Guo, Ma Ma and Ba Ba decided that we had heard the word "chink" too many times and moved us out of the creaky building.

This happened a week after I did a very bad thing. I took in a stray cat I had found outside the door and stowed her away in the vacant bedroom on the first floor. Before it became empty, someone whom Ba Ba called a "boat person" used to live there. Ba Ba explained to me that this meant that he had come over on a boat to escape hardship, and I wondered for years why he hadn't just taken a plane. In exchange for rent, the boat person took care of the old lady's husband. But one night an ambulance pulled up, its sirens lighting up the entire street, and men in identical outfits took the old man out on a bed with wheels.

The boat person left after that, and his bedroom stayed empty for weeks. The room was right by the front door and I always tried to turn the doorknob on my way in and out of the house. Most of the time it was locked, but one day I found it open and went in. The room contained only a bare mattress with a metal frame. Before shutting the door again, I ran up to our room to grab some tape, which I put over the part of the lock that clicked it in place. I had seen someone do this on TV once, and I was glad to find that it worked.

On the day I came upon a cat out in front of the house, rather than in the backyard like the others, I decided that she was mine. She was all black, with yellow eyes that beamed like the moon. Ma Ma said that cats were bad luck, and that black cats were even worse luck, and I thought back on my poor crab friends in China. No, I could not risk Ma Ma seeing my little Moonlight, so I did the only thing I could: I put her in the abandoned bedroom and returned every hour or so, telling Ma Ma and Ba Ba that I had to go to the bathroom, the kitchen, the backyard. With each visit, I stole from our neighbors' kitchen goods—a saucer of milk, a sliver of sausage—and slipped into the room. I sat on the bare mattress with its loose, loud springs until Moonlight came out from under the bed. Then I gave her my offering and, as she ate, I patted her on the head and stroked her back. As soon as she was done, she went right

back under the bed, not even leaving a tail out
to be pet. Toward the end of the evening, she
refused to come out at all, and I found myself
lying flat on my side on the floor, staring into
two moons, bright and full, at the back corner
of the bed.

I didn't get a chance to say good night to
Moonlight because on my last run, I told Ma
Ma that I was going down the hall to brush my
teeth. But Ma Ma came out of the room, too,
saying that she might as well brush her teeth
with me. I had already "used the bathroom"
several times earlier that evening, so there was
little I could do but diligently brush my teeth
by Ma Ma's side. She then marched me to bed.
I fell into a fitful sleep, full of nightmares of
Moonlight starving, crying, and shivering.

I awoke to screams and shuffles, following by
panting steps up the stairs, and then pounding
on our door. Ba Ba dragged himself out of bed
and opened the door. Through it, I saw the old
lady in her ghostly nightgown, hair splayed out
from her head like rays from the sun.

"Zen me me?"

"Xia bian! You ren!"

I jolted out of bed. The old lady had heard
something from the empty bedroom. She
thought it was a burglar. I took a second too
long to consider whether I should tell Ba Ba

about Moonlight. By the time I chickened out, it didn't matter anyway, because Ba Ba had already shut the door and run downstairs.

Ma Ma sat up in her bed and stared at me. All my life, she had a way of knowing when I was hiding something. I looked at Ma Ma and vomited the truth.

My memories of what came next are sleep-stained. Ma Ma and I lumbered down the stairs as if in a three-legged race. At the bottom, we came upon several open doors: the door to the room, the door to the broom closet across from the room, and the front door of the house. We darted toward the last one, following the noise. As we crossed the threshold, the hot summer air greeted us. I found Ba Ba by the sidewalk, holding a dustpan with various shaped poops, looking at a small black figure seated on the patchy sidewalk grass. There, looking back at us through her dilated yellow eyes, Moonlight sat carrying a gray and hairy clump in her mouth, a long tail trailing out just under her cheek.

I walked toward her, but this only caused her to bolt. She stopped only to turn around for a last glance before disappearing down the bend of the street. And just like that, there went another thing I cared about that I would never see again.

Turning back to the house, I caught Ba Ba watching me. Ma Ma had already retreated to our room, so I turned away to look at our landlady, who seemed to already be falling back asleep.

"Mao mao, hai yi wei shi ren ne," she said as she shuffled back into the house, chuckling with a flap of her vein-covered hand.

"Well," Ba Ba said as he dumped the contents of the dustpan into the well of a sidewalk tree, "it's a good thing the cat caught a mouse because she shat all over that room."

He paused for emphasis and stared at me.

"And the person who let her in would have been in real trouble."

* * *

Our new home was a little bigger, a little brighter, a little safer. It was on the first floor of a two-story house that was laid out as if on a railroad track, one long skinny line, with windows on one side only. Our landlords, a gentle couple with two sons around my age, lived on the entire second floor. They could afford the home because, as Ma Ma leaned over to whisper to me after our first meeting, they were among the workers in the sweatshops who sewed buttons, and they had been in America so long that both their sons had been born here. This gave me hope. Perhaps by the time I had my own children—who would be real, true

Americans—I might be able to afford to live on an entire floor of a house.

We had the three small connected rooms at the front of the first floor, with other tenants living in each of the two rooms at the back. Separating our rooms from theirs were the shared tiny bathroom and kitchen, this one modest, with no island. I realized only years later that the entire floor had been meant for one family, our rooms the intended dining room, living room, and sunroom, though that third room was useless because it was both too cold in the winter and too hot in the summer. We were grateful that the sunroom at least had a door to separate it from the two usable spaces. Between those spaces, we hung up a thin blue curtain we had packed from China.

I spent much of that first summer on our couch, melting my brain with the four TV channels available to me. Ma Ma and Ba Ba didn't think it was good for me to spend as much time at work with them as I did, so they left me at home with strict instructions not to go outside. They called every now and then to check up on me, but once I was confronted with a stranger when I expected Ma Ma on the other end.

"Ma Ma?"

"Hello! May I speak to your parents, please?"

"They're not home. Who is this?"

"They're not home! How old are you?"

"Who is this?"

"They shouldn't leave you at home alone."

I hung up with a slam. For the next few hours, I sat on the couch, immobile, waiting for the cops to break down our door and arrest me for being left alone at home, only to deport me once they found out the truth. At least they would have no way of finding my parents. They could torture me and I wouldn't tell them. They could tie me up and starve me, and I still wouldn't tell them. How much hungrier could I get, anyway? Would they ship me off to China? Would I be allowed to see Lao Lao and Lao Ye, or would I be stuck working as a slave somewhere?

I sat like this until Ma Ma came home, working out my plans and my answers and how I would scrimp and save if I were sent to live as a farmhand in the countryside.

I never did get to put any of those plans into action. Even so, I stopped picking up the phone.

By then, Ma Ma had stopped asking Ba Ba when we'd be going back to China. She also grew morose. Ma Ma and Ba Ba didn't talk so much anymore, and Ba Ba often came home late.

I worried that it was not good for my parents to be without me during workdays, but they said it was no place for a child. So I stayed at home, useless and selfish.

* * *

Ma Ma had many dreams. She wanted to make a change, break out of the illegal Chinatown market. One night, after returning under a cloak of exhaustion, Ma Ma asked me whether I thought she should do hair or nails.

"What do you mean?"

"You know, as a job."

It was easy. I thought people who painted their nails were weird, but everyone needed to cut their hair. "Hair!"

That answer set Ma Ma on a path. It took her a week to find a salon that was hiring unpaid apprentices, and the week after that she brought home a terrifying mannequin head that cost two weeks of our food budget and several nights of sleep for me. Ma Ma set the mannequin by the window in our bedroom. Late at night, the moonlight filtered into our room through the decapitated head, casting a large and terrifying shadow on the wall.

The mannequin had long golden hair that was as coarse as a horse's—at least according to Ma Ma; I'd never seen horsehair up close. The hair was so blond that I imagined it had come from the heads of the white people I saw on the subway. This was what their hair felt like, I figured, and apparently what horsehair felt like. Was my hair supposed to feel like that, too?

The mannequin started off with hair down to her imagined knees, but over the course of days, Ma Ma chopped and snipped in a meandering path, until the mannequin was left with no more than a scraggly, uneven buzz cut.

The biggest lesson Ma Ma learned from her apprenticeship went like this:

"Qian Qian, there once was a barber-in-training who had a really bad habit."

"What was it?"

"He spent months practicing close shaves with an expensive raw blade. Because he often cut his customers during the early months of his training, he started practicing on watermelons."

"Watermelons?"

"Yes, watermelons."

"Yummy."

"And whenever his mentor summoned him during his training, he stuck the blade right into the watermelon rind and walked to his mentor's station. By the end of each day, the rind would be all cut up."

"Could he still eat the flesh inside?" At this point I always drooled a little.

"But it didn't matter, because he never lost his expensive blade and every night, he brought home an easy-to-cut watermelon for his happy wife."

"So he **could** eat it! How great."

"Not so."

"Why not?"

"Habits form your character. Slowly, but inevitably and always. When he was finally ready, when he finally stopped making mistakes, he got his first customer and, guess what?"

"Uh-oh."

"Yes, the phone rang and, without thinking, he stuck the blade right into his customer's head."

At this she always laughed before continuing: "That's why, Qian Qian, we must always act as if it counts even when it's just practice."

The story haunted me. I figured that if it were true, Ma Ma's practice did not bode well for her customers. But at least she never stuck a blade into the mannequin; she just gave it choppy and asymmetrical cuts. Ma Ma tried to even it out, but one side always ended up shorter than the other. In frustration, Ma Ma finally buzzed the coarse hair off, leaving a shorn, pixie mess.

* * *

I got to visit Ma Ma's place of slaughter, the hair salon, late into the summer. When we stepped out of the subway station, I thought we were in Chinatown because there were Chinese people everywhere. It was the first time I learned that lots of people like us lived in Brooklyn, too. Ma Ma told me that the area was called Ba Da Dao, Eighth Avenue, a neighborhood I would later match up with that more commonly known as Sunset Park.

I remember two things about the visit.

The first was congee. I was less hungry during the summer because, having no reason to believe I was getting my meals at school, Ma Ma made sure to prepare food for me before leaving for work early each morning. I woke up every day to our little table full of dishes. Sunset Park was like that table, but stretched out across several streets. There were restaurants upon restaurants, each selling cheap meals. I slowed as we came upon one window front that had a sign advertising congee for sixty cents. Ma Ma nudged me in.

"Really?"

She didn't even have time to nod before I bolted through the door. I asked for congee, please, and a Cantonese woman in a hairnet used a ladle the size of her head to sop the white-rice soup, specked with pork and century egg, into a translucent container. As she capped the container, Ma Ma deposited two quarters and a dime into her hand. I had no idea that, all this time, we could buy heaven for so little.

I had never had southern Chinese congee before, only plain congee from the north. It was a delight to taste the rice, pork, and century egg all in one spoonful.

"Ma Ma, do you want?" My words exploded into the air, garbled through bits of meat, rice, and egg.

She shook her head. I recognized the look. She was determined and anxious to get to work. So I walked as quickly as I could while delivering spoon after spoon of congee into my mouth, spilling some onto my T-shirt.

We stopped in front of an all-glass storefront with barber stripes on the window and $10 HAIRCUT next to it. The glass was cracked in one corner, dirt caked at its edges. Ma Ma pushed the door in and we were greeted by wafts of shampoo, dyes, and blow-dryer exhaust.

The room was maybe six hundred square feet. Down one side, a row of swivel chairs with peeling leathery plastic sat before a wall of mirrors. On the other side, there were little tables with chairs around them. On that wall were not mirrors but small bottles of nail polish in different colors.

I saw that we were not the first in the shop, for through the curtain at the back came a woman who looked just like a witch. Perhaps I only remember her this way because of the many stories of unkind acts that Ma Ma had shared with me about her boss, but in my mind's eye, she held a broom and her hair was frizzy. Her lipstick was drawn way beyond her lip line. As she stepped forward, I retreated behind Ma Ma.

"Hao ke ai!" she gushed as I tried my best to look unafraid. After several minutes of me hiding in Ma Ma's skirt, resistant to her pleas, the Witch gave up and walked away. It took me a while longer to emerge from Ma Ma's shadow, and by then other employees were filtering in.

This led me to the second thing I remember about the visit. Cutting hair was not as glamorous as I had imagined. The customers who headed to the nail tables were mostly women, and they were either eager to chat with the staff or completely oblivious to them. But there were more men among the people who strolled in toward the hairstyling stations. They looked at Ma Ma and the other women strangely. They seemed to enjoy their scalp massage a little too much, and their hands had too many accidental brushes with the women intent on working on their hair.

During breaks in the back room—a closet, really, with some stools and a mini fridge full of food labeled with names—I heard Ma Ma chatter with the other women about how gross and cheap they felt, how much they dreaded the shampooing and scalp massages. Ma Ma was the newest, so shampooing and massaging was all she did, again and again, throughout her ten-hour shift. It brought me back to the fish-processing plant, how she had had to dip her fingers into wet, gross stuff until they came out purple, shriveled.

For the rest of my childhood, I carried in my heart the guilt of forcing Ma Ma into that job—not just through my existence and my need for food, but by simply giving her such bad advice.

Chapter 12

SHOPPING DAY

....

Shopping days came twice a week. We didn't always make it out both days, though we tried. We never knew what would be available and hated the thought of missing out. Spring was the best season. It rained often, but it was never too cold or hot. Plus, the rain left mist that stayed suspended in the night air, dew clinging to the mounds of the black plastic bags on the edge of the sidewalks. The sheen of spring's hopeful freshness blanketed all—the bags, the sidewalks, our lives.

Every night on shopping day, I wheeled our tottering cart out from its home between the sofa and the student chair. All three were treasures from shopping days past. The stains on the sofa were really not so bad. From far away, they made out what looked like an intentional design: flowers, maybe, or polka dots of various sizes. That's what we thought they were when we first came upon the couch under flickering streetlamps. It wasn't until we had carried it six blocks that the starkness of the room revealed the designs for what they actually were.

The student chair was my favorite. It looked just like the ones I saw in the schools on TV, down to the stray etchings in the wood and the dried gum caked onto the underside of the attached table. Someone had even carved on it the S made of six interconnected lines that my classmates and I were obsessed with. It mattered not that the table was designed for left-handed students, or that one of the legs had lost its rubber cap. I wedged it in between the couch and the wall and spent hours nestled in its cocoon, rocking back and forth on the unsteadiness of the shorter leg, playing at raising my hand as if I were one of the students in the schools on TV.

The shopping cart had rusty liver spots. Each time I retrieved it from its napping place, more spots appeared. It unleashed cantankerous squeaks every foot or so. The protests grew in the cold weather, when the snow, sleet, and salt attacked the arthritic wheels. Sometimes pushing it on the winter sidewalks was so strenuous that I closed my eyes and pretended I was on my very own lawn, somewhere rural and rustic, pushing one of those red mowers that I sometimes saw on TV.

When it came to selecting items on shopping day, Ba Ba was specific: they had to be portable, they had to be practical, and we had to be ready to leave them at a moment's notice. His admonitions were my mantra. **Never forget, Qian Qian, that we might have to leave at any second.** But that was not tragic, he told me. What was tragic was our attachments. I listened to Ba Ba because he knew just how dangerous attachments were. He had lost things, over and over again. But he also never truly lost them because he carried them with him still. I saw them in his eyes.

Ba Ba told me this and I in turn carried it in my heart: so long as we didn't stake claim to what wasn't ours—the things, our rooms, America, this beautiful country—we would be okay.

* * *

Ma Ma and I came upon a plastic lawn chair one shopping day. I sat in it and quickly found that it was one of those lightweight chairs that was too flexible, too empathetic, moving with my every motion. This particular one used to be white, but now it was brownish gray. It had a crack in its back that was long but did not go all the way through. It met all of Ba Ba's requirements: it was easy to carry, we could sit in it, and the crack made it impossible for us to get attached. It was perfect because it might fall apart any day.

We lifted the lawn chair onto the top of our groaning cart, already stuffed with a broom, a handful of recyclable cans—worth five cents each!—and a folding chair. I was pushing the cart, excited to return home and show Ba Ba our proud bounty, when I came face-to-face with a boy from school, walking with someone who might have been his older brother. What they were doing out in Brooklyn, I didn't know. I had never talked to him—his were one of the many sets of eyes I avoided in the hallways and in our classrooms. The shock of recognition took lease of my face and I choked in a gulp of air. He did not slow his steps, and for a second, I hoped that he had not recognized me, but as he neared, his face twisted into a smirk.

It took ten years for my face to stop burning. I didn't dare look at Ma Ma as we waded through silence down the block. Around the corner, we came upon the elderly couple who lived down the street from us, the only other Asians in our area. As always, they wore beaming smiles on their prune faces as they strolled along with their young cart, which still had FOODTOWN stamped across its chest. As our cart groaned, theirs boasted of its mountain of cans, all of them **clack-clack-clack**ing against one another as the virile wheels bounded across the sidewalk terrain.

"See," Ma Ma said. "We are not the only ones who collect cans."

We were doing exactly what the prune couple was doing, it was true. But that made me sadder. They were happy to be collecting cans while we were ashamed. What was a source of light for them seemed to be only the pit of darkness for us.

* * *

Actual shopping was an exercise in willpower. We had no budget beyond what we had to spare for food, which really meant we spent as little as possible, ideally nothing. At any given time, my wardrobe contained four T-shirts—baggy and long to double as nightshirts and so I could grow into them—three to five of Lao Lao's scratchy, stiff sweaters; and two or three pairs of jeans from Conway. In the winter, we kept all of our clothes folded in a stack along the windows. That way, when they weren't keeping our bodies warm, they protected us against the draft.

I got a new pair of shoes every September. During each annual visit, I spent hours at Payless ShoeSource, poring over my options and making sure my selection was something I would love for the next 365 days.

The love never lasted that long.

For the first four months or so, I cherished my

shoes. I tiptoed around puddles and stopped off in the school bathrooms to give them careful wipes with wet paper towels. The subsequent season saw me acting more or less like a normal kid, not giving the shoes much thought. But for the last few months, when my growing feet bulged against the fabric, blackened and gaping at the seams, I rejoiced in my boylike freedom to kick trash on the sidewalks, jump into mounds of mud, run in the rain, and act like a feral cat.

* * *

My favorite shopping day of all time came in the summer, the worst season for shopping. The Brooklyn summer was the tiger mother I never had. She was in every sidewalk crack, on every black plastic bag, and in every pungent smell. It did not matter where I went. She was forever in my face, telling me to sift faster, to ignore my discomfort, all the while squeezing thick, salty sweat out of every pore.

It happened on a typical summer's shopping day, as I labored with my tiger mother looming over me, sweat sweeping across my forehead and down my back. My parents and I had split up to minimize the time we needed to canvass the area; they had grown tired of fighting my insistence that I was old enough to go off on my own. I crept farther from our street, knowing from experience that the farther I went, the better my finds would be. I had long learned that everything was segregated by neighborhood, including trash. Where we lived, trash was trash. It smelled bad, looked bad, and was worth nothing. But forage outward, and trash was marvelous.

I would have no sense of just how beautiful trash could be until over two decades later, when I walked my two dogs in the Upper East Side on what I still thought of as shopping day. I was aghast at what my neighbors threw out: a fully functional elliptical machine; a handcrafted desk in pristine condition; a child's basketball set, with a perfectly inflated ball. As one of my dogs lifted his leg to unleash a yellow stream onto a sturdy bookshelf, I reminded myself that none of the objects fit the bill anyway: they were not portable, they had only frivolous uses, and most of all, I most definitely would have become attached to all of it.

I could not fathom any of these riches in Brooklyn at age eight, of course, as I made my way down Chester Avenue. Drops of sweat trickled down my back, staining the shirt that I was to wear for another three days. At least, I consoled myself, the smell was not too bad tonight. My tiger mother loosened her grip a little bit that evening. She even rewarded me every now and then with a gentle breeze. I surveyed the clumps of bags, hypothesizing where the treasures might be. A single white Rite Aid bag stopped me. It was a white pearl sitting in the black sea. It was rare for true trash to be left out in a bag like that, and if it was, it was usually bathroom trash—the worst kind, containing used toilet paper, bloody pads, and cakey, dried rubber things that I would not recognize as used condoms until many years later. Opening those bags was always a bit of a thrill; a lottery of sorts.

This particular bag was different. Through the translucent plastic, I could see the candy colors of plastic cases.

Could it be?

It couldn't.

I held my breath as I untied the bag with disbelieving hands.

It was.

In the bag were six Polly Pockets—the same toys I had watched my classmates play with at recess. I had gotten to borrow them every now and then, but only for a few minutes, and only to hold. I had committed to memory their commercials; when they came on TV, I kept my eyes wide open, unblinking, hungry to absorb as many morsels as possible of the pastel cases and the homes and dolls. I memorized their shapes and colors so that when I closed my eyes late at night, they danced before me and carried me into sleep.

And now here they were. Six of them, each a different shape in different colors, all for me to hold—to play with! To keep!—for untold minutes. Here was a purple pentagon with a restaurant inside. There, inside a book with a clasp, a mermaid's underwater world. Next, a round one, a ballerina's theater, with a beautiful white girl spinning center stage for all to admire. And then an octagonal yellow one, a beauty parlor and hair salon, with girls, all white, lined up for glamorous hairdos. But there was still more: A full house with separate bedrooms for each resident! A camper van that unfolded to reveal its own private kitchen!

Each was a portal to a different world, one where shopping day didn't exist—or, perhaps, where every day was shopping day; was that how it worked?—and all I had to worry about was what dress I would wear and how I would style my hair.

I wondered if I was dreaming. Surely, this was too good to be true. Six Polly Pockets? **Six** Polly Pockets? If it was a dream, I was okay with prolonging it awhile. I scooped all six Pockets—all six perfect Pockets—back into the Rite Aid bag and walked back home, the rest of my shopping expedition forgotten.

Chapter 13

McDONALD'S

....

It was at the hair salon that Ma Ma met James Lombardi, a name that to me remains synonymous with McDonald's.

James Lombardi was an old man. Ma Ma often cautioned me against men who looked "dirty," but I didn't know what she meant, not really, until I met James.

James was a regular at Ma Ma's hair salon. But he did not have a regular stylist. He preferred to try the newest, "most appealing" worker of the day. He came only during off-peak hours, so he had easy pick of the women who worked there.

I cannot claim to remember James with any objectivity because the very thought of him causes my body to tense. My memory of him cannot be decoupled from fear, for James was my first reckoning with the fact that as women, and Asian ones at that, Ma Ma's body and mine would never escape the colonizing stake of white men's eyes.

As I remember him, James was fat and balding. He always smelled faintly of onions and seemed to spend all of his days eating Chinese food and trawling for Chinese women in Sunset Park. I can't even remember what he did for a living before retirement, so steeped into his bones was his way of life. He always had at least one used napkin in his pockets. I knew this because he had a habit of taking everything out of his pockets every now and then, as if looking for cash. But no cash ever appeared; instead, it was just more of those napkins, tinged with yellow, brown, and red relics of meals past.

Later, the sight of Jack Nicholson in **As Good as It Gets** never failed to recall to me James Lombardi, and no matter how many years had passed, the smell of onions would pass through my nostrils.

On one of the days that James showed up at the hair salon, Ma Ma had the misfortune of standing by the door, sweeping the floor. I imagine it went something like this:

James sees Ma Ma and asks her boss, the Witch, whether she can do his hair. The Witch responds, "Don't be silly! That's our newest apprentice. Only the best for you, Mr. James."

(The Witch does not care one whit whether James gets the best or the worst. She cares only that he pays full fare for senior stylists, which he rarely does, so drawn is he to the younger, newer workers.)

"Well, let's give her a chance. There's not much left that you can cut on me, anyway."

The Witch pulls Ma Ma aside, settling for a sale, even a small one, and Ma Ma responds along the lines of: "No way. I'm not touching that old pervert."

A debate ensues, with Ma Ma succumbing as always to the promise of tips and a promotion that would mean higher wages.

Ma Ma puts down the broom and takes James to the shampoo area, where she lathers his sparse strands and proceeds to the scalp massage.

Not all of this came from my child imaginings, for later that day Ma Ma came home to me, crying and saying that what she did at work made her feel like a prostitute. I had no idea what prostitutes did, but I thought from Ma Ma's face that it must have been very bad.

I myself did not meet James until weeks after he had met Ma Ma. One Sunday, Ma Ma said that James would be coming over and driving us to McDonald's.

Would Ba Ba come, too? I asked. Yes, he would, she assured me, and for some reason that made me feel better.

I had never been to a McDonald's in Mei Guo. I still remembered the one in Zhong Guo, with the clown who had the scary giant red mouth. But eating at a restaurant—any restaurant—was not something we got to do anymore, so I got dressed with alacrity.

When James arrived to pick us up, I saw that he drove an old car, long and square. Ba Ba leaned down toward me and whispered, "That's a Lincoln Town Car!"

James did not get out; I could see through the windows that his belly was wedged nicely between the steering wheel and the seat. Some of the hairy flesh peeked at me through the gaping buttons of his shirt. He waved us in. Ba Ba got in the front and Ma Ma and I went into the back.

The first thing I noticed was the smell. It was old-man sweat, mixed with onions and musk that had a tang to it.

The second thing I noticed was the ceiling of the car. A thin cloth clung to it, but was so loose and low in places that it touched our heads. Here and there, staples pushed the cloth back in place. But the areas without staples draped down like little balloons. Other than the taxi from the airport, my memories of which were fogged up by exhaustion, I had never been in a car in Mei Guo before. Was this how they made them here?

"So nice to finally meet you, Vincent, and you, too, Chan." James tried to turn around but his big belly and thick neck allowed him only to look at me through the corner of his murky eyes.

"Crane has told me so many wonderful things about you two!"

Ma Ma and Ba Ba had adopted Americanized names, because, they said, lao wai had thick tongues and could not handle the delicate elegance of our language. I stayed with Qian. Why should I have to change what I was called just because their tongues were too clumsy?

James started talking to Ba Ba about China, how long we'd been here, how good his English was. It was the ritual dance Ba Ba was forced to do with every white person he met. But where Ba Ba would have been short with another Chinese person, he was always gracious with the lao wai. I couldn't tell if it was because he respected them more, or thought they were dumber people who needed more coddling.

I took this opportunity to collect several of the staples from the ceiling. They came out of the foamlike material easily, ready to bite with their straight metal teeth. As more of the staples came out, more of the ceiling draped down onto us. The da ren did not notice, probably because James had moved on to talking nonsense:

"You know, 'Vincent' is another name for 'James.' This means we have the same name, Vincent."

I would have rolled my eyes but I was preoccupied with sticking the staples back in the ceiling just in the area directly above my head. The staples went in as easily as they had come out, and, placed together, they kept the ceiling fabric up nice and tight, like they had been in the cars I had ridden in in China. I had one last staple in my hand, but as I raised it to the ceiling, one of its teeth latched onto my hand.

"Ah!" The cry emerged from my mouth before I could stop it.

Ma Ma turned and caught me staple-handed.

"Qian Qian, bie nong."

I sat still for a few minutes until she looked away, slipping back into conversation with the old man. Then, just as we pulled into a parking lot with a giant yellow M overlooking it, I stuck the staple into the remaining part of the ceiling. After that last handiwork, the ceiling—my part of it, at least—was nice and smooth. The rest of it billowed in the air.

We walked into the restaurant behind a waddling James. Once we were through the doors, the smell of greasy fries and cleaning solution greeted us. James sat down at the nearest booth and slid his way in, squeezing his belly against the table. He opened the wallet in his hands and extracted two twenty-dollar bills. Before he closed the wallet up again, I saw at least five other twenty-dollar bills in his wallet. My breath caught in my throat. I had never seen that many American dollars in one place. This guy was rich!

"Order whatever you'd like for yourself and Chan. I'll have a Quarter Pounder. Chan can wait here with me."

Ma Ma and Ba Ba nodded and walked off, talking about what they might be able to get with all that money. I followed them with my eyes and then looked back at James. He had little hair on his head indeed, but he did have much more hair coming out of his ears. Why did it grow there, I wondered. I reached my right pinkie into my ear to see if I, too, had hair there.

"So tell me, little girl—what do you know about China?"

At this, he placed his clasped hands on the tan table. His knuckles were hairy, as were his forearms. His head was the only place short on hair.

"I dunno," I managed to squeak out, uncomfortable under the watch of his murky eyes and wishing I had gone with Ma Ma.

"Tell me," he persisted. "Do you know Maw Chit Ton?" With these last syllables he sounded like he was choking on regurgitated food, just like each time he attempted my name.

"Who's that?"

My response seemed to suffice, because he

stopped looking at me, and instead retrieved from his pocket a stained napkin—the first of many that he would produce in my presence—which he unfolded and refolded before wiping it across his brow. I took the opportunity to feast my eyes on all that was around, and let my gaze linger on a window on the other side of the room. It looked into another room with nets and slides all over it, plastic balls filling the floor. There was a little Black boy in the room, diving into the balls and then reemerging, his ebony face poking out from the pink, blue, and yellow plastic.

I debated asking to go into the room, but concluded that I wouldn't know the right way to play anyway. Plus, I probably wasn't dressed properly. My jeans were tattered and lined with dirt and markings from last winter's street salt. My sneakers, which had been white when Ma Ma and I bought them almost a year before, were now brown from daily wear and had holes with loose thread coming out of them. When I took them off, they filled the air with the smell of sweat, rainwater, and unwashed socks.

No, I could not go into the ball room even if I did know how to play. I would stink up the place.

When Ma Ma and Ba Ba returned with plastic trays full of food, the ball room fled my mind.

Ma Ma had gotten me the same order as Ba Ba: I was going to get to eat a whole Big Mac meal, just like a real grown adult. Ma Ma had gotten the fish burger, she said, because she figured it was the healthiest option. James's Quarter Pounder was huge, and as he rammed it into his mouth, my brain clicked into place why he had so many stained napkins.

As we were all chewing in contentment—I most of all—James frowned and made as if he had something very important to say to Ba Ba.

"Vincent, I must tell you, I am very concerned about Chan."

"Why's that?" Ba Ba gave me a look that I returned with a blank.

"It's important for her to know her culture. She doesn't even know Maw Chit Ton!"

I thought he was choking on his burger this time, but I realized that he was just trying to speak Chinese again.

Ba Ba looked puzzled, too. He took a bite of his Big Mac, which squirted its orange-yellow juice onto a corner of his mouth. Ma Ma remained focused on squeezing ketchup from a neatly opened mouth of a packet, drawing a thin red line onto each individual fry.

"Qian Qian," Ba Ba spoke in Chinese, "you don't know Mao Zedong?"

"Oh! Is that what he was trying to say? Mao

Zedong?" I intentionally responded in English. "Of course I know him. He"—with this I pointed a finger at James—"can't pronounce Chinese names."

When this emerged from my mouth, all three da ren chuckled. But I could tell from the tone and length of Ba Ba's laughter that I would soon receive another lecture about saving face and giving face, especially for old lao wai like James. I knew what I would respond with, though: Why were we expected to speak English perfectly while praising Americans for even the clumsiest dribble of Chinese?

James fixed on me his cloudy eyes, now full of suspicion.

But why would I lie and pretend to know something I didn't, I thought as I bit with bitterness into my Big Mac. The food was good, but it wasn't worth sitting under James's scrutiny.

* * *

As it turned out, Ma Ma thought the free burger was worth it. We saw James again a few Sundays later, for our next outing to McDonald's. By then, he had already earned the moniker of Lao Jim in our household.

Ba Ba said he had to work that day. When Lao Jim's car arrived, I saw Jim in the front passenger seat, with a younger Chinese woman next to him, behind the steering wheel.

When we got in, I noticed that the car smelled not like onions but like Rite Aid's perfume section. My attention then turned to the fact that someone had removed the constellation of staples in my corner. They were now distributed again, balloons billowing throughout the ceiling.

"Crane, Chan, this is Mimi." With each word, Lao Jim infused the air anew with onion and old-man smell.

Mimi adjusted the rearview mirror to make eye contact with Ma Ma. She waved a few slender fingers at me without turning around.

"Hello," she said in English.

She was not pretty, not really, but I was confused because she acted like she was. She was skinny and wore tight clothes, but her eyes looked sly. She reminded me of a fox. She looked graceful but, like with everyone else, I knew I couldn't trust her. And who was she to speak English to us when we were all equally Chinese?

Ma Ma returned Mimi's greeting while I stayed silent. Mimi put the car into drive and, unprompted, told us the story of how she had met Lao Jim. I settled into tuning her out and reconstructing my staple masterpiece. I looked away from the ceiling only when a song came on the radio that elicited a squeal from Mimi. She turned the volume up and started singing to a voice that sounded like it belonged to a very skinny and hungry lao wai.

When the song hit its crescendo—and the whiner on the radio demanded what sounded to me like "spread your lemon fly"—Mimi lifted her butt slightly and started moving it from side to side. Ma Ma did not notice, but even from where I sat, directly behind him, I could see that Lao Jim had shifted his entire body to stare at Mimi's flat, bony butt.

It was the most disgusting thing I had ever seen.

Once we were in McDonald's, Mimi insisted that she order for everyone. Lao Jim opened his wallet and retrieved the same sum he had given Ma Ma and Ba Ba—two twenty-dollar bills— but Mimi sauntered closer to him, almost kissing his ear as she said, "Jimmy, you know that's not enough."

I had never before seen a woman in such command of a man. Without a word, Lao Jim opened up his wallet again and handed her three more bills. He beamed, apparently proud of being manipulated.

Mimi walked away without asking what any of us wanted to eat. I pleaded with Ma Ma for permission to go after her—I had never seen the counter or the menu—and after a pause, Ma Ma gave a small nod. I ran after Mimi's tight light-blue jeans. Turning the corner to the cashier, I was greeted with lights, bins of fries, a colorful menu, and a display case indicating that it held the "Limited time only!" toys that came with the Happy Meals. Inside the case were little Barbie dolls that were supposed to be from across the world, to represent the Olympics: the white one with her blond hair in a ponytail was the only one who wore an official red-white-and-blue gymnast uniform, while the others wore outfits from their culture. There was an Asian doll who wore a kimono, but she had a lao wai's facial features, and looked nothing like me. In any event, I knew that I wanted the blond one, because that was the "regular" Barbie, the only one who got to wear a real Olympics uniform. I got as close as I could to the plastic case, marveling at the fact that I could get a whole Barbie for free with a meal. The figurines were much smaller than the Barbies I had seen my class-mates play with, but they were close enough, and more than I had ever expected for myself.

My time was limited. I turned to where Mimi was standing before the cashier, who was point-ing to the menu items high on the wall behind him. I hustled over to her and implored, "Mimi, may I please have a Happy Meal?"

She looked at me for a second and turned back

to ordering. I worried that she hadn't heard me until she said in her broken English, "And Happy Meal, for girl."

Curious as to just how much everything cost, I paid careful attention as Mimi chose the Chicken McNuggets for me and then moved to pay. When the cashier was done pressing button after button on the register, Mimi handed over two of the twenties and kept her hand out for change. I gasped. Happiness cost almost twice our weekly food budget.

Mimi stuck the change and the other two twenties in her front jeans pocket and we stood on the side of the counter, waiting for our food. Mimi made no effort to talk to me and instead fixed her eyes on the wall of advertising inviting us to "Supersize it." As for me, I had much to study on the menu, converting the prices into ratios of our budget.

Soon, the cashier started filling up two trays with our food, and the golden fries with browned edges and little clear crystals of salt had me salivating at the thought of the crunch giving way to its warm, soft center. I caught the drool that was dripping out of my mouth just as Ma Ma appeared at the counter, gesturing to another cashier.

"Jim needs"—Ma Ma stumbled over her English words—"he needs, nei ge, nei ge, nei ge . . .” In her frustration, Ma Ma was reverting to the Chinese word for “um,” which we tended to repeat in quick succession when we were at a loss for the right word.

The cashier took offense to this. She pulled her head back and spat out, “**What** did you say?”

Ma Ma seemed to realize something and chuckled with nerves. “No—not that. Not that word. It’s a Chinese word.” But the lady continued to look at Ma Ma with the same suspicion that Lao Jim wore when I told him I had known who Chairman Mao was all along.

I did not understand what was happening, but I zipped into action anyway, helping Mimi remove Ma Ma from the area and then apologizing to the cashier for whatever it was that had happened. When at long last I was able to get what Lao Jim needed—mayonnaise and napkins to grow his collection—we sat down with our trays of food. Mimi handed Lao Jim the single dollar bills, and I caught him frowning at the trays and then his hand, mentally counting the missing money. Just as quickly, though, Mimi deployed the fluttering high voice she seemed to reserve for him: “Look, Jimmy, your favorite: Quarter Pounder.”

Silence fell upon the table, interrupted only by chewing. As I stuffed my face with the nuggets, I freed my new blond gymnast from the red

Happy Meal box. She was perfect, but I was less happy with the nuggets, which were tiny, dry, and tasted nothing like chicken.

Ma Ma was eating the fish burger again, the golden fried patty covered with a white sauce. Some minutes later, as I was combing through my tiny athlete's hair with a single finger, wishing I had ordered an adult-size meal so I wouldn't have to sit there with my stomach growling, Lao Jim got up and went to the bathroom across the room.

Mimi checked to see that the bathroom door had fully closed behind Lao Jim before declaring: "You know he's disgusting, right?"

Ma Ma opened her mouth in surprise, but I didn't know if it was because Mimi had finally spoken Chinese or if she was just shocked at what Mimi said.

"Who?"

"Him. James. He's filthy. He has nasty thoughts about everyone. Even"—at this, she gestured toward me by moving her chin up and then down—"her."

Ma Ma turned and stared at me with new eyes. I had no idea what "nasty thoughts" were but I did not like how they made Ma Ma look at me.

"He has diabetes but he still comes here every weekend. It's the only way to get people to spend time with him. Can you believe that?"

She paused for Ma Ma's response but, receiving none, she pushed on.

"Anyway, you should make the most of it. Eat more."

A squeak announced that Lao Jim was out of the bathroom and on his way back to the table. We finished the meal and rode home to the sounds of Lao Jim's burps and my stomach's rumblings.

We continued to go to McDonald's with Lao Jim after that, but Ba Ba always made sure to come with us. We never saw Mimi again.

Chapter 14

SLEEPOVER

....

Third grade was a welcome change. Though it was a new class and a new teacher, I immediately felt like I belonged. Miss Pong was Chinese but didn't speak Cantonese or Mandarin, so I was no more foreign to her than my Cantonese-speaking classmates. And she had a kind face that set me at peace. I found home in her approval, which became my daily goal. Looking back now, I realize that Miss Pong must have been just a few years out of college. To me at eight years old, though, Miss Pong had more power and wisdom than did any other adult.

A few months into our time together, Miss Pong called me up to her desk as the class filed out to recess. She produced a book with a colorful cover depicting a girl, a pig, a sheep, and a duck, all staring up at a spider in its web.

"Qian, I love how much you enjoy reading. You remind me of myself when I was a little girl."

I beamed. There was no greater compliment. I thanked her for the book—my third gift in America—which I tore through that week.

After that, Miss Pong became for me the noble, guiding influence that Charlotte was for Wilbur, that Miss Honey was for Matilda. Unlike Ma Ma and Ba Ba, Miss Pong was always the same. She never raised her voice, she was never distracted, and she always listened to what I had to say. I adored her.

Over the course of that year, Miss Pong and I exchanged letters and cards, correspondence that I would come upon again more than two decades later, when my parents abruptly moved out of their home and dumped what little remained of my childhood—report cards, medals, vaccine records—in my apartment. Among that pile remained **Charlotte's Web**, yellowed but in otherwise pristine condition. The first page bore Miss Pong's note: "Qian, this was my favorite book when I was your age. I hope you enjoy it as much as I did." And my response, which she never received because I wrote it in the book itself: "Thank you, Miss Pong, I did!"

* * *

Miss Pong was a large part of why I felt more anchored in the third grade, but there were other reasons, too. I was pretty much fluent in

English by then—as fluent as any other third grader who had been born here, who had always been in America—and that gave me a certain sense of safety. I also had a new best friend, Elaine. Much to my relief and hers, Janie was no longer in my class. I grew so removed from my need for her translations that I don't even remember seeing her around the school after second grade.

Elaine was sweetness personified, with an easy smile, big eyes, and the thickest, straightest hair I had ever seen. She was the first friend that I really trusted. It was not that I hadn't trusted my friends in China, of course— I had trusted them in the same way that kids untouched by immigration and poverty trusted everything around them: without question and by default. Elaine, though, was the first person I made the conscious decision to trust. She was the youngest and most easygoing of three sisters. Even though their parents were immigrants who spoke little English, all three of them had been born in Mei Guo. Their parents worked at sweatshops, too, but they were among the ones who sewed buttons.

A few months into third grade, Elaine and I started to have sleepovers. It almost made me feel like a normal kid. Looking back on it now, I have no recollection of where she actually did the sleeping, so small were our rooms. Nor do I remember being ashamed of our home, and though Elaine must have been surprised, her sweet nature kept her from betraying it. At the time, I assumed that because she was Chinese, her home in America was just like mine, completely different from the lao wai palaces shown on TV.

Elaine was the first and only person I ever had join me in the bathroom my family shared with our roommates. It was my sanctuary and place of peace because it was the one room where I was away from Ma Ma's worries, where I could be alone with my thoughts and my books. When Elaine was over, we hung out there and talked, she sitting on the edge of the bathtub and I on the toilet, ostensibly pooping. If she found it at all odd, she did not let on—at least, not until I began to actually poop.

Invariably she would begin to wince, and ask through a pinched nose, "Can I leave now?"

"Why?"

"—Smells so bad!"

"You are such a baby." Sometimes I would not have the chance to get this retort out before she ran out the door.

Elaine slept over at my place several times before she asked that I sleep over at hers. The suggestion shot trepidation through me, and

I put it off, hoping that she would forget. Spending the night at her place meant that I would not be around to take care of Ma Ma, give her advice, or protect her. I couldn't risk that. Plus, I shuddered at the thought of entering a new household and family. There had been too many new things in my life, few of them good. I could not handle much more.

Unfortunately, Elaine did not forget, and the days counted down quickly to the night I had doomed myself to spend away from Ma Ma and Ba Ba. This might have taken place as late as over summer break, because I remember that we had no school that day and Elaine's second oldest sister, Wanda, was to fetch me from my dad's office and take me to the very different part of Brooklyn where their family lived. Wanda was in high school, so she had the authority of a real adult. She also was the scariest person I had ever met. She had the steely feel of—as I would only later understand—girls who dared to have a mind of their own. Physically, though, she looked pretty normal, aside from the fact that she rivaled only Ms. Zhu in the amount of makeup she wore.

The friend Wanda brought with her was another story entirely. Although Wanda was the scariest person I had ever met, her friend was just scary-looking. She may have grown scarier in my memory over the years: I see her vividly before me in thick black eyeshadow, thicker face piercings, and what I later knew to be gauged lobes, but what I then perceived to be severe ear deformities. Ba Ba must have thought the same thing, because the minute Wanda and her deformed friend came into the office, he stopped talking and froze. He had a cigarette in his mouth that fell to his desk, which he quickly retrieved, dusting off the ashes in embarrassment. I looked up at Ba Ba and back at the girls, who stared until Wanda stepped forward.

"I'm Wanda? I'm here for Qian?"

Ba Ba barely collected himself before pushing me and my bag forward with a clumsy hug goodbye.

On the way out, and then the entire way home, Wanda and her friend said not a word to me. It was just as well, though, because I was preoccupied with eavesdropping on their conversation.

"Omigod, he was so cute!"

Elaine had not told me that Wanda had a boyfriend, so I leaned in closer and stood on my tiptoes, trying to figure out who she was talking about.

"But, omigod, did you see how much I freaked him out? I told you I shouldn't have gone up with you."

Gone up where? Who was freaked out? The

only people who were freaked out by the holes in Wanda's friend were me and Ba Ba. I was not a "he." And Ba Ba was not "so cute."

I faded out of eavesdropping for the rest of the trip home, puzzling over this mystery and excited to bring it to Elaine, who would surely help me solve it.

Many stops later—so many that by then the train was above ground—Wanda's spooky friend got off, and Wanda and I rode the rest of the way in silence.

When we finally got to their apartment, I paused at the entryway in awe. I had been wrong about all Chinese having similar homes in America. How could I have made Elaine spend so many nights in our cramped rooms? Elaine's family lived in the nicest apartment I had seen so far in America, though it was still much smaller than the white-people homes on television. A TV, couch, and dining table filled up the living area. The dining table led into a galley kitchen, which they had all to themselves. Next to the TV was a room blocked off by a bunk bed that served as a makeshift wall. Inside that room, another bunk bed stood perpendicular to the first. The two beds corralled the sunlight flowing through the only window in the living area. Next to that was Elaine's parents' bedroom, which I never went into, and the little bathroom. The bathroom was about the size of ours, only their family did not have to share it with anybody else.

The weirdest thing about Elaine's home was that the living area was too small to allow the couch to be placed facing the TV. Instead, the couch sat perpendicular to the TV so that all watching had to rotate their heads to the left. Elaine explained that there were special rules for sitting on the couch. The person sitting at the end closest to the TV had the best view, but could not move around freely since that would block everyone else sitting on the couch. The person in the middle could move a bit, but not too much. The person at the farthest end, meanwhile, could make up for the poor view by gesticulating to her heart's content.

There were many rules like the couch rules at Elaine's place, and I found it all very strange. Her parents were warm, like mine, but I thought it was weird that they controlled their kids so much. Elaine's mom's hair was shorn short and she was small and skinny in a way that made her look much younger than she was. She spoke neither English nor Mandarin—only Cantonese—but she was so loving that I needed no language to understand just what kind of mother she was. She reminded me of Ma Ma and she worked in the sweatshops like Ma Ma had, so in her presence I felt at home.

My memory of Elaine's father is fuzzy. This was probably because he was rarely home from work. But from what I did experience of him, I remember a gentle, quiet, and somber presence, loving but distracted by the demands of life.

By the time dinner came around, I had relaxed into myself. Except for the additional siblings and the lack of roommates, it had not been so different from being at my home. All afternoon, Natalie, Elaine's eldest sister, and Wanda watched me with amusement. Even as Elaine and I played with her dolls, I felt their hot gaze on my neck. They continued through the meal, but I was so hungry for the steaming hot noodles and beef strands that the moment Elaine's mom placed the plate before me, I lost all self-consciousness.

An eternity passed as I waited for everyone to be served. And then, when we were all ready, I let loose, slurping up the noodles, making whooshing sounds as I stuffed strand after strand into my mouth with my chopsticks. I kept my eyes down at my plate and did not notice the family's curious stares until I looked up again. It was then that I realized for the first time that Ma Ma and Ba Ba must have taught me to eat noodles the wrong way.

I spent the rest of the night in unease, muscles stiffened to ward off wrong movements. I did not know what else Ma Ma and Ba Ba had taught me wrong, so I questioned every one of my instincts. After dinner, we watched a cartoon. I can't remember what it was about, only that it was something I had never seen before. Mostly, I sat on the couch with my neck turned to the left and my face pointed at the TV while soaking up the shock that at Elaine's house, it was not the children's job to wash the dishes and clean up.

Then it was bath time, during which Elaine showed me that she showered like we did in China—sitting on a stool while using a little cup to scoop water from a plastic water basin. I waited politely until she was done and then said I was fine going straight to bed. I was not used to showering more than once a week, and that seemed to me a better way to save water, but I figured I had probably been doing the showering thing wrong, too.

Even my pajamas felt wrong. They were long bottoms that were so thin from wear that I could easily see the blue edging of my underwear underneath. On top, I had a T-shirt Ma Ma had bought from the 99-cent store. I had already worn it to school for days on end the year before. It had started out as much too large on me, but had since shrunk down to only slightly large and tattered. Elaine and her sisters had matching pajama tops and bottoms, the special kind that were just for wearing in bed, the kind that I had only ever seen white people wear on TV.

I was to take the upper bunk of the second bed, the one above Elaine. I had long dreamed about having a bunk bed and a sister to share it with. But suddenly, the thought of falling asleep so high up from the ground, without Ma Ma and Ba Ba anywhere nearby, felt terrifying, sad, and final. A well of tears formed in my eyes. Natalie and Wanda looked up at my bunk, first startled, then amused again. Eventually, Elaine's mother emerged from her room, in a similar matching set that she clearly wore only to sleep. She spoke to her daughters in the sharp tones of Cantonese.

"What's wrong, Qian?" It was Elaine who ventured first.

"I miss my ma ma and ba ba." I must have been somewhat comprehensible over my sniffles, because Natalie and Wanda started chortling.

After some shushing and translating, Elaine's mom ushered me to the phone. I remember little of the phone call or of the rest of the night, only that I asked to go home and that, when told it was far too late, I asked my parents to pick me up as soon as possible the next morning. After I hung up, the pinching in my stomach continued, and I knew, as I did whenever I was away from Ma Ma and Ba Ba, that something bad would happen to them while I was gone. I would never see them again—I just knew it. I would look up at the sky and say, "That's where they went," only there wouldn't be an airplane; I'd just be looking up at heaven. I fell asleep clutching these thoughts.

The next morning, everything was a little more mortifying, a little less necessary. I regretted that Ma Ma and Ba Ba were coming because Elaine's mom had taken the day off to take us to the aquarium. Under the safe light of day, I no longer missed home, but having made such a grand show the night before, I had no choice but to stick to my word. So I followed Elaine and her mom to the subway station, where Ba Ba was waiting on the other side of the turnstiles. I hugged Elaine goodbye before she and her mom got on the train on the opposite side of the platform, the one headed for a fun day at the aquarium.

Chapter 15
TRAPDOORS

....

That year, as flowers bloomed and the sun grew brighter, Ma Ma and Ba Ba decided that I was old enough to go home on my own after school. I did not know whether it was because they could no longer deal with me after school, or whether I had proven myself responsible. In any event, the decision changed my days: in the mornings I was a child, riding the subway with Ba Ba, my hair unkempt, my teeth unbrushed, and my stomach growling with hunger, but in the afternoons I emerged from my schoolroom cocoon a full adult. I stood a little taller, my chin raised a little higher, and I acted as self-possessed and unflappable as I imagined that I might one day feel. The last part proved difficult. I never knew what to expect on the subway, and it would be years before I became one of the many who felt safe enough to pay attention only to the book in her hands.

The subway was its own world, rife with characters who seemed like they could not survive aboveground. One man boarded my afternoon F train at East Broadway with such regularity that he created for me a real-life game of **Where's Waldo?** I made sure to spot him on the platform every day before boarding the train, and then took care to keep my distance but remain close enough so we always got on the same car.

He was disheveled—even more than I was—and he wore a trench coat that was several sizes too large, spotted and stained with coffee drips and mud. His body was hairy and, despite that he was half bald, the remaining hairs on his head still managed to be unruly. He wore a pair of sunglasses that were black but fogged over with dirt. He also carried a peeling black walking stick that had a tennis ball at the end.

Invariably, he sat in a two-seater at the end of the car. This was not always easy, but on occasions when the seats were full, he would stand and wait, poking his walking stick here and there until some too-kind fool took pity on him and gave up his seat.

It was a good act.

Once seated, he always managed to find the nearest young woman. If there were several around, he had an uncanny way of zeroing in on the prettiest one.

It always began the same way.

"Excuse me, excuse me . . ." He gestured with his walking stick.

There would be a long, awkward pause as people reshuffled themselves to accommodate his gesticulations. Some people simply walked to the other end of the car, but everyone stayed quiet.

"Won't anyone take pity on an old blind man?"

I was almost taken in during our first encounter. What stopped me first was my new shyness. Second, of course, was Ba Ba's voice reminding me to trust no one.

What stopped me next, though, was my sneakiness. I could never help but notice the smallest of details. Indeed, the details often came to me before I consciously registered them. For instance, I knew, before recognizing that a police officer was standing on the corner of a street, that something was amiss, that I should walk the other way. It was as if I monitored my surroundings without even noticing it, and my body knew what to do long before my brain caught up to all that it had processed. But Ma Ma and Ba Ba often told me—and thus I half believed—that I did not have an astute intuition, that I was just a know-it-all kid.

All I knew was that after ten seconds with the blind old man, my body told me that he was not blind, and that he was not to be trusted. He moved his head and directed his field of vision with too much precision and accuracy. I had zero experience being blind; for all I knew, that was how all blind people acted. Still, I decided not to engage, instead staying silent and far away from the old man.

Watching it happen for the first few times was like live television. Inevitably, the poor pretty target—for there was always a pretty target—took pity on him.

Yes, hi, sir—what do you need? The one I remember had long blond hair and blue eyes. I remember her because I had learned by then that those were all the traits that made someone beautiful. This made for easy criteria, because I still could not tell one blond-haired, blue-eyed woman from the next.

Oh, thank you, you kind, young thing. Please, can you tell me, what's the weather like outside?

He was blind. He wasn't numb. Why did he need someone else to tell him what it was like outside? Didn't he have to walk outside to get to the train? I had never been blind but I was pretty sure that, even with my eyes closed, I could feel the sun on my skin.

Well, it's warm. Sunny.

How warm?

Really lovely. Warm and comfortable, not too hot.

Really? That warm? You must have a thin, flowy dress on.

Every time I watched him, he was right about what the woman was wearing. And at this point some hesitation would start to dawn in the poor pretty woman's eyes.

Well . . . yes.

Please, can I feel the material? To see how warm it is outside?

At this point, the woman usually said no more and moved to the opposite end of the car.

* * *

The subway was the reason people-watching became instinct for me. I learned quickly that the underground tunnels held many trapdoors that would swallow me up if I didn't stay observant, if I didn't keep my distance, if I let just anyone stand next to me.

The first time it happened, I did not know what I was looking at. I wondered if it was just a fat, weird finger poking out of a coat. I told myself it was, but a sick ache in my tummy said otherwise.

It was as if a switch flipped on after that first time. There was no telling where the finger would pop up. Here it was, by the crosswalk on my way home from school. And again, here, standing next to me on the platform. It started following me everywhere I went. I knew somehow that it had to be my fault. Each time, it was my fault. I should have kept my eyes to myself. I should not have looked up from the two square inches on the ground just in front of my feet. I should have known better. I was a bad, shameful girl.

I felt grateful that when it appeared, the finger lasted only a few seconds. Then it snuck back behind the zipper. Sometimes it happened so quickly that I convinced myself that I had only imagined it all, with my bad brain and my bad thoughts.

Then there were other kinds of trapdoors. More dangerous ones.

I almost fell into one.

I was seated in my usual spot near the car door, reading a Baby-Sitters Club installation, when I felt my skin prickle. Keeping my face directed at the book, I spun my eyes around in their sockets and surveyed the car. They fell upon several fellow passengers who survived scrutiny: an old lady chewing on the edge of a red-bean bun; a smiling man engrossed in his boom box, bopping his head to the beat; a tourist looking constipated and unsteady.

None of this was reason for my skin to prickle, so I continued my examination until my eyes hit upon a man at the other end of the car, pale and slovenly, his shirt yellowing with age, his hair sticking out in random directions. His face has since faded in my memory and merged with those of the many other men I've encountered in the subway since.

The train was just pulling into York Street station. The man kept his eyes on me. The doors dinged open and the usual commands from the operator followed. A Chinese woman hurried out with her son, about my age, in tow. In sauntered a grown-up couple, hands all over body parts, oblivious to the rest of us. I looked over at the man, who returned my gaze. His eyes had a glint I had never before seen. That glint set my body into action before my brain realized what was happening. As if controlled by someone else, my legs straightened and carried me out the door. My book stayed open in my left hand, fingers pinching the page I had been savoring before I realized that I had an audience. I set foot on the platform for but a few seconds before shuffling into the next car and walking from one end to the other.

I should have known better than to think that I was safe, but for a second, that was what I believed.

But then a flash of yellow-white caught my attention. It was at the same end of the car where I had entered. My stomach turned into a rock.

He had followed me.

He had **followed** me.

My brain jumbled to all the stories Lao Lao and Da Jiu Jiu told me about Mei Guo, of the madness and the chaos. Out of nowhere, I longed for my dolls and my bike, all decomposing in the little storage unit.

I reopened my book and stared into the black ink, not comprehending a single word. By the time the train pulled into the next station, my hands had numbed and he had edged half a car closer.

Maybe I should try it again, I posited to myself.

He'll just follow you, I responded.

Should I tell an adult?

What if he's undercover, here to deport me?

Just stay put. You're safer if you stay put. There are people all around.

A hundred mes shouted at one another but I could not afford a long debate. I shuffled to take a seat next to the door by my end of the car, my eyes still on the page.

The doors opened and no one stepped out. I counted my breath, willing myself not to look over at my white-yellow shadow. The doors dinged again, declaring that my chance to run was slipping away. Still, I stayed seated, counting. Face still pointed down, I flipped the page I had not read, hoping that my shaking hands and dry mouth would not be visible from down the car. Out of the very edges of my eyeballs, I saw the metal doors emerging from their sheaths on either side, like a chewing jaw.

Then, as if propelled, I burst up and out of the opening, so fast yet so late that my backpack just avoided getting pinched. Once on the platform, it took me a few seconds to slow and steady myself. By then, the train was already roaring into motion. I inspected the platform for the white-yellow hue, moving my head around pillars. I found only people looking wearily into the tunnel at the other side of the platform. No white-yellow shirt. No glint.

I sat on the wooden bench and directed my gaze onto the page, not reading a word. As I flipped a page every so often, I looked around. I was terrified that if I moved, he would reappear. So I stayed put even as another train pulled into the station and then departed. I debated walking home or taking the bus, but neither seemed safe. As another train lurched into the station, I willed myself to stand up and step on while still choking on my palpitating heart.

Between that stop and my home station, I switched cars twice, looking each time to see if anyone followed me. I swiveled even as I climbed the steps out of the Church Avenue station. On the walk home, I crossed the street and then crossed it again. Unlocking the front door was the ultimate test: my cold hands shook so much that I could not guide the key into its slot. These efforts were made all the more difficult by the fact that I could not keep myself from looking down the street to make sure no one was coming.

I don't know how I got the key in place that day, but I must have at some point, because I remember standing in the hallway on the other side of the two layers of bolted doors, gulping in gasps of air that swallowed me whole.

* * *

I may have lost that man that day, but his specter stayed with me. From that day forward, he crept behind me on every street I walked on. He was in every subway car, every moving crowd, every thought that urged me to move a little faster, be a little smarter, trust a little less. He was in every dark corner, promising that he would get me. I never forgot that he would eventually get me. It was only a matter of time.

Chapter 16
SOLID GROUND

....

I found that it took more and more for me to be enough for Ma Ma. She was perpetually anxious now, and I was the little doctor who was on call around the clock, ever ready to jump in and soothe her. My only time off was when I was sitting on the toilet, which I took to doing occasionally for thirty minutes at a time, reading, thinking, and savoring the peace. Every now and then, I took so long that a roommate would knock angrily, at which point I cleared my throat, gave a flush, or turned on the faucet to appease him, only to go on reading one of the three Baby-Sitters Club books I made sure to bring into the bathroom.

Ba Ba was home less and less, and Ma Ma frequently told me that she thought there might be other women. I didn't know what this meant at first, but one day I walked into his office after school to see a woman sitting so close to him it looked like she was on his lap. I ran back out, down to ground level and onto East Broadway before allowing myself to take another breath. Ba Ba had not seen me, and I was never able to see him the same way again.

Still, I told Ma Ma during her morose times that I was sure there was nobody, that Ba Ba was good. I must not have been convincing, though, because it rarely worked.

One afternoon, Ma Ma met me at the front door of PS 124 just as I was walking out. Her face was gray, her eyes sucked of all light.

"Ma Ma, what's wrong?"

"I almost jumped," she mumbled to the floor.

"Jumped? Where?"

She looked like she was on the edge of collapse. As classmates filtered out in clumps, some laughing and some looking at us, I ushered Ma Ma to the steps at the corner, sitting her down with me after checking to make sure there was no gum.

Over the course of the next several minutes, I pieced together that Ma Ma had tried to dodge subway fare to try to save money. On that particular day, she was coming back from the Thirty-fourth Street station. She had gone in for a free photo shoot after a random woman stopped her on the street to say that she might be a good catalog model.

The "shoot" had not gone well. They said that before they could begin, she needed to pay fifty dollars for the "free" photos. After Ma Ma explained that she could not spare several weeks' worth of family groceries, they said she didn't have what it took, anyway.

On the way back, all she could see was the long carpet of meaningless jobs that unrolled before her. She was so distracted by this vision and so upset that she had traveled all that way that she did not notice the man standing by the steps down to the platform, watching her as she moved to duck past the turnstile.

The man approached Ma Ma with swift steps and flipped open a badge. In her recounting, Ma Ma took for granted that he was a cop, and thus so did I. He asked her questions, but she was too flustered to remember what he said and what she responded. He had given her the wrinkled paper ticket that she now gripped in her hand. She expected him to put handcuffs around her wrists and send her off to be deported, but he only lectured her in tones that she could not comprehend before finally letting her go.

I smoothed out the paper, careful to not smudge the ink with my small hands. I gulped down each word as if it were a morsel. The ticket demanded that Ma Ma mail in a fine. I do not remember the number, only that it was large. And it must have been more than the photo shoot cost, because Ma Ma kept saying that if she had only stayed for the shoot, she might have avoided it.

After being handed the ticket, Ma Ma found some coins in her purse and bought a new fare, walking down the stairs as the cop continued to stare at her back. It was not until she was on the platform that she looked down at the piece of paper in her palm. Everything washed over her in that moment. Her spirit capsized, and as a train pulled into the station, she wondered what it would be like to hurl her body before it.

The only reason I didn't do it was you.

I'm glad you didn't, Ma Ma.

I paused to find more to offer and came up short. My words were meager. Paltry. Not enough.

Just like me.

* * *

Ma Ma changed after the incident. I did not understand then that there are few things more activating than the quiet desperation of a dignified woman.

It happened gradually. It must have. But so attuned was I to Ma Ma's every move that in my recollection, it felt seismic and immediate.

After I started fourth grade and as the weather grew colder, Ma Ma started studying in our shared kitchen every night as I began getting ready for bed. The kitchen was the warmest part of our apartment, and the residual heat from cooking, coupled with the incandescence of the lamp, best protected her from the night's chill as she tried to stay awake. Our roommates barely used the kitchen, particularly at that late hour. Plus, Ma Ma welcomed the short break of someone entering to microwave his frozen meal.

Ma Ma's goal was the TOEFL, which she was very nervous about. When she first told me about it, she explained that her English was so poor that she could barely touch the minimum score demanded by even the worst graduate programs.

"You're going to graduate school?" This was the first I had heard of it, and I was the first to hear of everything in Ma Ma's world.

"Yes," she said. It was our only route to a better life.

"I cannot live like this forever," she continued, and I thought about her on the subway platform, gripping that ticket.

"Will they let you? What if we get caught?"

But Ma Ma had looked into it already. She had a friend in a similar situation. The friend told her that it was fine as long as she was careful with the school she chose.

The friend must not have known that Ma Ma was always careful.

"City College, they don't check or ask any questions, just like your school."

I let out a breath that I did not even know I had been holding. Perhaps there would be college for me after all.

"What will you study, Ma Ma?"

"Computer science, as I was always meant to. As if I'd never left China."

I did not ask what she was going to do with the degree. I did not remind her that we never dared to apply to the real companies that I saw only on TV, the ones with offices high up and big windows overlooking Central Park, with watercoolers and huge mahogany desks. For their bright light would shine too brightly onto our Chinese passports, revealing the hole where our American paperwork should have been.

Before we left China, Lao Ye gave me a little keychain. It was not just any keychain. It had several tools in it that made me feel safer in America whenever I had it with me. The keychain was in the shape of a foot, and it had a metal center with a brown plastic shell. On one side, it had a small pocketknife, with the tiniest of blades. On the other was a small pair of scissors. Both folded into the metal center. Four characters were written on the foot in white font: Jiao ta shi di. Feet on solid ground.

"What does it mean, Ma Ma?" I had asked after running to show her my new shiny possession.

"It means taking it one step at a time, Qian

Qian, being grounded and looking at just what's in front you."

The message of Lao Ye's keychain served me well in our life in America. I learned to focus on just what was right before me, and in this instance it was supporting Ma Ma in the only pursuit that had managed to inject hope into her face since we walked out of that JFK terminal.

The hard questions, I saved them for myself.

* * *

Ma Ma studied over the course of the rest of the winter and early spring, using books that we got from the library. But she said the books were outdated and made it difficult to know if she was really preparing for the test she would be taking. She approached the end of spring with caution, like a rabbit darting past a sleeping lion.

The test came and went quickly. The results were slower. I froze every time Ma Ma opened the black metal mailbox just outside our front door. In those moments, anything was possible—our lives hung in the air, just under that ballooning cloud of poverty.

One day, I watched with disbelieving eyes as her hand resurfaced from the depths of the mailbox with the envelope. She ripped it open, nearly tearing the thin letter within. She looked at it, and then at me.

I don't remember the score, only that she started laughing.

Which caused me to start laughing. Then jumping. Then cheering.

Soon, we were laughing through tears, the sidewalk passersby looking at us and then pretending not to see us, two lunatic girls from mainland China.

The cloud dissolved. I closed my eyes and felt the rays of the middle-class sun on my face.

Things would be different. Things would change. One step at a time.

* * *

When we packed for America, I slid the foot keychain into an external pocket of our checked luggage. I didn't know why, but I felt that we might need it on our journey. Ma Ma had hooked the foot onto a spare nail clipper, so that came with us, too. Once we got to New York, I hung the foot and the nail clipper from a zipper on my backpack. I figured that was where my only keychain needed to go, since it was the place where plush happy faces and bright troll dolls suspended from my classmates' backpacks.

Over the years, I moved the foot keychain from one backpack to the next, and then finally to a storage bin where I kept nail clippers and files. The foot shed its parts over the years, first losing one brown plastic piece, then the other, until it was just a metal chunk with vestigial spots of dried glue. I have the keychain to this day, and though it is now barely identifiable as a foot, its message shines as clear to me as the day Lao Ye handed it to me, white characters on shiny brown casing and all. No matter where I wanted to go, I only needed to worry about one step at a time. Feet on solid ground.

Chapter 17

AUNTIE LOVE

....

Ma Ma began to step a little lighter, buoyed by new hope. Soon, she told me, she would start school. Before that, though, she found a new job at a warehouse.

The new job seemed to be an improvement over the hair salon. The warehouse stored supplies for restaurants, and her second week of work, Ma Ma returned home with a canister larger than her head, full of shaped yellow wafers that I had never seen before. Ma Ma told me that white people thought they were Chinese and called them "fortune cookies."

"Here," she said, her eyes not quite focusing on me. "You can have it all."

That entire container became my dinner for the night, and I was not even hungry in school the next morning because I was still sick from all the fortune.

A few days after that, Ma Ma returned with a box full of toothpicks with colorful paper at the end, suspended throughout by little match-like sticks. With a push, the paper unfolded and opened out to a mini parasol. There were two colors: pink and green, each with flowers and leaves drawn on them.

"Ma Ma, zhe shi gan shen me de?" They did not seem to have a purpose.

"Xia wanr ba." Something silly to play with.

Within the week, our two linked rooms were filled with little paper parasols, taped onto the walls, sticking out of the fabric of the armrests of our couch, standing in the slats of our TV set.

As I filled my stomach with fortune cookies and stuck toothpick parasols into every crevice of our home, Ma Ma mumbled on and on about her new boss, Henry Yee.

"Henry Yee treats me like a servant," she said as soon as she got home. "I have to wash his dishes and get him tea."

"Henry Yee doesn't do anything," she talked into the chopping board as she cooked our dinner. "He just sits there and reads his newspapers while barking out orders."

"Henry Yee is a racist," she mumbled over her chopsticks as they suspended stir-fried string beans over her bowl of white rice. "He has no proof but he keeps saying the Black guys in the warehouse steal.

"Then why hire them?

"Because they are cheaper.

"Because he is cheap.

"Because he is racist.

"Because he is a cheap racist."

Always it was Henry Yee, not Henry, not Yee, but both names together in one. It seemed as if he was not her boss if he was not both Henry and Yee.

There was a woman who worked with Ma Ma at the warehouse. She was also Chinese but she was older, Ma Ma said, and she was in love with Henry Yee.

"Isn't he old?" I asked.

"Yes," Ma Ma affirmed, even older than the woman.

"How could she love something so shriveled," I marveled.

"Loneliness makes people odd," Ma Ma mused almost to herself.

I was lonely, too, but I would never, I thought, be in love with someone racist and wrinkled.

From then on, I started to think of the woman as Ai Ah Yi: Auntie Love.

* * *

One Saturday, the weather grew so hot that Ma Ma got permission to take me to work. She did not want me stewing all day in our tiny place. There was a little air conditioner in the window of the office, Ma Ma said. She shared that office with Ai Ah Yi and Henry Yee, though, so I would have to be good and quiet. I nodded with my solemn face, and hid my disappointment at having to miss a day of freedom, full of books and TV and no worries but my own.

On the first morning I went to the warehouse with Ma Ma, she led us out of the subway at Canal Street, a station that I'd never seen before. It was at the opposite end of Chinatown. There were also Chinese letters everywhere there, but unlike on East Broadway, there were not as many Chinese people. The area had many white people who did not look quite right, though it took me a few minutes to figure out why. I concluded finally that they must have all come in from out of town, because they were fatter, clumsier, happier. They also dressed as if they were mimicking characters from TV shows set in New York. They looked like they were uncomfortable and not used to wearing those clothes, which were either all black or much too bright, and which did not look like they were meant to be worn together in the same outfit, much less by the people wearing them.

As we continued walking, the excited, chubby white people thinned out and the crowd turned normal—gaunt New Yorkers wearing shabby clothes and exhausted faces. The surroundings started to remind me of Brooklyn, for though the streets contained warehouses, they were also covered with graffiti.

Ma Ma slowed down at one of the warehouses and I saw that the door was raised off the ground, a big, levitating mouth that opened right up against the butt of the truck parked against it. We took the steps that led up and into the mouth. Several men, Black and Latino, were gathered in the warehouse, some lifting and moving boxes, others sitting. They did not have uniforms on but wore similar outfits—black T-shirts, stained jeans, tan boots. They greeted us with warmth and seemed to know my name, but I froze. I had learned by then to be guarded around all new men, and especially the ones who were not Chinese, as Ba Ba had taught me. But Ma Ma seemed comfortable around them, and she was almost never comfortable anymore. This prompted me to give a quick, shy smile before Ma Ma led me to the stairway at the back of the large room.

There were many stairs, and as we climbed them, I felt Ma Ma's hand tense up again. The stairway spat us out onto another floor of the warehouse. We walked past dark shelf after dark shelf before coming to an office, which just looked like another warehouse room, with bright tubes of light dangling from the ceiling, just under the metal pipes.

On the floor were two rows of tables leading to rusty, large windows. The tables were each covered with stacks of papers and one feeble computer apiece. The table surfaces were made of wood so rough that my hand hurt from splinters at just the sight of them.

Ma Ma and I were the last to arrive. At the seat closest to the doorway was a lady whom I assumed was Ai Ah Yi. Her appearance recalled the "pancake face" story from the recesses of my memory. She looked at us but did not smile before turning back to her computer. She wore such a serious and focused expression that, had she not blinked, I would have thought she was a mannequin. She also looked as if she had a Very Important Job, even though I knew that couldn't be because she had the same job as Ma Ma.

Next to her, separated by wide, tall stacks of papers, many of them wrinkled and yellowed, was Ye Ye. He was not Ye Ye, not really, but so much time had passed since I'd seen Ye Ye that I had started to spot him everywhere: on the subway, eating a mooncake; at a restaurant, bussing tables; on the sidewalk, walking with a woman who was not Nai Nai.

The sight of Ye Ye brought to me a glow of joy and love. But when Ye Ye turned to look at me, I realized it was not him. The man was not unfriendly, but he kept his distance and his face did not burst into rays of happiness. So this was Henry Yee.

I did not have much time to stare because Ma Ma told me to follow her down the hall. One of her morning tasks was to make tea for Henry Yee. Gripping a metal mug, Ma Ma took me to the other end of the warehouse floor, where there was an exposed little sink attached to the wall with a single leg supporting it, and a rusty metal spout and matching rusty handles above it.

Instead of turning the handle and rinsing the mug with water, Ma Ma spat into the mug three times and turned it to move her spit around. She then turned to the other wall, where she bent over to pick up a sad black kettle covered with dirt. She filled the kettle with water and plugged it into the wall.

I stood a few steps behind Ma Ma and surveyed the area. Next to the kettle was a microwave that looked like its sister: black and filthy. On the floor, by the sink, was a yellow box that looked to be as old as Henry Yee. It had the word LIPTON written on it. Propped up on the wall next to that was a broom from China. I knew it was so because it was made from many loose bamboo sticks tied together, not like any broom I had seen since leaving home.

When the kettle sang, Ma Ma flicked it off, pouring steaming water on top of her spit. She unwrapped a bag from the Lipton box and dunked it into the mug without ceremony. We then walked back through the darkness and into the fluorescence of the office.

I settled into a folding chair next to the window, as close as possible to the air-conditioning blast. Ma Ma sat in front of the computer and the stack of paper that apparently belonged to her. She stayed this way until Henry Yee barked out his next command, at which point she got up. The rest of the day passed much in this way: me following Ma Ma back and forth, from the lit room through the dark channel to the grungy cooking area and back. She stayed silent. I longed for the time when I was not just a dangling thread on her dress, chasing her to and fro as she catered to the whims of an old man who turned out to be nothing like Ye Ye.

Henry Yee left at around five p.m., according to the big round face on the wall of the office. Periodically, though, the phone rang and Ma Ma ran across the room to answer it. Ai Ah Yi remained as she had all day long, seated at her desk, flipping through papers and typing endlessly, breaking only twice for the bathroom.

Ai Ah Yi did not look at me until around eight o'clock, when she gestured for me to walk over. I hesitated, turning to Ma Ma for guidance. But she only kept her eyes on the screen before her, oblivious to my plea.

I walked over but crossed my arms in front of

my torso, braced for battle. I stopped just ten feet in front of Ai Ah Yi and then turned around to Ma Ma, who still had not noticed.

"Lai ya, zai lai ya." My gaze whipped back at Ai Ah Yi's command for me to approach closer.

I shuffled my feet, hoping that she would not notice how small my steps were.

"How old are you?"

This was an easy question, but her bottomless eyes made me worry that I might give the wrong answer. Again, I turned to Ma Ma for help. She remained absorbed in the screen before her.

I had no choice but to answer truthfully.

"Nine! My son might have been nine, too." She looked away, in the direction of the windows.

I took this opportunity to scamper back to my chair, where I dared not look up from my library book until Ma Ma told me that it was time to leave.

When we walked out, Ai Ah Yi was still sitting at her desk, typing away, and every now and then, looking up through the windows.

* * *

Many peculiar things happened during Ma Ma's time with Henry Yee. One night, Ma Ma came home to tell me that she had found a nest of little baby mice—pinkies, Miss Pong had once said they were called. Ma Ma told me that she did not see a mommy mouse, so she had to flush the babies down the toilet.

The story filled me with sadness. For nights after, I had dreams of little baby mice, scrambling against the tide of the spinning toilet water and flailing their pink paws and legs before going limp and getting sucked into the hole at the bottom of the toilet bowl.

A little while after that, Ma Ma came home with a wan and sallow face. She reported that Ai Ah Yi had collapsed just as Ma Ma got up from her table to go home. It was just Ma Ma and Ai Ah Yi in the room when it happened, and when Ai Ah Yi did not respond to Ma Ma's voice, Ma Ma ran downstairs to find that all the warehouse men had left, too.

She ran back upstairs, toward the hope that Ai Ah Yi had awakened while she was downstairs.

No luck.

Ma Ma at that point knew she had to call 911, so she did. But rumors of immigration raids and detention were strong kindling for the fear that pulsed through each of us. Ma Ma knew she had no choice, but still, she was terrified that the cops would arrive only to arrest her, pay no attention to Ai Ah Yi, and leave her there to be eaten by the pinkies' mother while Ma Ma was sent off to China.

Awaiting the shrill sirens, Ma Ma alternated between sitting with Ai Ah Yi and making sure she was still breathing to tidying up her own desk and packing her stuff, so convinced was she that she would be deported, never to step foot in the warehouse again. As she tells it, time froze and the paramedics took an eternity and a half to arrive.

But once they were there, things moved quickly. Two paramedics stormed up the stairs and into the office with a stretcher. Even under the bright bulbs, Ma Ma was unsure of the text on their uniforms, knowing only that she was breaking every instruction she had given me by staying in the same room as them instead of running away.

As they assessed Ai Ah Yi, the paramedics—Ma Ma never described them to me, so in my mind's eye their faces are white blanks with black outlines of moving, drawn-in mouths—asked Ma Ma to describe what had happened just before Ai Ah Yi's collapse. While Ma Ma stumbled over the few English words that she was able to summon on such short order, Ai Ah Yi opened her eyes. It was Ma Ma who noticed first, and she pointed to the blank-but-open eyes. The paramedics turned in unison and began speaking to Ai Ah Yi all at once.

"I didn't catch all that they were saying to her," Ma Ma recalled to me. "I remember only that they asked her who the president was."

"What did she say?" Why did they ask that? I thought. Is that how they determined who was here legally? I made a mental note to always have the president's name at the ready.

"She answered, 'Henry Yee.'

"Then they said, 'No, the president of the United States.'

"And again she answered, 'Henry Yee.'"

Ma Ma was looking off into the distance as she recounted this. It was an impressive impression of Ai Ah Yi.

"Then what?"

"They put her on the stretcher and then got her in the ambulance. I sat with her the whole way there and waited while they took her in. They asked me some more questions, but they didn't let me in."

"Then what?"

"Then I came back here. I don't remember how, though. It's a blank."

* * *

Ma Ma came home late a few nights later. She had gone to visit Ai Ah Yi. I was just getting into bed, and Ba Ba was watching TV on the other side of the curtain, in the living room.

"How is she, Ma Ma?" Tales of Ma Ma's day were my lullabies.

"She had a stroke. She didn't recognize me at

all. Her head—it was swollen to double what it used to be."

"What will happen now?"

"I don't know. And I don't think she had any other visitors."

There had been nothing in Ai Ah Yi's hospital room except a large basket of flowers that Henry Yee had sent her, Ma Ma recounted.

"Didn't Henry Yee visit her?" He was racist and wrinkly, but she still loved him.

"I don't know. I don't think so. She doesn't recognize anyone anyway. But the flowers, a nurse put them right next to her, and she kept turning to look at them."

Later that week, Ma Ma learned that Ai Ah Yi had died. She had to clean up Ai Ah Yi's desk, but she had no relatives to send her things to. Ma Ma placed the box of items on one of the warehouse shelves.

"What was in her desk?"

"Just papers, things that had her notes on them. I couldn't bear to just throw all of it out. Her whole life was working for that man, Henry Yee."

"What about personal stuff?"

"She had a mug for her tea. That was it. I put it in the box, too."

"She didn't even have a photo of her son?"

"What son?"

"Didn't she have a son?"

"I don't know. I don't think so."

* * *

For many years following Ai Ah Yi's death, I was plagued with a recurring dream:

Ma Ma, Ba Ba, and I are on an old Chinese train, the kind that Ma Ma and I once took to Shanghai. We are running from men in uniform. We run from one car to the next, and then the next, and then the one after that, until we are in the first car, the one that is the head of the train. We look through the window on the door to the conductor's cabin. We see not a conductor but a uniformed man with beady eyes, staring back at us.

I scream but Ba Ba covers my mouth. Then he turns to open a side door in the car and we three jump out, all at once, into a grassy clearing. It does not hurt, and we roll in unison before standing up. We turn around and see uniformed men behind us, jumping out of the train, one by one. We start running again, but every time I turn around, the field holds more men. Soon, it is no longer green from grass but from the uniforms. I run as fast as I can, slowing only when Ma Ma and Ba Ba can't keep up.

After some time, always after some time, as exhaustion crawls up my legs and into my torso, we see a fence that stretches the full horizon of the clearing. From afar, the fence looks like it has bulbs and balloons in the gaps between its links. We have no choice but to continue running until we close in on the fence. The uniformed men follow.

They always follow.

And then, just as I turn around to see them reaching their arms out to grab Ma Ma and Ba Ba, the world fills with the sound of popping.

Bursts of liquid fall onto my face.

I turn to the uniformed men, but they are gone.

I turn to Ma Ma and Ba Ba, but they, too, are gone.

The field is empty and I am alone, always alone, when I realize that the grass is no longer green. It is now red.

I turn to the fence and realize that those are not balloons between the links.

They are human heads, bloated and engorged with blood, water, pus.

Each looks at me with lifeless eyes and then off into the distance behind me.

I stand there, unable to move, as, one by one, they pop and burst onto my face.

Chapter 18
NORMALCY

....

As my nights began to fill with dreams of horror, my life slipped into a sort of normalcy that I didn't think was possible in America. It was this that scared Ma Ma: she started saying more and more that we needed to change something, we needed to move and leave this place that refused to recognize us. But even this refrain—along with my weak assurances that it would take just one step at a time—became a mundane routine of sorts. My memories of those days started to blur into one another, as I imagine that memories of uneventful childhoods tend to do.

I do remember, though, that fourth grade was the first time I realized I could be smarter than some adults. And one adult in particular: my teacher that year was Ms. Glass. I thought of her as a grandmother. She had orange-red hair and the frenetic energy of someone who could never hold on to a single idea long enough. She seemed to be forever chasing after the train of thought in her mind. The knowledge that I was faster and more intelligent than the adult in charge of me was exhilarating. I almost always knew what Ms. Glass was going to say before she stumbled her own way there. This helped me develop awful classroom habits that would follow me for the rest of my schooling. I spent most of my classroom hours daydreaming, doodling, and counting down the seconds and stomach rumbles to lunchtime.

For at least the early part of the year, home life was much the same. I took the subway home and did my homework in front of my PBS Kids family: **Wishbone** and **The Magic School Bus**. Other than the days when he stayed out late, Ba Ba often came home first. He asked me about school before taking over the television.

If Ma Ma came home first, she, too, would ask me about school before sharing her day with me: her fears about Ba Ba's dalliances, her longing for our lives to change, her anxieties about school. That last part included Ba Ba's objection to her going to school at all. This went on until Ba Ba came home, at which point Ma Ma headed into the kitchen to cook dinner in silence.

I preferred when Ma Ma came home first because even though Ma Ma and Ba Ba spent the same amount of time listening about my day, with Ma Ma it felt closer and less selfish because she also shared her day with me and asked me for advice.

By this point, we must have been doing better with money. This was clear to me only in hindsight, for Ma Ma's school cost a little bit of money, and Ba Ba joined some sort of gym where he went on Sundays. Plus, Ma Ma had come upon a new recipe for chicken and, every now and then, we had a whole smoked chicken for dinner. I did not notice it, however, in the moment. Other than the smoked chicken, my life was very much the same, and for that I was grateful. I longed for some sort of continuity, even if it had to be in the form of a life that Ma Ma hated.

After Ma Ma prepared dinner, the three of us sat at the rickety communal table in the kitchen, the one with the rusty metal legs and a white top with green and blue specks. Ma Ma and Ba Ba fought more and more, propelling their cutting words across our dinner table. The argument was always the same: Ma Ma wanted to leave, to move, and Ba Ba said no. Where would we go? We are just as American as the next family. This would make Ma Ma spit out something mean, like, **What's so great about this America of yours, where they treat us like shit?** and **What kind of coward are you that you're so terrified of change?**

Me, I stayed silent, head down over my plate to keep from crying, mouth stuffed with white rice and stir-fried potatoes.

Other times, better times, Ma Ma and Ba Ba got mad at me instead. They spent those meals berating me about having gotten so chubby and having grown messed-up teeth that made my entire face look crooked. Once they got to this topic, they stayed on it for the entire meal, and sometimes, for the remainder of the night. I was never going to make anything of myself, they said, with that fat and asymmetrical face. And no one else would ever tell me the truth but them. It was their job to tell me my flaws, Ba Ba said, because who else would do it? I could not trust the rest of the world. Everyone else would only lie to me out of politeness.

Those dinners were confusing; I never knew how to feel. A big part of me was glad that, for once, Ma Ma and Ba Ba were on the same side. That was rarely the case anymore and I found warmth and safety when they were aligned, even if it was against me. At the same time, though, I never felt more alone than when Ma Ma joined Ba Ba in his critiques of me, for it was often the case that just minutes before, she had been sharing with me all the ways in which Ba Ba was bad and selfish.

Those dinners marked the only times that I

could not finish eating. I got upset but I had to swallow that feeling until it became a stomachache that squeezed out hunger. Seeing this, Ma Ma and Ba Ba would pivot to how spoiled I was. How dare I not finish the meal they offered to me? Didn't I know that food cost money, and that we had none? I was too spoiled for my own good, they said, and I received too much love.

This only added more to my confusion and stomach pain. If I was fat and we were poor, why did they want me to eat more?

I believed everything they said at those dinners, as I did everything Ma Ma told me. It never even occurred to me to think that they might have been wrong. But looking back, I had not gotten fat, not really. I continued to skip breakfast and depend on the free lunch at school and any free scraps I managed to find, either on my way home from school or in our communal kitchen. But I had bloated from weekly binges on free McDonald's with Lao Jim. The hour after those excursions marked the only time of week that I felt full—almost approaching the kind of full I had once felt in China.

The photos of my face back then recall a cartoon I had once seen on television in China. A boy squatted over a frog on the ground and tapped it with a chopstick. At each tap, the frog's chin grew bigger and bigger. The skin grew tauter, looking less green and more white with each tap. That was my face: large and growing larger with each McDonald's visit—not from nourishment but from malnutrition. Indeed, I was chubby in the way that only the poor could be: from too much sodium, too many canned goods.

As for my teeth, by this point I had not seen a dentist in nearly three years. I was grateful that most of my teeth were straight except for the bottom right canine that protruded (and protrudes to this day), locking my jaw in whenever I closed my mouth.

Nor had I seen an eye doctor. At school, Ms. Glass's writings on the chalkboard grew fuzzier by the day. I relied on tablemates to read out words and numbers to me.

Many nights, I awoke to pain in my legs so piercing that I could not move them. I could only clutch them and roll around, doing my best to keep quiet until Ma Ma awoke, which she always did, assuring me that it was only growing pains, that I would be done with them soon. As she said this, she moved to the edge of my bed, where she sat and massaged my legs. I would fall asleep again only under the blanket of her soft whispers and strong hands.

Our family was closest in the face of pain.

* * *

We passed some weekends and holidays with two other families from north China who were also stranded and could not go home to be with their real families. Ba Ba had gone to school with the mother in one family and the father in another. After each time we saw them, Ma Ma and Ba Ba said that they would not have chosen to be friends with those people if we were all still in China. But we were in America now, so what were we to do?

The other two families each had one son. We were all doomed to be sibling-less, thanks to the one-child policy we had left behind. One of the boys was a year younger than me, smart, quirky, and nice enough. He was short and had the look of a mad, talented artist who was always pondering some grand idea. The other was several years older than me and an utter idiot. I rarely had anything to say to either of them, but Ma Ma said that we didn't get to pick our family when we were so far away from home. Maybe, I consoled myself, this was what having real brothers was like.

Our get-togethers were never fancy. The three families took turns hosting. One lived in Brooklyn, like us, and the other lived in Queens. Inside, our apartments were nearly identical: two-room setups, sparsely furnished with sidewalk treasures. What made each a home was the savory smells that told of northern Chinese home cooking. Our gatherings in the winter were more often at the other homes, because both of those families had their own private kitchens (and bathrooms, for that matter) and the kitchen was where we gathered to stay warm in the cooking heat. We—kids and adults alike—would sit in a circle on folding chairs around a dining table. The table was often so full of potlucked snacks that it threatened to topple over. Sometimes there were peanuts and sunflower seeds and, if we were lucky, even small pieces of chocolate. The kids sat quietly as the parents went on about how great life had been in China, how hopeless life had been in China, how much they missed it, and how they did not miss it at all.

The adults did not notice us kids, and least of all me, the girl. When they did notice me, it was nothing like it had once been in China. No one ever commented on how pretty I was anymore. Mostly, they talked about how smart I was, how well behaved and mature. Guai. Dong shi. It was the only value I had in America.

I took this as further evidence that Ma Ma and Ba Ba were right: the other adults could not say that my face was fat and crooked, so they had to talk about something else. They didn't think that I remembered that in China, no one could stop talking about how pretty I was and how I would surely be on TV one day. I carried this silent loss with me from room to room, home to school, nursing it and resolving to make up for what I had lost in looks with determination and hard work.

I got this idea partly from the show that we watched with the other families. **Beijing Ren Zai Niu Yue,** or **Beijinger in New York,** had been a hit book and series in China even before we left. It was not until we got to New York, though, that we had watched it, renting the VHS tapes one by one with money pooled together from the three families. The series featured a young man from Beijing who followed his wife to New York City. It showed them living a life similar to ours, mediated somewhat by the gloss of television. We watched them struggle with English, money, and new American ways of living. We watched them interview for, and work at, the same odd jobs that Ma Ma had. The main character even had the same last name as me and Ba Ba.

"Ma Ma, what is the point of watching our own life on television?" I asked during one such gathering.

"Well, isn't it nice to know, Qian Qian, that we're not alone?"

But I didn't think it was nice at all. It didn't seem right that there were many more people out there feeling alone and homesick and hungry in the same moments when we were feeling those things. Hundreds of lonely people, I figured, was far worse than three lonely people.

As the television played a scene of people bullying Wang Qiming, the main character, the "us" on the show, Ba Ba shuffled his folding chair over to me and whispered, "You see, Qian Qian? Qiming was on top in China but now he is on the bottom in America. Just like us."

At this point I wondered: Were we that far from the top in America? Everyone around me seemed to be living just about the same life we were. I had given the worst Secret Santa gift, but I figured that had just been my fault, that I had been too selfish. Sure, my classmates had toys and better clothes and even fancier pencils. And they never seemed to be very hungry, nowhere as hungry as I felt. But aside from Julia and Jennifer, they didn't seem so much richer that I thought they were at the top and we were at the bottom. I considered Elaine's home. Yes, it was cleaner and bigger and the family talked more, but it was strange there. I knew how my home worked, at least. Theirs had strange rules. Was that what being on top in America meant?

I much preferred the later episodes of **Beijinger in New York**, because they showed that after many years of hard work and chi ku, swallowing bitterness, Wang Qiming became so rich and successful that he lived in a house with more than two rooms, and no longer needed to beg for odd jobs. This turn in the show energized me. As the screen panned around Wang Qiming's fancy new home, all bright with sunlight, I turned to Ba Ba and said, "Wang Qiming is on top again, Ba Ba. Like we will be, right?"

I did not say this quietly enough. All the adults around the room heard me and chuckled. An odd look took over Ba Ba's face, like the time he told me not to say the word "chink," and I waited for him to scold me again. But he stayed silent.

Later, turmoil found Wang Qiming and his family again, even despite their success, hard work, and wealth. I saw this as no mirror. I had been a close study of television since arriving in America, and I knew that it always had to make things difficult for the characters. Money, I thought, protected people from everything. In China, we had money and no problems. In America, we had no money and only problems. Money was the cure.

* * *

Around that time, I decided that I would become a lawyer one day. My reasoning was simple. First, lawyers had money. Lots of money. The ones I saw on television were always wearing fancy suits and talking quickly about money. I didn't mind that they were always white men. In my early days in Chatham Square, I had come upon and gulped down condensed biographies of Ruth Bader Ginsburg and Thurgood Marshall. Ruth and Thurgood showed me that lawyers didn't have to be men, and they didn't have to be white.

Second, I knew that I was going to do what Ruth did. She made it so that no woman would have to endure what she went through. That was what I was going to do for immigrants like us. But I just didn't know how that was going to happen. I had wasted time: I was already nine. I hoped I had enough time left to figure it all out. Ba Ba had once told me that Harvard was the best school, and it was where the lawyer who gave me the ladybug had gone. So I fixed my sights on Harvard. There, I would figure it all out.

I clung to this plan. Nobody liked it when I shared it, though. My classmates said it was boring and lame, not like their dreams of becoming astronauts and dancers. But even more so than the other kids, the adults really didn't like my plan. Sometimes they laughed, but not in a positive or happy way. It was always more of a chortle. Other times, they frowned. They rarely said anything in response.

When I told Ba Ba and Ma Ma, they were quiet for so long that I wondered if they had heard me.

Then Ba Ba pierced the silence. "It's great to have big dreams, Qian Qian, and to work toward them. That's even more important than accomplishing the dream itself. It doesn't matter if the dream doesn't come true, so just don't be too sad when that happens."

The last adult I shared my plan with was my new fifth-grade teacher, the first male teacher I ever had. His name was Mr. Kane, and he had very short hair and small blue eyes that hid behind rectangular glasses. He made many jokes and talked so much it almost seemed as if he had no one to talk to at home. I didn't know this for sure, but I did know that if I didn't have Ma Ma to speak to, I might have tried to get more attention in school.

Although Mr. Kane shared many words, they were light, like fluff floating in the air, impossible to grab or hold on to. They were nothing like words from Ba Ba and Ma Ma, which were made of heavy metal, which you stored in your pockets and balanced on your shoulders.

When I told Mr. Kane my great plan, he paused and then chuckled. He said nothing and after waiting for a while, I walked back to my desk, cheeks hot, blood in my ears. It wasn't as if I had told him I wanted to be a lion when I grew up, I thought.

I couldn't make sense of any of it. After that, though, I stopped sharing my plan. But I clutched it hard and close, carrying it against my chest like a hidden compass. The chortles and chuckles followed me, but I didn't mind. They reminded me that I had an audience to prove wrong.

Chapter 19
MARILYN

....

I began to talk a lot about pets. I wondered often about what it would be like to have someone always on my side. Someone who saw me and noticed me and got excited when I came home. Someone who didn't need me for advice, someone who was just there for me.

In fifth grade, I had a friend who had a hamster. One morning before school, she put his cage in the sun so that he could get a tan—his belly was too white, she said. But when she came home, she found him immobile at the bottom of the cage, next to his wheel.

She said she opened the gate and reached in to wake him up, but he was hard as a rock.

"At least you had a pet at some point," I responded when she recounted the experience to me. "I've always wanted one but the one time I asked, my parents told me that they can't even afford to feed me."

"Your parents don't feed you?"

At this, I bit my peeling lips. I had said the

wrong thing. We would be deported now, as soon as someone came to investigate why I didn't have enough to eat. I kept talking, hoping new words would squeeze what I had just revealed out of my friend's skull.

"In China, I sometimes got little chicks who followed me around the house, all in a row. But they never lived longer than a day or two." I thought back on running to the cardboard box on Lao Lao's balcony upon returning from school. The images came to me all at once. Three little unmoving puffs, yellow feathers matted and tinged with brown. Tiny eyelids in pink-brown leather, refusing to wake up no matter how hard I shook the box. Warm teardrops blanketing the cardboard, the feathers, the beaks.

"They died," I said. "And then there was a bunny rabbit, so cute and white, with black spots around her eyes." There I paused, as that memory simmered. "She disappeared. Da Jiu Jiu and I came home and she was gone. But a few days later, I walked around the corner of our building and there was a man sitting on the street, selling all kinds of animal skin. One of them was a rabbit with black spots around her eyes."

In response, my friend declared, "China sounds weird."

She was Chinese, too, but not Chinese like I was. So much of my life had been coming home to find things gone. She didn't seem to know anything about that kind of Chinese life.

* * *

It happened on just another Sunday. I brought into Lao Jim's car, and then McDonald's, my library book of the moment, a book I could not put down about a girl around my age who came into possession of a litter of kittens. She named each of the kittens after a Hollywood star, like Audrey Hepburn and Vivien Leigh. Lao Jim asked me about the book as he chewed up his Quarter Pounder.

"Do you like cats?"

"Yes, I would like any pet, a cat or a dog or even a rabbit or mouse."

"Would you like to have a cat?" Lao Jim did not look at my parents as he asked me this. He kept his eyes trained on me and I wasted no time nodding my head until everything in sight began to shake.

"We don't have room for—"

"We can't afford to feed—"

The fast protests from Ma Ma and Ba Ba piled on top of each other.

Still, Lao Jim kept his eyes on me, and for once I didn't mind. "My sister has a cat. She would be perfect for you. I can bring her next week."

Then, looking to Ma Ma and Ba Ba, he said,

"We can bring some food. And if it doesn't work out, you can bring her back to us."

Time passed glacially after that. I found seven books from the library that promised to teach me about caring for a cat. But as soon as I started reading, I realized that I could not do any of it. Why did they recommend things like buying cat beds and cat toys, I wondered, when no one could afford them?

My only hope was finding something on the sidewalks, and I approached shopping day with more fervor than ever. My mission failed each time, but I always came home with the sense that next time, I would succeed.

Meanwhile, I contented myself with stealing Q-tips from our roommates' bathroom storage and taping them together in bunches as makeshift cat toys. I hoped that it might be enough for Marilyn—for that was what I had already decided to name her, after Marilyn Monroe, who Ba Ba told me had been the most beautiful star of all of Hollywood. He showed me a photo of her once and I was awed by the perfect paleness of her skin.

Sight unseen, I already knew that mine would be the most beautiful cat in the world.

When the day finally came, I awoke at eight a.m., my stomach in little twists and knots. I had never gotten up so early before, and was happy to busy myself with watching morning cartoons for the first time ever. Although I was eager to see what the fuss was about, I discovered that I could not process anything that I was watching. It was as if the scenes before me went in through my eyeballs and out the back of my head. All I could think about was how slowly time was moving, how many commercials there were for toys I no longer cared about.

The sounds of the TV pierced the curtain dividing our rooms, and Ma Ma and Ba Ba roused, marveling that I was already awake. Ba Ba always commented that my sleepiness in the morning and alertness at night—zao chen bu qi, wan shang bu shui—would be the "end of me," as would my slovenliness. He said this no matter how well I made my bed and cleaned up, even when I woke up early before school to do it all. The few times I shared with Ma Ma how much Ba Ba hurt me with his words, she told me not to be so emotional or to take them so seriously. After all, she said, Ba Ba was known for guarding his warm heart with cold words.

Ma Ma didn't seem to notice that no matter what I did or how hard I worked, there was Ba Ba's voice, flowing out of his head and getting lodged in mine, reminding me that there was little I could do but march toward the "end of me." I did not know what it meant, not really, only that the phrase brought about images of me thrashing under a crescendo of gray-blue waves, fighting to survive despite never having had the chance to learn to swim.

That morning, though, Ba Ba simply said nothing. It was a brief reprieve, and one that I savored.

By the time afternoon arrived, I was bouncing from the corners of the room, sticking occasionally to the window of the tiny sunroom. When I saw that familiar Town Car round the corner, envisioning with my mind's eye the gray ceiling fabric swaying with the motion of the wheels, I bounded into the hallway and out the two front doors.

That day, Lao Jim had brought his sister, a nun. He had three sisters. They all lived together in the Brooklyn home where they had grown up. He had said that all of the sisters were nuns; I remember this well even though I have no memory of what Lao Jim himself did before retirement, maybe because I worried that I would one day meet his sisters only to find that they were the same monsters in black cloth that I had seen five years before in the Beijing airport.

As Lao Jim and his sister stepped out of the car, I was relieved to find that she was wearing almost normal clothes. I could see her full face, and as she approached, I registered that her eyes were not blue but a murky brown, like Lao Jim's. Lao Jim retrieved a cage from the backseat. I was surprised that they did not just carry Marilyn out, or put her on a leash, but then I realized I did not know what people did with cats, least of all what white people did with them.

"Ma Ma! Ba Ba! Kuai lai ya!"

I could barely believe that my parents were acting as if it were just a normal day. We were welcoming a new family member— nothing would ever be the same.

Ba Ba and Ma Ma waited in the hallway as Lao Jim and his sister walked through the front doors and into our living area. Earlier that morning, I had set out a folding chair so there would be enough seats for everyone. Did the cat need a seat? I had pondered this for a second before realizing that she would just be sitting on my lap.

Lao Jim groaned into the couch and set the cage on the floor. I peered into it and met with a flash of black, white, and tan fur, and round eyes aglow. Lao Jim's sister bent over the cage. She was thin and moved easily; it was as if Lao Jim had done all the aging for her. She pinched the two metal bars in front of the cage door, and then, at long last, out came my Marilyn.

She was a skinny little thing. Through the

black fur coat, I could see the ripples of ribs. She walked in a straight line and assessed me with doubt. Her face was a collage of black down one side and a swirl of white and tan on the other. Her eyes were dark, full of mysterious intelligence. With a swish of her long black tail, she came over and rubbed her head against my ankle, leaving strands of black hair on my jeans. Next, Marilyn studied Ma Ma, who looked back at her with reciprocal suspicion. I knew from Ma Ma's gaze that she did not like that Marilyn was mostly black, with an unbalanced face. I had by then drifted pretty far from Chinese culture, but even I knew that such asymmetry, such darkness, was considered very bad luck.

"She likes you." Lao Jim smiled.

By the time Marilyn reached Ba Ba, I could tell that his mind was made up. "They must have gotten this cat off the street." He shared this in Chinese while keeping his smile intact, his tone gentle, so as not to betray what he was saying. "Look at it. Its face is all asymmetrical. What horrible luck to bring into our home. We can't afford a curse like this."

Ma Ma nodded while continuing to smile at Lao Jim as my heart crumbled. I must have appeared okay, though, because Lao Jim's sister began speaking to me with her quiet voice and pursed lips.

"I understand you'll be the one taking care of . . . Marilyn, is it?"

I nodded solemnly.

"Well, then, let's walk you through what you need to do."

She talked me through the litter box and the food as I tried to focus while blinking back tears. There was so little I could do to keep my parents from doing the inevitable.

"Will you come visit her?" I asked. My parents would not lose face and throw Marilyn out if Lao Jim and his sister were due for another visit.

"Only if you like, dear. This is her home now."

I looked to Marilyn, who had started to clean herself while sprawled on the floor.

How cruel it was that home could be so temporary.

* * *

Marilyn was even more incredible than I imagined. Our living area had the thinnest, narrowest of moldings protruding from the wall less than a foot down from the ceiling. Marilyn could leap from the floor to that molding with a single push of her hind legs. She then walked around the perimeter, observing us from above. She also learned to fetch the Q-tip bundle, though often she leapt up to the molding with it in her mouth. I watched her walk around with it, sometimes following her around the room, hoping that she would drop the bundle in my hand. I would do this until my neck started to hurt, and then I would look down for a while before following her again with my eyes.

Our room was a warmer place with Marilyn. She wasn't a lap cat and she was never particularly excited to see me, but still, as I had imagined, it was nice to come back to someone who was there just for me. I spent hours watching her jump from here to there, tracing the muscles and bones that grooved under her skin. I enjoyed watching her eat most of all. Once we ran out of the food from Lao Jim, Ma Ma bought the cheapest dry cat food from the store. I always mixed it, though, with whatever rice and chicken I could find. With my elbows on the ground and my hands cupping my face, I watched on as Marilyn crunched through the hard food using one side of her mouth, and then the other. This brought me more delight than any eating I could have done on my own.

The moments I spent watching Marilyn were the rare times when I did not worry about Ma Ma, her trouble with Ba Ba, our impending deportation, or how I would find my way to Harvard. No, when I was watching Marilyn, it was just me and her in all of the world, a little girl and her first real pet.

Ba Ba did not like Marilyn from the start,

but it only got worse. Marilyn never cuddled, and this went against what Ba Ba thought a cat should do. One night, Ba Ba placed Marilyn on his lap, but with a swish of her tail, she leapt off. It was her signature move, one that I had come to expect. But Ba Ba never gave up on anything. He grabbed her again, and with another swish she was gone. The third time Ba Ba grabbed her, she hissed and ran under the couch. Only her tail was visible from under the spotted fabric, slapping with annoyance against the floor.

This only made Ba Ba madder. He walked out of the room and I held my breath, hoping that he had gone to take a walk but knowing better. He reentered just a few seconds later, with our broom in hand. We had found the broom on one of our shopping days, and it had a green plastic covering on the stick that peeled and stuck to our hands in bits and pieces. The bristles at the end stuck out every which way, making it impossible to collect all the dirt in one spot.

Ba Ba directed the bristled end under the couch. Marilyn's tail disappeared and Ba Ba stuck the broom even deeper, moving it about. Marilyn emerged from the other end, and I said nothing, hoping Ba Ba would not notice. I did not know what he was going to do to her, and my chest felt as if it were sandwiched between two cleavers.

Ba Ba noticed the black of Marilyn's tail just as she disappeared into the cold sunroom. He ran in, still holding the broom, and shut the door.

"Stop!"

He ignored my plea.

"Stop, please, Ba Ba!"

I did not follow into the room, but instead ran over to the couch where Ma Ma sat frozen.

From the sunroom came only the sounds of Ba Ba thumping the broom against the floor, followed by Marilyn's hisses and the scrape of her claws against the hard floor. I buried my face into Ma Ma's chest and put my hands against my ears. Ma Ma wrapped me in a tight embrace, still saying nothing. For the first time in a long time I was close enough to breathe in the comforting smell of soap on her skin.

I don't know how long this went on, but I aged decades in that time. At some point, the door creaked open with a thump of the broom and I saw Marilyn's black paw emerge from the corner between the door and the frame. In a flash, she ran out and into our living room, leaving with each step little streaks of red.

"She's bleeding—Ma Ma, she's bleeding."

Ma Ma's eyes traced the floor before her body came awake. By this point, Marilyn had run under my bed, toward which Ba Ba was now directing the broom.

Ma Ma rushed over, with me following. When she opened her mouth, I was not braced for the fire that blazed from her throat, the volume of her voice.

"Xing le ba, ni. Xiang xiao hai zi yi yang." That's quite enough. You are acting like a child.

Ma Ma gripped the end of the broom that protruded out through Ba Ba's arm and torso and pulled it away from him. Ba Ba turned around and I saw that he had the devil in his eyes— that was what Ma Ma and I called it when he became truly mad. I covered my face, fearing what he might do next but also knowing that I needed to stay close and stop him if he directed his rage at Ma Ma. In a blink, though, the devil flickered and died. Ba Ba let go of the broom and walked out of the room.

I fell to the ground to look after Marilyn under the bed. She was huddled at the corner where my bed met the wall, a mess of fur, bones, and blood. Ma Ma sat on the bed, motioning for me to rise.

"She will come out when she feels safe."

I wanted to ask what it meant to feel safe, but I knew somehow that Ma Ma and Marilyn both needed me to stay quiet. So we sat, I with my eyes directed at the floor, Ma Ma with her face colorless, the fire extinguished.

Ba Ba was gone for a long time that night. A

little while after he walked out, long enough to make sure, perhaps, that he was not returning with a bigger broom, Marilyn emerged from under the bed. Ma Ma gathered my poor Marilyn in her arms as I dabbed at bloody paws with more of our roommates' Q-tips. Most of the bleeding had stopped and caked up, and my stomach finally untied itself at the sight of Marilyn drifting off to sleep on Ma Ma's legs. This was what it took for her to become a lap cat.

By the time we went to bed that night, Ba Ba had still not returned. But for the first time, Marilyn had crawled into bed with me and stayed there, between my torso and the crook of my arm. Ma Ma tucked us both in with a kiss on our foreheads. The thought occurred to me that this, of all nights, was the first time I had felt protected in a long, long time. And then, in as much time as it took for me to give Marilyn a squeeze and a kiss, I was asleep.

Chapter 20

GRAFFITI

....

Ma Ma's new classes were at night, so she did not get home until long after Ba Ba cooked and served dinner. When Ma Ma returned through the front doors, she did not even stop by our room. Instead, she walked down the hallway, heading directly into the kitchen. Then, with a flick of the switch on our little lamp, she started studying.

I had never had so much alone time with Ba Ba since he left China, and I was surprised to find that we still had fun together. He really only knew how to cook one dish: stir-fried tomatoes and egg, with bits of scallion in it. It was the recipe that no one could escape in northern China. I would stand in the kitchen with Ba Ba as he cooked, watching him beat the eggs, slice the tomatoes, then scallions, and throw them all into the big frying pan we shared with our roommates. We chatted about the people he dealt with at work and how each of them came to be so far from home. Then I ranted about all the things that my new best friend, Christine, did to annoy me and about how Julia was so spoiled that she bought a Good Humor strawberry shortcake ice cream bar from the vending machine every day after school. I knew because I had developed the masochistic hobby of following her out of class and watching each time as she put the sixty cents into the coin slot, salivating as she made her way through the pretty treat, covered with pink and red dots.

It was nice but strange to go all evening without hearing about Ma Ma's worries. I felt guilty for not being there for her and for having so much fun with Ba Ba, especially when he was the source of so many of our troubles. This guilt showed its face in the moments when I was laughing hardest at Ba Ba's jokes, which I would cut short, remembering that Ba Ba sometimes had the devil in his eyes and that I should be careful not to get too close.

When she was home, Ma Ma started telling me that she had stomach pains. I figured they were the same as the pain I felt when I waited, starved, for lunch. But Ba Ba and Ma Ma said it was Marilyn's fault, that her black coat and her asymmetrical face had cursed us. I knew better, though: we had had bad luck ever since Ba Ba left for America. And I knew I could prove them wrong if I could just give Ma Ma a little bit more to eat.

At the end of each dinner, I made sure to put some of my meal onto a plate just for Ma Ma, placing on the edge one of the napkins Ba Ba regularly pocketed from the dispensers at McDonald's. I wrote on the napkin the message "Do not touch!"—just in case our roommates got any ideas.

Ma Ma never ate the food, though. She went directly to studying at the table, never even looking in the fridge. After Ba Ba fell asleep one night, Marilyn and I climbed out of bed and followed Ma Ma to the kitchen. There, I brought the plate out to where Ma Ma was seated, peering through her big square glasses at a thick textbook full of numbers and formulas. Marilyn jumped to the table, fixing herself under the lamp, always the warmest place in our home.

"Ma Ma, you have to eat something."

Ma Ma waved me away.

"Ma Ma, you have to eat something." Persistence was my strong suit.

"I don't have time," she muttered, "and you should be in bed."

I was guai and dong shi, a good and mature girl, so I did what Ma Ma said. On the way out of the kitchen, though, I looked back to see her holding her stomach with her left hand as she flipped through the textbook with her right.

Back in bed, guilt gnawed at me. How could I go to sleep while Ma Ma studied, hungry? At least, I thought, Marilyn was there with her, taking care of her. I fell into spurts of sleep, awaking several times to look over at Ma Ma's side of the bed. Each time I saw that it was empty, I stayed awake for as long as my guilt could carry me, before backsliding into drowsiness again. This continued until finally I awoke to see that Ma Ma was in her place in the bed, coiled on her side, facing me and away from Ba Ba. I wondered where Marilyn was, scanning our bedroom just as the faint glimmers of sunlight began to sneak in through the windows. The skein of black, tan, and white fur coiled into itself under Ma Ma's bed was the last thing I had time to see before meeting restful, deep sleep for the first time that night.

* * *

I began to get sick around this time, too. I often felt like I was going to throw up, especially after I vacuumed into my mouth everything that was on my lunch tray and then piled on top of it gulps from the milk carton. Usually, nothing came of the nausea and it passed by dinnertime. A few times, though, I actually did throw up. The first time happened on the subway after school. Each motion of the train brought another cresting wave in my stomach's rocky seas. I managed to hold on until the train began to pull into the Church Avenue station. Then, just as I stood to rise, I felt the sea bubble up. Through the carbonation, a balloon rose from my stomach and floated up into my throat. I swallowed hard several times, hoping to push the balloon down, but failing. Just as the train doors dinged opened, I felt the balloon burst and erupt hot air into my mouth. Only it wasn't air. It was chewed-up bread and sloppy joe, even sloppier on its way up than it had been on the way down. I barely had time to register the flush of red heat that swarmed my face and the brown and orange pile that sat on the floor before the train doors dinged a second time, announcing their impending closure. I jumped over the pile and walked through the door, dodging eye contact with the other passengers, all too aware of the smells I was leaving behind.

Then, on the platform, another balloon rose through my stomach and burst in my mouth. I left pile after pile throughout the station and on the sidewalk, a trail of bread crumbs that followed me all the way home.

Pretty soon, it began to feel as if the balloons were always in my belly, just waiting to pop. They were there even when my class went on a field trip to the Brooklyn Bridge. I felt them start to emerge as Christine and I walked along Centre Street, past the fancy courthouses that had many steps leading to them. We were near the front of the line formed by our class, and Christine was driving me crazy. We had become fast friends because I was drawn to her open, smiling nature, and because she was very pretty and thin, with large, bright eyes and a perfectly symmetrical face. She had none of the physical flaws that Ma Ma and Ba Ba had identified in me, but because she was so accepting, I sometimes got away with saying mean things to her like Ma Ma and Ba Ba did to me.

On that particular day, Christine had spent the entire walk to the bridge fawning over her new sneakers.

"Look how bright and white they are! I'm going to keep them like this forever."

I ignored her, but I squeezed my toes in secret. It was early spring, and my sneakers for the year were nearing the end of their life. My toenails had already dug holes in the layers of fabric, so I had developed a habit of clenching my toes to keep them from rubbing against the holes even more.

The toe clenching slowed our walking, and as we got onto the bridge, the rest of the class caught up with and then passed us. The plan was to walk to the Brooklyn side, and then turn around and walk back.

It was a free field trip, and I was grateful for that. Later in the school year, we were to take a trip to a fancy movie theater by Lincoln Center and watch **Mulan,** my very first Disney movie. But to do that, Mr. Kane had collected a lot of money from all of us. It had cost Ma Ma and Ba Ba money that would have fed us for several days. And it wasn't even enough, because Mr. Kane told us to bring more money on the day we were supposed to go to the theater so we could buy popcorn, which elicited many cheers from my classmates. I had never been to the movies in America before, and wondered why everyone was so excited about popcorn. In China, we ate sunflower seeds in the theaters, the cracking sounds playing backup to the movie soundtrack, the floors slowly filling with empty, open shells.

Earlier on the Brooklyn Bridge field trip, the free one, my class had walked by Ba Ba as we snaked through lower Manhattan, just before we hit the courthouses. Ba Ba seemed to be coming from one of the brown government buildings that he always told me to stay away from. He was alone, dressed very nicely, with his dress shirt and dress pants and shiny shoes with thin laces.

I had no idea what he was doing there but ran over to hug him anyway. He waved hi to Mr. Kane. They had met before, at parent-teacher conferences where Mr. Kane told Ba Ba that I was a diligent student, but that I needed to be less shy and that I needed to change my clothes more often.

I was grateful only that Ba Ba was well dressed when we ran into him. I tried not to think about what he had been doing in those government buildings.

After that, the balloons emerged. They bubbled up slowly and stayed afloat just above the waves. I didn't even notice them float up until they pushed through the doors of my throat. Instead of ugly words, ugly food emerged— another school lunch, this time chicken nuggets, flooding out of my esophagus and onto Christine's brand-new sneakers.

"My shoes!" Christine exploded, but I had no time to feel embarrassed, because she started gagging. A few other classmates joined in within a few minutes, and Mr. Kane had to walk back several steps to find all of us huddled together, heaving around my vomit.

"What the hell happened?" The best thing about Mr. Kane was that sometimes he forgot that he wasn't supposed to swear around us.

"Vomit—" Heaves muffled Christine's words. By now, she had covered her face with her hands. "It makes me throw up."

Mr. Kane herded all of us away from the scene and back the way we had come on the bridge. As we shuffled toward Manhattan, our gags subsided. I fought the residual waves in silence. By the time we stepped off the bridge, I felt almost normal, thankful that I did not throw up again. But as nausea retreated, shame mounted. I had nearly caused my entire class to throw up on the Brooklyn Bridge. And because of me, we never got to see the Brooklyn side. I mulled over this on the rest of the walk back to school, avoiding others' eyes and keeping my gaze on the ground. Christine tottered beside me, her shoes coming into my line of sight every now and then. For the rest of the school trip, I saw only the gray pavement, interrupted every so often by the white of Christine's sneakers, now marked by brown splashes and orange chunks, the graffiti of the human body.

Chapter 21
JULIE

....

I became a habitual liar. Alternate lives spewed out of my mouth before circuiting my brain. I started small but soon advanced to bigger, more extravagant creations.

"I was born here," I ventured once at the lunch table. A few of my friends grunted in recognition, but none looked up from their hamburgers.

That was my gateway drug.

"My dad is a cop," I tried next.

This got a friend's interest. "Does he have a gun?"

"Of course," I replied without looking up, donning a mask of cool nonchalance. "Sometimes I get to hold it."

"Where does he work?"

"Can he come to school and show us?"

"He works in Chinatown." It seemed safest to go with the only neighborhood I knew well.

"He's part of the Dragon Fighters." I had conflated Chinatown's firefighters with its cops, but none of us knew any better.

"Maybe he can come to school one day," I risked, "but he's very busy."

I wasn't just talking about these lives. In those moments, I lived them. I was no longer Wang Qian, the bloated girl weighed down with daily worry, the skittering cockroach who turned and walked the opposite way whenever anyone in uniform appeared. In those moments, I was the person who actually deserved the silent awe my friends bestowed upon me at the lunch table with wide, shining eyes.

I grew braver with my lies.

"I'm half-white," I declared during another field trip, this time to the Museum of Natural History. Mr. Kane was a big fan of field trips. It meant he didn't have to teach, which was a treat for all of us.

Christine didn't respond. I turned to see that she was not enthralled by my makeshift, half-prestigious heritage, but instead fixated on the fossils arranged into a triceratops.

"My dad, he's a white CEO," I said as I examined the tiny arms of the Tyrannosaurus rex towering over us, careful to hide my exuberance at finally deploying the term I had once heard on TV and earmarked for later use.

"I thought your dad was a cop." Christine perked up. "And we saw him on that trip! He's not white."

The problem with Christine was that you never knew when she would be paying attention.

"Look, Christine, a triceratops in the same room as a T-rex! That makes no sense! He'll be eaten."

"I thought your dad was a cop. A Chinese cop."

Memory like an elephant.

"He—he is. I was just testing you. You passed!"

* * *

Ma Ma grew sicker. When she wasn't in school or at work, she was in bed. We never went window-shopping anymore. Not to the nearby Thirteenth Avenue, where we got free samples of sunflower seeds and nuts from the Jewish stores. And certainly not to our favorite area, Herald Square, which had both stores where we could actually shop, like Conway, and stores where we could only dream to one day shop, like Macy's.

Instead, our outings were to the only Chinese doctors who were safe to visit. Their offices were in their homes, their basements. Ma Ma told me that many of the doctors were "hei" like us; they had been doctors in China just as Ma Ma and Ba Ba had been professors in China, but now none of them could do the things they were good at. Not openly, anyway. It was safe this way, Ma Ma said, because they couldn't report us and we couldn't report them.

"What if they do something wrong," I said, "and they make you sicker?"

She replied with one of those questions that was really an answer: "Could it be worse than not seeing a doctor at all?"

* * *

The "friend test" worked well for me. Anytime I was caught in a lie, I had a way of flipping it and turning it into a "gotcha." It gave me control of every situation.

My lies grew beyond who I was and where my parents were from. They budded and flowered in even the most banal scenarios.

As best friends were required to do, Christine and I always went to the bathroom together, using adjacent stalls. If no two adjacent stalls were available, we waited. Who were we to question the rules of friendship?

Christine loved to slam the toilet seat down onto the bowl the minute she got into the stall. Because I was always next door, it hurt my ears. But of course I did not tell her that.

"Christine, my mom said that if you do that a hundred times, you will go deaf."

"I've done it thousands of times. I do it every day."

"I know." I kept my voice measured and calm. "I was just testing you. You passed."

"Sweet!"

I was smarter than Christine. But she was happier because she celebrated all victories, real or false.

* * *

It didn't matter who the doctor was. We met with them all. The safe ones, anyway. They all told Ma Ma the same thing.

It's just a stomachache.

Eat better.

Go get some of that pink liquid medicine from the stores.

None of it worked.

* * *

As with fourth grade, I spent most of fifth grade daydreaming, alternating between staring at the chalkboard and at Mr. Kane while my mind roamed. It was weird to have a white man for a teacher. PS 124 was good like that. Even if they didn't speak Mandarin, most of the teachers, like the students, at least looked a little like me.

Mr. Kane looked nothing like me. He was the white kind of pale, with a lot of red underneath. His skin reminded me of the steamed buns with the pink dots in the center. Except his skin wasn't taut and tender like a bun's. It was a little saggy.

I had no idea how old he was, only that he seemed old with a capital **O**. This may have been due in part to the fact that Mr. Kane looked like he was a million feet tall. It was confusing, though, because sometimes Mr. Kane was fun and playful, just like one of us, and other times he seemed to look down at us.

I seemed to confuse Mr. Kane, too. Once, he called me up to the front of the class, as everyone else got to get a head start on homework.

"Qian." His face twisted in confusion. "What is with your overalls?"

"What?" It was all I could muster.

"Why do you wear those every day? We're not on a farm."

It seemed like a question that wasn't really searching for an answer. I knew those well because Ma Ma asked them often, so I stayed silent and returned to my seat. I took my time walking back. I didn't want to give him a chance to see my tomato-red face but was pretty sure he got a good view of the color from the back of my burning neck.

* * *

Ma Ma got very sick one night.

Ba Ba was not home. I had just taken an extended break in the bathroom, where I had caught up on the latest Baby-Sitters Club book and vented about Christine in my diary. I knew something was wrong the minute I came back to our room. Ma Ma was not in the living area, and the curtain dividing the sleeping area had been untied, blocking my view of the beds. Part of me did not want to lift the curtain. Instead, I wanted to run back to the bathroom and keep reading my book. Another part yearned to call Elaine and ask to sleep over at her house, where both of her parents were home and the children didn't have to do the dishes and where there were rules for everything, like how you ate and where you sat on the couch.

I lifted the curtain.

* * *

Mr. Kane taught us the ways of the world. He stood at the front of the classroom and beamed at us one day.

"Did you know that there are many sweat-shops in Chinatown?"

Most of our parents worked in one.

"Most of your parents are uneducated. They can only work in sweatshops."

That wasn't the reason.

"Not Shirley's mom, though. She comes to PTA meetings in suits. Or Qian's dad. You remember, we saw Qian's dad in a dress shirt by the government buildings when we went to the Brooklyn Bridge."

Mr. Kane also believed in limits. That is, we all had our limits and needed to be reminded of them. We also needed to accept them, without asking questions.

The limits applied more to some than to others. And we were to be grateful for this white savior who taught us our limits early and often. It almost felt as if he thought he was protecting us.

Writing had always been my strength. I always thought that if an adult read my writing, she would get to see into my soul, and I would get to prove that I belonged in America just as much as any other kid.

Mr. Kane was the first to tell me that my talent did not fit my shell. It was not part of who I was supposed to be, what people expected of me. One day, he asked me to talk to him again at the front of the class. My face was already red by the time I got to his desk, but I clutched a bead of hope that it might be about something positive this time. Maybe he was touched by my essay. Then I looked down and saw that I was still wearing the same overalls.

"Qian." He was holding the essay from the day before. "Did you write this?"

Was it a trick question? Maybe it was another question that was actually an answer.

"I don't think you wrote this, Qian."

Maybe it was one of those jokes he loved to make but that no one got.

"Then who did?" I squeaked out.

"This is . . . this is not the type of writing I see at PS 124."

"But I did write it."

"Are you sure?"

"Yes." But under his eyes, somehow, I wasn't.

"I'm very disappointed in you. Go back to your seat, please."

It was the first of many similar encounters I would have with white teachers to come. For the rest of my time in Mr. Kane's class, I made sure to add spelling and grammatical mistakes before handing anything in.

* * *

Ma Ma was rolling back and forth on the bed.

Ma Ma, zen me le?

Her face was gray and tears flowed out of her eyes, squeezed shut from pain.

Ma Ma?

What if she had passed out? What if she couldn't talk? What could I do? Were our roommates around? I sat dumbly by her side, wading through these questions and rubbing her stomach.

Qian Qian. When she finally spoke, I thought I imagined it. But I turned around and there she was, her eyes open, looking at me. **Qian Qian, call 911.**

What? What's going on, Ma Ma? What if they deport us, Ma Ma? What do you need?

Guai, ting hua, hao hai zi. We can't worry about that right now. It hurts—it hurts so much. I'm scared.

Whenever Ma Ma said those words, I knew I had to be the adult. I could not be scared when she was. I firmed up my face just in case any of my horror showed.

Tell me what you feel, Ma Ma.

From there, the night blurred. Words tumbled out of Ma Ma, and though I didn't quite understand what they all meant, separately or together, my brain gripped on to everything she said just in case I had to recount it all to someone else later. She said something about being afraid that there was a hole in her stomach. I had no idea that was even possible. I thought about my toenails rubbing holes into my sneakers. Was that how it worked? It sounded dangerous, so I grabbed Marilyn from the bed and locked her in the sunroom.

I ran down the hall.

Silence.

Our roommates were gone.

Then I ran up the hall, slamming open the first front door, shoving my thumb onto the doorbell for our landlords with all my force. I held down on the button and did not let go.

Please be home. They spoke no English but they were adults, and that was all that mattered. They would know what to do. They had to.

Please be home.

Please be home.

Please be home.

They were home.

They rushed down the stairs, their genial faces furrowed in worry. I told them what Ma Ma had told me and then they sat with Ma Ma on the other side of the curtain as I dialed 911 and talked to a lady whose stern voice came through the phone a little too loudly, hurting my ears.

The ambulance came quickly. I noted with a sigh that there was no police car. The two paramedics came into our room with a skinny bed, long and narrow, on wheels. With them and the rolling bed there, our home felt small. I tied up the curtain so it was out of the way, but still, it was hard to breathe.

The paramedics wore uniforms and at first I thought they were police officers. They asked me question after question as they examined Ma Ma and looked around. I waited for them to ask to see our papers or demand whether I knew who the president was, but they never did. Maybe that would come later, I thought, after they arrested us and put us in handcuffs.

I don't remember how or when, but at some

point, Ba Ba came home. He looked at me with startled eyes as he entered the room. Ma Ma had once told me that when she was very pregnant with me, earthquake tremors had taken over our home in China. Ba Ba had told her to stay put before he went down the five flights of stairs to investigate. He did not return until over an hour later, when the small earthquake had passed.

The problem, Ma Ma explained, was that his childhood left in him a fear so big that it eclipsed everything, even the people he loved most. Especially the people he loved most.

I was glad he decided to come home this time.

And then, just as quickly as everyone had showed up and packed into the little room that burst at its seams, they were gone. Ba Ba left with the ambulance and the kindly landlords offered me some food before returning to their home upstairs. It was at this point that I remembered that Ma Ma had been cooking dinner for us before I went into the bathroom, before she had collapsed in bed. I walked into the kitchen and found a meal awaiting a family that would never arrive. I packed the dishes away into the fridge and walked back to our room, where I turned on the television and let down the dividing curtain again before crawling into the bed with Marilyn in my arms, the phone by my head.

I closed my eyes and willed myself to sleep.

Everything is fine, Qian Qian, I mumbled. Ma Ma is just on the other side of the curtain, watching television.

* * *

In fifth grade, I decided to become a new person entirely. No one could ever pronounce my name. There was always that inevitable pause, at the beginning of the school year and whenever I met anyone new, when the spotlight insisted on shining down on me and my weird name.

"How do you pronounce it?"

"The **Q** makes a what sound?"

And worst of all: "How interesting!"

One day, in better times, before I had to call 911, I took my routine walk through Rite Aid after class. It had become my daily ritual to drool over new Lisa Frank stationery, and visit with all the fine-point pens in their assorted colors. That day, though, a rack of rubber stamps stopped me from getting to Lisa Frank. Each stamp was for a different name, organized alphabetically from **Anna** to **Zane**. They were all purple, each with a heart-shaped holder and a silver sticker that declared the name it would mark.

There were no names beginning with **Q**.

There was, however, one for **Julie**, that Chinese puppet from **The Puzzle Place**.

Julie had shiny, long black hair like mine.

She also had eyes that turned up at the outer corners, giving her a catlike, slanty look. I didn't look like that, but still, she looked more like me than anyone else I saw on television.

Julie's last name was Woo, and she was Chinese American. Other than her eyes, she was no different from her friends. She spoke perfect English. She didn't seem stressed out or hungry. She never lied. And all the puppets wore the same clothes all the time, so it didn't matter that she did, too.

She fit in.

The stamp was $4.99, a fortune I could just barely afford with the pennies remaining from my sweatshop days.

I grabbed it and walked to the cashier.

* * *

Ba Ba did not come home until four or five o'clock in the morning. I know because I looked up every hour to check for Ma Ma and Ba Ba in their bed, and then to check the clock. I did not sleep that night, not really. I just closed my eyes and tried to ignore the fluttery ache deep in my tummy. I was awake the minute I heard Ba Ba's key in the lock of our room door. Exhaustion pulled at his face.

Ma Ma was not with him.

"What happened? Is she okay?"

"She just has to stay there for a little while." Ba Ba directed his eyes at me but did not see me. "She will be okay. We waited a long time to see someone."

"How long will she be there?

"What's wrong with her?

"Did they ask us to pay?

"Did they ask for our paperwork?

"Are we deported?

"Should I pack up?"

By then, Ba Ba had stopped hearing me. He walked to his bed and lay down, slowing only to take off his shoes. I had so many more questions—endless questions, none of which were destined to meet their answers.

"Go to bed, Qian Qian. Guai, hao hai zi. You have to get some sleep before school."

I closed my eyes but the questions played on.

What did sleep matter? What did school matter? What did any of it matter, now that I had failed to protect Ma Ma?

* * *

I used my new stamp on everything. I stamped the walls, Marilyn, my hand, and most of all, my assignments, under which I wrote in smaller print, "Qian." I loved the exhilarating moment after each stamp, when the ink on the surface was still wet and shiny.

It felt good to mark things as mine.

A few weeks after I donned my new name with my new stamp, Mr. Kane called me up to his desk again, and I again made the walk with a flushed face. I clenched my fists and dug my nails into my palms. I knew I should have put more spelling mistakes in the last essay.

"Qian, I just realized that this essay with a big 'Julie' stamp on it also has your name."

"Yes."

"I've been giving the credit for all the home-work with this stamp to Julia Huang."

Not her again. Didn't she have enough? I turned to look at Julia, who of course had on another new outfit. She looked like Snow White, perfect and dutiful as she copied notes from the board. She was always good. She was always nice. She was never accused of plagiarism. I hated her.

I turned back to Mr. Kane to find him staring at me. I batted back the tears welling in my eyes.

"You have to decide. You can be Qian or you can be Julie. Which one is it?"

I stared back at him, shrinking into myself with each ticking second.

"Qian," I finally said, but I didn't know if he heard me. Even to me, even in the depths of my own head, my name came out as a squeak.

* * *

Ma Ma was not there when I returned from school the next day. When Ba Ba appeared several hours later, he told me that Ma Ma needed to have surgery soon, but that we had to wait until a doctor was available. They had done a scan of her and it showed what he called a large mass. Ba Ba explained that this was like a big rock, and it was where her liver and gallbladder were. The surgery was going to last more than ten hours and it would be the only way to find out what was going on inside and whether Ma Ma had cancer.

I had a lot to say and a lot to ask: She has a rock inside her! How did that happen? What is cancer? How do we find a doctor? Can we ask one of those Chinese basement doctors? How long do we have to wait?

All this went on inside my head as I stayed silent. There was no need to talk or ask anymore. I didn't need to say anything to know that Ba Ba didn't have the answers.

And anyway, none of it mattered. Because I had failed. It was all my fault.

In healthier days, Ma Ma had reminded me that worrying was a talisman to keep the worst from happening. "If you worry about something," Ma Ma said, "it won't happen. It's the things we don't worry about that are dangerous." And so I knew: I had not worried enough to ward off Ma

Ma's sickness. I had not worried about whether she would be healthy enough to see her graduation and to see us living her dream—leaving this awful, beautiful country for a different place, a world where we were just as human as everyone else.

Chapter 22

HOSPITAL

....

Going to the hospital went against everything I had learned since leaving China. As Ba Ba led me into the lobby of St. Vincent's Hospital, past the huddle of uniformed police officers and doctors in white coats, I fought every muscle's urge to run out the door and into the underground subway tunnels.

The hospital was different from the ones I'd gone to in China. The smells were much stronger, as if American doctors used more chemicals. And there were machines all around us, plastic seats everywhere. The seats were padded, and though it was a hospital, everything felt more luxurious. We went into an elevator and then through a set of doors, before going down one hallway and then another. There were so many turns that I wondered whether we would ever see Ma Ma. As we followed the twisting corridors, I pictured me and Ba Ba, turning this way and that, up these floors and then down those steps, walking forever in circles in the science fumes, never to arrive at Ma Ma's bed.

* * *

The hospitals in China were spare in contrast with American hospitals. I once snuck a look into the hall closet at PS 124 and it reminded me of the hospital where I had gotten my shots before we boarded the plane: the walls were unfinished, as were the floors, and both had random black markings on them going every which way. The closet was purely utilitarian and it looked that way—there were hooks for brooms and dustpans, cubbies for the janitor's items, and nails from features past. Nothing was painted, and nothing was any more adorned than it needed to be.

In our years in America, I had seen a doctor only when the school required me to get shots. Since we could not get those shots recorded by the Chinese basement doctors, Ba Ba took me instead to the free kids' clinics around Chinatown. We found out about the clinics only because they had been advertised on ratty papers stuck on the telephone poles around PS 124. Those papers promised us that the clinics were always free and that no one there ever asked about immigration status. We couldn't be sure that it wasn't a trap, but I needed the shots so Ba Ba had no choice.

Going to those clinics gave me a little taste of what it must have been like to be normal in America: Ba Ba and I walked in and up to the receptionist as if we were regular people who had nothing to fear. After filling out forms, we sat down and I played with the toys on the table—usually wooden blocks meant for babies but sometimes Connect4 or checkers. With the games I played both sides, pretending that I was playing against my own twin, both of us American, as our American ba ba stared off into the distance of the opposite wall. I became so engrossed in this make-believe that I barely even looked up whenever the door opened. It was almost as if we were not waiting for an officer to walk through the doors and place us under arrest.

And then, when the receptionists finally muttered my name—always incorrectly, even in this normal version of our lives—I walked up and in through the back doors with Ba Ba. Our legs betrayed only the slightest hesitation, tensing at the doorway in case an ambush awaited us. And then, just as quickly, we fell back into our normal stride, and it was almost as if I had no worries other than the impending stab of a long, thin metal thing. To the nurse who did not know any better, I was just another poor kid, bloated on sodium and fat, dreading the judgment of the scale.

* * *

At the hospital, when we finally did enter a room, I wondered if there would only be another connected hallway that we would have to turn down. I thought this because the first face I saw in a bed did not belong to Ma Ma, but to an old white lady, who had blanched skin and closed eyes that were curtained by wrinkles.

But it turned out that there was no hallway from there. Beyond the bed was a curtain and as we walked toward it, I felt the kiss of sunlight. Under the strong rays casting in through the window, it took me a few more steps to see that the sleeping figure in the white bed was Ma Ma. She was a raisin of herself, and her eyes opened just as I threw myself onto her.

* * *

I visited Ma Ma regularly, finding my way to St. Vincent's by subway after school. My fear of being found out and captured at the hospital lost a decibel each time I walked by an officer in the halls only to be ignored. Over time, it became but a dull murmur in the background of my visits with Ma Ma.

Instead, I became more preoccupied with the fear of losing Ma Ma. My new fixation actually eased my previous stomach discomfort. There were still bubbles that led to throw-up, but they came and went, receiving little attention, like Mr. Kane's teachings at the front of the class. My anxiety found its full throat whenever I was not with Ma Ma—all during school and for the entire night the minute I left her hospital room. What if they wheeled her off to surgery without me? What if I never saw her again? What if she needed me when I was not there?

It felt to me just like that time the plane took Ba Ba. And like the time Ma Ma and I got on it and our whole family and world were taken away from us. Only this time, I didn't have the hope or innocence I did before. I knew that new awful things were waiting, and that there was nothing I could do to keep it all from unfolding. My short life was replaying, but each time it promised to spin into worse and worse dimensions. I spent hours wrapped in this miserable thought, sitting on the metal chair next to Ma Ma's hospital bed, my homework dutifully on my lap, my eyes fixed on her sleeping figure.

For days after, Ma Ma's classmates came with arrangements of flowers in colors and shapes I had not seen since we left China. To this day, thoughts of the hospital recall to me the smell of lilies, bleach, and rubbing alcohol, all kneaded up into one terrifying ball.

Only one thing had me leave my metal chair

during visits. Three rooms down from Ma Ma stayed an old lady who had the bed by the door. I first saw her when I was walking with Ma Ma down the hall. I held on to Ma Ma's right hand as her other hand gripped the tall pole from which hung a bag of liquid whose tube was connected to a needle, which was in turn jabbed into the inside crook of Ma Ma's left arm. Ma Ma and I had just eclipsed the third door when we heard the word "Nurse" trickle out. When I turned, I saw the old lady looking back at me, unblinking. Her eyes were foggy with cataracts, her short hair white and wiry. She reminded me of the poodles I'd seen often on my walk from the subway station to the hospital, in shock at how many more dogs there were in white neighborhoods.

My first thought was that I was looking into death's withered face. My second thought was a question: How did she get a bed bigger than Ma Ma's? But then I realized that it was just an illusion: so small was the lady that, even seated in her adjustable bed, she barely appeared to have a neck or torso. She was just one balloon head, huge compared against the rest of her, eyes staring at me through a smoggy shield.

From then on, I checked on her every time I walked by. I would hold my breath before passing her room and cross my fingers that she would be there. Only when I saw that she was would I let myself breathe again. On my way in, I had to pass the lady's room before reaching Ma Ma's, and this became a game of superstition: if the lady was there, Ma Ma would be okay. So from the moment I got off the elevator to the minute I stepped past her room door, I whispered my mantra under my breath as fear shrieked in my head: **Please be there. Please, please, please be there.**

The old lady never had visitors, but one day, just as I let out my breath in front of her door, I found her clutching a gray-brown stuffed bear the size of her two hands. We had by then developed a routine: she shouted "Nurse" into the hallway until Ba Ba or I looked in on her, at which point she would stop. She didn't smile, not really—she would only look back us through her papery eyelids, her mouth slightly curved and open, bones and veins visible on her hands through the veneer of spotted skin.

I never talked to her. But it was warm comfort to see her every day. In those moments when our eyes held each other, it felt as if we were family, as if neither she, nor I, nor anyone else in that hospital was quite as alone as we actually were.

* * *

Ba Ba was still working at the lawyer's office, but he was now haunted by all the many places he had to be. As I did after school, he took the subway directly to the hospital after work, and there the three of us would share Ma Ma's dinner, which arrived on a tan cardboard tray. When the generous worker was on duty, he would leave us two or three extra meals, a feast. Ma Ma always saved the Jell-O cups for me. I had never had Jell-O before, and when I brought a piece out on the spork and shook it until it danced and wiggled, it felt as if I were just another rich, white American kid who could afford to play with her food.

Walking past the cops at the hospital never seemed to get easier for Ba Ba. His hand always squeezed mine harder at the sight, as if he needed to remind himself that we were still there, together and safe. Even after we passed a cop, Ba Ba never resumed talking, instead keeping his eyes turned just over his shoulders, watching for figures behind us, listening for quickening footsteps.

But when he wasn't running from his own shadows, Ba Ba liked to make me laugh. He multiplied his efforts during the time when Ma Ma was in the hospital, perhaps because my smiles grew so rare. It was as if I had lost the muscles for them.

We didn't have much at our disposal, but Ba Ba knew that my laughter sat on the shoulders of the cheapest inventions. One easy favorite came from the simple mechanics of plumbing: Ba Ba would go to the bathroom and leave a nice, sizable creation in the toilet without flushing. The first time he pulled this prank, he came back to our room only to say, **Oh! I forgot my book by the toilet!** before asking me to retrieve it. I walked to the bathroom with my nose in my book, and did not look up until too late, until I was right in front of the toilet bowl, in full view of the glorious brown mess. Then came Ba Ba's snickering from outside the door, and his declaration that, oh, sorry, he must have forgotten to flush.

And then, of course, there was our song, **Xi Mou Hou.** We started dancing to it again at night, after returning from our visits with Ma Ma and after Ba Ba locked the door to our rooms and waited long enough to be sure that no footsteps were coming. When at last his shoulders loosened and dropped, my feet found the tops of his and the two of us swayed to the rhythm carved into our bones. It was my lullaby, sweeping me away from the beeping of the hospital machines.

* * *

As Ma Ma's time in the hospital ticked by, I created many more solitary and superstitious games. I made little bets, like if I could get to this crosswalk or that building before the light changed or before the next car honk, Ma Ma would be okay. It was also then that I tripped over my own feet more. I even began to hit doorframes as I walked out of rooms. It was as if my arms had all of a sudden grown too long, had started swinging too widely. I repeatedly hit them against other people, objects, and all that surrounded me. The more I willed myself to walk quickly, to move smoothly, to save Ma Ma, the more I stumbled and failed, my goal collapsing just before my outreached hands.

One particularly bad fall took place during lunch recess. I don't remember what I was doing or how it even happened, only that I had been moping around the fence, far from my hopscotch-playing friends. I was contemplating how stupid it was to jump on one leg and then the other, from one box to the next, when there were people out there in the world who were so sick they had to stay in bed with needles stuck in them. And then, out of nowhere, I tripped on nothing and fell, landing on my twisted right hand and wrist. I pushed myself up as quickly as possible. In my haste, I pressed the back of the hand, which was already turning blue, farther into the ground.

No one had noticed my stumble, or at least no one came over. I didn't dare look around. If someone had seen, if someone had laughed, I didn't want to know. I spent the rest of the afternoon staring at the gradations of blue and purple as my hand rose like yeasted dough. Within an hour, it became impossible for me to grip a pencil or write. I still could not read anything off the board. In fact, my eyes had gotten worse. So I sat still and nodded every now and then, trying to act normal while committing to memory what I would have to do for homework later that night.

I was lucky because that week I was wearing my pink sweater, which was several sizes too big. I was meant to grow into it as I wore it, but the weave of the stiff, acrylic yarn had already loosened. The space between the threads of yarn got bigger and bigger, gaping until the sleeves draped well over my hands. It just happened to be the perfect cover for my swollen stump.

I said nothing to Christine or anyone else when class was over. Instead, I strode toward the door and down the hall into the bathroom, pausing only when my hand brushed the doorframe—my clumsiness persisted—shooting shards of pain up the hand and into my wrist, now also swollen.

I hoped that running water on it would help.

But, as it turned out, a taro-bun hand did not feel like a normal hand. Even after I adjusted the temperature to extreme cold and then extreme hot, the bump felt nothing. By this point, my classmates were catching up to me, so I draped my sleeve over the swollen hand once more and walked out of the bathroom, hoping no one would notice the dripping water.

I spent the whole subway ride to St. Vincent's fretting about hiding my hand from Ma Ma so she would not have to worry. By the time I reached the hospital and walked past the old lady's room, I still had not come up with an excuse. I was so focused on my hand, in fact, that I did not realize until after I had already passed the old lady's door that I had not even checked to make sure she was there. A bad omen.

It was a bad day for Ma Ma and she had no time to notice me. When I arrived, a nurse was already in Ma Ma's room, explaining that because all of her easy-to-find veins had been used too much for the IV drip, they had to start using long, scary needles now that poked into the top of Ma Ma's feet. The needle meant that Ma Ma could not walk around, so she was left in her bed to think about nothing but her pain and anxiety.

I forgot about my hand until Ba Ba and I left the hospital. It wasn't until I reached to swipe my MetroCard that I remembered that it hurt to hold things now. Ba Ba didn't notice: his eyes had that far-off glaze that told me he was battling his shadows again. After swiping through the turnstile with a grimace, I returned my hand to its sleeve, just in case Ba Ba came back to me.

Chapter 23
MOTHERS

....

Ba Ba started having me stay with family friends over the weekends. He told me it was for the best, that he had to be with Ma Ma at the hospital, but it was not good for a little girl like me to spend so much time in such a place. I wanted to believe him, but doubts poked at my brain from all directions. I was Ma Ma's sentry, her little doctor. Was I failing her by listening to him?

It didn't matter, because at the end of the day, I was a good girl who did what her ba ba said, even if it meant betraying her ma ma at the same time, even if it meant crying and embarrassing herself, as I had at Elaine's.

I stayed with Ba Ba's friend Yang Ah Yi first. She was the mother of the younger of the two boys I was forced to spend time with when all our families got together. Though I liked her son, I feared her. They looked a lot alike, with small chins that gave their faces a rounded look full of curiosity. They were both very dark, looking as if they had been roasted. Yang Ah Yi's son was very kind. But Ma Ma and Ba Ba insisted that in China, dark faces were seen as bad luck, and they once told me that some of Yang Ah Yi's darkness was on the inside, too. I didn't know what any of this meant, but I kept a good distance from Yang Ah Yi all the same.

Yang Ah Yi's husband didn't seem good or bad, but he reminded me of Lao Bai and his flexible morality. He always did just what Yang Ah Yi told him to do.

As I recall, they had then just moved to a two-bedroom in Queens—either Forest Hills or Elmhurst; the two blur together in my mind. It was the nicest American apartment I had ever seen outside of TV, even better than Elaine's apartment. The kitchen connected to the living area, so they had room to fit an actual dinner table, around which sat matching chairs. Outside of China, I had never seen such nice furniture in person.

Yang Ah Yi picked me up and brought me to her fancy apartment just before dinner, and I spent much of the time before the meal marveling at the dining set. From the meal itself, I remember only three things. First, I had to ask for a fork. My hand was still a swollen ball; I had not been able to use chopsticks for several days, and I had forgotten to pack the plastic spork I had pocketed from the hospital. Second, everything on the plates was tinged brown, and when I managed to get the food to my mouth, I was disappointed to find that it all tasted the same—salty—and had the chewy quality of overcooked school lunches. I missed the trays of hospital food and hoped that, without me there, Ma Ma would still remember to save the Jell-O cups for me. Third, I was left out of the conversation entirely. Yang Ah Yi and her husband talked as if I were not there at all. Though the son tried to involve me a few times, he was shy and had already developed the preteen hatred for his parents that I had yet to grow into. He and I sat on our side of the table, chewing, chewing, chewing through the salt as the adults droned on about one thing or another. It was not until after dinner, when I was doing the dishes, and the son was back in his room, that Yang Ah Yi spoke to me for the first time.

"Wang Qian," she said, her mouth mirthless, "did you know that people say that my family is low-income?"

I didn't know. I hadn't realized that people talked about other people that way. But she was scary, so I nodded.

"In fact, we are all called low-income, all of your father's friends, even though we did pretty well in China."

The nodding continued.

"Well, not you and your family."

Another nod, slower this time.

"Because if my family is low-income in America, then you are no-income."

No one had ever said anything like that to me. I had trouble understanding it at first, and the shock offered some padding for the sting. But later that night, as I lay on the stiff couch in the living room, willing myself to sleep, the words came back to me. I didn't feel an urge to cry, as I had at Elaine's, because I was too busy unlocking the puzzle formed by Yang Ah Yi's words. What did it mean, that we were no-income? Ba Ba and Ma Ma made money. I had seen the money. I had earned some of the money, too. I had not imagined it all. But I knew that Yang Ah Yi was better off than we were. Just look at this couch, that table. Plus, Ma Ma had told me that they were rich because Yang Ah Yi had found a way to hold on to her visa all this time—something, she said, that Ba Ba had been too dumb to do.

When I got home on Sunday night, I told Ba Ba that I wanted to stay with someone else the following weekend.

"Why? They have such a nice place. I bet you ate good food."

I didn't want to tell Ba Ba that we were no-income. He didn't need to know.

"I don't want a fancy place. It was too sad there."

Ba Ba didn't ask any other questions and his

eyes drifted off to a faraway place again, but the next Friday, Ma Ma's friend Wu Ah Yi picked me up from the hospital.

Wu Ah Yi was one of Ma Ma's new friends from the master's program. She was not quite scary like Yang Ah Yi, but I didn't like her, either. She had an odd, floaty quality to her. The very sight of her recalled to me what Ma Ma had told me years before: that a woman could be beautiful without being pretty, but a woman could not be beautiful without having dignity.

When Wu Ah Yi came to retrieve me from the hospital, she had a face so full of makeup that it reminded me of the attendant on our flight so many years before. I don't remember exactly what Wu Ah Yi wore, only that it was bright and silky and had a logo design that I had seen on the subway, on women so classy and elegant that they set into stark relief the dulled graffiti on dirty aluminum.

Ma Ma shrank a little lower in her hospital bed at the sight of Wu Ah Yi's extravagance, and in that instant, I wanted to tear the logos apart with my hands. All Ma Ma had on was a white hospital gown with a little blue pattern on it, like the top of the table we had found and dragged back to our kitchen. The gown gaped in areas where there were no strings keeping them together, the seams rolling into the fabric, aged from repeated laundering.

Every time I was around her, Wu Ah Yi was either talking about how pretty she was or asking others to confirm that they thought she was pretty. I once asked Ma Ma why she was friends with someone who only seemed to care about one thing. Ma Ma had responded that Wu Ah Yi was very kind deep down, but that the world had taught her to measure herself by her appearance, by comparison against every woman and girl. "Try to understand her instead of judging her, Qian Qian," Ma Ma had said. "You are luckier than her because you know you are worth more than that." I tried to keep this in mind, but it was hard to be truly understanding of something I did not yet comprehend.

Wu Ah Yi had a daughter, Feng Feng, who was two years younger than me. I had been disappointed to find that her mother had given her the same floaty disease. When she was well, Ma Ma had forced us to spend time together, admonishing me time and again to be "understanding" and "nice." But I could never pay attention to anything Feng said. No matter how much I forced myself to like her, I wound up with the same conclusion: Feng was dull. Plus, whenever we passed by windows and glass doors, Feng's head swiveled as she walked, eyes following her own reflection until it was gone. Wu Ah Yi was the only other person I'd seen do that.

As Wu Ah Yi cooked in her kitchen the first night I stayed over, Feng and I stood around, mandatory audience to her stories about beauty. They were stories I had already heard, but it didn't matter.

"Wang Qian, you know, when Feng Feng was in China, one of my friends said a horrible thing to her, that she was not as pretty as I was!"

I knew from the first time I had heard this story that Wu Ah Yi wanted me to be surprised and insulted in response, so I supplied those emotions to her, opening my mouth and wrinkling my face in indignation.

"No, no, it's fine, because you know what Feng Feng said?"

I shook my head, as I was expected to do.

"It's incredible! I can't believe she said it! She was only five at the time!"

Feng beamed now, as she had in previous tellings.

"She said to my friend, she said, 'You're not as pretty as my ma ma, either!'"

At this, the two broke into peals of laughter. They were well rehearsed. It almost felt organic.

It was then that I examined them for the first time. They both had fine features, but neither of them was good-looking, not really. They both lacked the kindness and gravitas that made Ma Ma beautiful. But Wu Ah Yi nevertheless found it important to remind Feng repeatedly that night, while I was in earshot, that her mother's eyes were bigger and prettier than my mother's eyes. But then Wu Ah Yi also said that Feng's own eyes were nowhere as big or pretty as hers.

Eyes are the ultimate gauge of beauty in Chinese culture. The larger her eyes—the more they looked like white people's—the more beautiful a woman. And it was true that Feng had eyes so small that I wondered if she and her mom were actually related. I would not realize until I was in college that Wu Ah Yi had gotten eyelid surgery, the same kind of surgery that the blueprint of her childhood destined Feng to undergo. It was almost as if she believed that by slicing the flesh of her monolids, she could dig out the insecurity that her mother had buried in her all those years.

In the moment, though, as I listened to Wu Ah Yi berate Feng, I could not help but travel back to my own dinner table, where Ma Ma and Ba Ba made such sport of dissecting the innumerable flaws in my own appearance. It made me want to like Feng—really like her, not just because Ma Ma commanded me to, but because we had something big in common. But camaraderie over the callous, brutal pelts that fired from our parents' mouths was not enough to give root to real friendship. Try as I did—and boy, did I try that weekend—I could not get around finding her boring. It made me start to wonder whether Ma Ma had missed something in her equation: that maybe, even more than dignity, beauty demanded substance.

None of this kept me from growing homesick during my stay at their home. It was the back-and-forths between Feng and her mother, the comments and eye rolls and nudges that recalled to me a safer time when Ma Ma and I were always side by side. In those moments, I was an orphan, with no one to love or protect.

Wu Ah Yi was interested in only one other topic: my academic performance. She grilled me about my grades, and after each response, she turned to Feng and said, "Can you do it, too, Feng Feng? Can you?" Feng never responded.

It didn't make her dislike me, though. For at her core, Feng was good. She followed me around like a baby chick, chirping nonstop questions. She even waited outside the bathroom, clocking my pee times.

This compounded my troubles. I was never able to poop in a toilet other than the one in our shared bathroom, and even there, I took a long time. I never even bothered to try at school or at Elaine's, but on Sunday morning, after a second full night at Wu Ah Yi's, I felt heavy and close to exploding. Feng, of course, followed me to the bathroom and waited outside. She continued her prattle through the door, so I gave it a good five minutes before emerging in defeat.

A little while after breakfast, Feng fell into deep conversation with Wu Ah Yi and I thought I would use the window to try again. She did not follow me at first. But then, after a few minutes, she came pounding on the bathroom door, berating me for not telling her where I was going.

"I would have come with you, Jie Jie, just tell me next time."

Feng had taken to calling me "older sister," but I felt like her chained monkey. If I had not already had so much sitting on my shoulders and hanging from my neck, perhaps I would have enjoyed the presumptive intimacy she felt. But as it was, I felt only annoyed that I had yet another person looking to me for guidance. Another person whom I would fail.

"Go away. It's going to be a while."

"It's okay, Jie Jie! Take your time. I'll wait."

My fate was sealed with that, and after taking the perfunctory steps of flushing the toilet and washing my hands, I opened the door to find Feng seated cross-legged on the floor.

"That wasn't so long, Jie Jie! What do you want to do now?"

When she ran to the kitchen to declare to Wu Ah Yi that we were playing checkers, I also heard her whisper, "Ma Ma, do you think Jie Jie ate something bad? I'm worried. She's going to the bathroom a lot. Should we give her some medicine?"

When Feng returned to the living room, I said nothing, pretending not to have heard what she said, pretending not to be bloated, homesick, exhausted. We set up the checkers board. To make up for all that I couldn't give her, I let her have the red pieces, the color of happiness and prosperity in our culture.

* * *

After Wu Ah Yi's, I begged Ba Ba to let me stay with him on the weekends. I could even stay home, I said, if he didn't want me to go with him to the hospital. I could take care of myself and it was less exhausting that way, and I wasn't alone, not really, because Marilyn was there.

Ba Ba's brows scrunched toward each other and he opened his mouth gradually, as he did when he was forced to talk about a topic that he had put off. "Well, about Marilyn—"

I knew in that moment that what I had dreaded for months had finally come, that Marilyn's time was running out. I had to stop him before he could say it. Because if he didn't say it, maybe it wouldn't be true.

"Hao de, hao de. I will stay somewhere else this weekend, but please take care of Marilyn while I'm gone." I hoped that Ba Ba would accept this as my barter—he could send me away for the weekends if he would just put up with Marilyn a little bit longer.

It seemed to work. Ba Ba didn't bring it up again, and I was due to be shipped off somewhere else on Friday. But just in case, I started feeding Marilyn a little more of my food every night.

* * *

Lin Ah Yi's home was the poorest of all. Like Wu Ah Yi, she was a new friend, having met Ma Ma in the school. I don't even remember where she lived, but I know it was somewhere far from Manhattan, because it took a long time to get there by subway.

Lin Ah Yi's home was in a basement. It reminded me of the hallways in the hospital, with all of its lights buzzing, so artificial and bright that they gave me an instant headache. I figured that this meant Lin Ah Yi's family must have been really poor, maybe no-income, like us.

Ma Ma, Ba Ba, and I had almost lived in a basement apartment. When we visited the place, we saw that it had gray walls and pipes everywhere that banged and clacked. There was only one little sink and one portable stove, like the ones we had used to eat hot pot at Lao Lao's. Ma Ma had said that there was a good public school in the area that made it worth it, but I said nothing was worth this, and so that was that.

Lin Ah Yi's home was not as bad as that basement apartment; it was finished with white walls and had only a few white pipes, but still, it was a basement. The neighborhood did not seem like it had a good school, either, because all of the doors and windows had bars on them. It reminded me of the area where we first lived when we arrived in America, the place that taught me that we were chinks who would be attacked by dogs as their owner stood by, laughing.

Lin Ah Yi had a son, Ting, who was the same age as Feng. I was grateful that he seemed to find me boring and never followed me around. His friendly apathy was a wide-open window on a stifling summer's day.

The only time Ting and I spent together was when Lin Ah Yi took us to the library. Even though it was the first time we met, Ma Ma had told Lin Ah Yi all about how much I loved books, and that I never felt alone when I had one with me. So before my arrival, Lin Ah Yi had looked up the branch nearest to her home. It was still pretty far away, so after picking me up, Lin Ah Yi took me and Ting to find the branch, turning down this street and then the next, Ting running ahead of us and chattering about his games and toys while Lin Ah Yi asked me about school and the graduation that was to come. It was the most focused attention I had gotten to myself since Ba Ba had left China. It was nice, but I also felt uneasy, as if I were being too selfish, taking too much. But then we were at the library, and I peeled off like Ting, grabbing at books and checking out eight Baby-Sitters Club editions, a personal record.

When we got back to the basement, I learned that for the first time in my life, I had my own room. The apartment was a long railway, like ours, except the family did not have to share with anybody. At the front was the kitchen, which was also the dining and living area. It was the only room with a window, a small, dusty thing at the very top of the wall. Next came Ting's room, or what would be my room during my stay, for he was going to bunk with his parents. It was a square box with a humming fluorescent tube on its lid. Next to that was the bathroom, then the adults' room. I was so enthralled with the idea of my own room that I rarely bothered to venture into the other spaces—not even the bathroom, my habitual place of safety. My room was spare, with all white walls, a full-size bed, and a stool that doubled as a nightstand. To anyone else, it would have suggested a sterile examination room, but to me it was heaven. As soon as I saw it, I sank into the giant bed with its marshmallow comforter and began devouring the books, not getting up until I was called to dinner.

Dinner was steaming and yummy, with lots of dishes like the ones that Ma Ma made— stir-fried bell peppers; tofu and scallions; pillowy white buns that reminded me of the bed that awaited me. Lin Ah Yi's husband did not say much to me, but he had a benevolent face that smiled back at me every time I looked at him. Ting seemed excited to have a new person in the house but not overly so, speaking with zeal to his parents and me about school and the library and his friends. As for Lin Ah Yi, she was love itself, making sure I had enough of everything to eat and asking whether I might like to go to the store with her to buy a white dress, as was required for my graduation.

It was at that creaky table, under the flickering lights and the tiny dusty window, that I noted how full I felt. Out the door, the world remained the same, with Ma Ma in a hospital bed, awaiting an uncertain fate, and Ba Ba in an unknown place with unknown company. But in that basement, underneath the surface of the sidewalk, how everything had changed for me. For once, I had space.

Lin Ah Yi refused to let me clean up after dinner, so I returned to my room, to my marathon of books. I started off on top of the comforter but made my way under it after Lin Ah Yi came in to say good night. I slipped lower and lower in the bed, until I slid into sleep with an open book on my face, the overhead lights still humming.

I was so at peace that I did not even come close to feeling homesick that night. The horrible truth was that, in that moment, Ma Ma was nowhere near my mind. She appeared only in stomach pangs that pulsed every now and then, so anxious was I about hearing bad news when I got back to Ba Ba.

Peace was still there when I awoke the next morning. The clock on the wall informed me it was ten—early!—so I opened my book up again, savoring the freedom that came with four walls and a door all my own. Beyond the door, I heard the family rousing: the telltale beeps of Ting's handheld game; Lin Ah Yi's frying of you tiao, savory long doughnuts that brought a drool to my mouth; her husband's humming to the Chinese tunes sounding from the boom box. And still I stayed cocooned in the comforter, even as the wafting kitchen smells cradled me. I did not leave the room until a full hour later, when I felt like it, at which point Lin Ah Yi greeted me with a meal she had kept warm for me on the stove. There were no words about how pretty she was or how little money Ma Ma and Ba Ba had. There was only good food and flowing music.

The rest of my weekend passed just like that—doing what I wanted, shutting the door to my room when I felt like it, carrying no concerns other than what book I would start next. And though worry about Ma Ma and guilt for being so selfish popped up every now and then, they got buried under the sentences and pages and chapters and the new ease in my body.

* * *

I was sad when Ba Ba came to pick me up. Ba Ba and I spent the subway ride home catching up on our weekend—Ma Ma was better, though he stayed silent about Marilyn when I asked after her—and through it all, the low hum of peace from Lin Ah Yi's home buzzed through me. It stayed with me until I stepped through the threshold to our room, disappearing only when I realized something was wrong.

I gasped.

There was no tail swish to greet me, no little black figure who rubbed and leaned on my ankle.

I didn't need to ask. Ba Ba launched into a series of explanations, as if it were a choose-your-own-adventure book where I got to read all the potential routes and pick my favorite—not that it mattered; not that any of it would end with Marilyn back in our room; not that it would change the fact that I had to once again live without the one being who was there just for me.

"I had to set her free, Qian Qian. The doctor said it would not be good for Ma Ma . . . plus, Marilyn's asymmetrical face, it's bad luck . . . and we barely have any money to feed you, we can't afford all that food . . . be a good girl . . . be a big girl."

I caught only snippets of his pathetic offerings, so heavy was the pounding in my head, my throat, my heart. The things I loved, they always went away.

We had not even gotten to say goodbye.

I did not look at Ba Ba or acknowledge his weak words. Instead, I dropped my backpack on the ground and dove past the curtain, straight into bed, back in a world where the only four walls I had to myself came from my unwashed comforter.

For the next few hours, until sleep relieved me, I thought about what happened when people and animals died. Where did this brain go that carried so many fears? Where did this heart go that pulsed with so much pain?

Chapter 24

SURGERY

....

When at long last the nurses and doctors realized Ma Ma could not wait anymore, no matter how many rich people demanded that their operations come first, the surgery came. I remember little of the day, only that Ba Ba and I waited eleven hours on the stiff metal chairs in a white room that smelled like bleach. Ba Ba said that we had to stay there the whole time in case something happened. When I asked what could happen, he didn't respond. Ba Ba's body stayed next to me but the rest of him was far away, leaving me to study the gray-white tiles on the ground, counting them one by one, and then restarting each time an indolent adult walked across the floor and disrupted my survey.

It was important that I got an accurate count of the precise number of tiles on the floor. Ma Ma depended on it.

All around us, there was chatter and beeping and phones ringing. The chemical smell was stronger than ever, my nose under attack. And the ceiling lights were brighter than anything had ever been in the history of the world. I don't remember there being a window in the room, though there very well may have been one. I remember only staring at the ground, whiteness all around.

By this point, my hand was less blue and swollen, settling into a deep-red plumpness. It did not hurt as much as it had before, or maybe I had just gotten used to it. I had developed small techniques that grew normal over the weeks: I squeezed the toothpaste tube with my left hand; I wrote in lighter strokes, giving up my tight pencil grip. I learned to keep the hand shriveled in a sleeve, a pocket—though squeezing it in was often painful—or hidden behind my back, just in case it drew a worried glance. I had the closest call at Lin Ah Yi's, where I dropped my chopsticks during dinner, causing me and Lin Ah Yi to reach for them at the same time. I reached stupidly, reflexively, with my right hand, and she grabbed my wrist to examine the rump, no longer purple but then blue-green with a yellow halo.

"What happened?"

"What? Oh, this? It's always like this."

"Really?" She looked deep in my eyes and it was all I could do to keep my face from twitching.

"Yeah."

She looked at my left hand, a normal size and color, and then turned back to the right, pressing her thumb into the fattest part of the rump.

"Does this hurt?"

Acting normal demanded all the discipline in the world.

"Not at all."

I was in particular danger in the hospital. There were too many professionals; they would know something was wrong and I wouldn't be able to trick them like I had with Lin Ah Yi. We couldn't afford to treat it, I knew, and anyway, it was getting better. So I wrapped my hand in my sleeve and returned to the book I had been trying to read for hours. It was a special edition: the Baby-Sitters Club was traveling across the country in RVs, which I had just learned were mini homes on wheels. I had started to fantasize about having one. How great would it be, I thought, to have all my possessions in one place and have it all to myself? Marilyn would be there, of course, and I would drive her from place to place and keep her safe. Perhaps I could even take her to the East River, which I saw in person once on the Brooklyn Bridge field trip, and otherwise only on TV and through subway windows. There, she might be able to catch a fish. And Ba Ba wouldn't have to leave me at random homes. As much as I liked it at Lin Ah Yi's, having a home of my own sounded even better. Plus, I would be able to drive Marilyn around in a radius around the hospital, so that we would never be too far away from Ma Ma. And if we were caught, I would just sneak Ma Ma out and we would drive far away just like she dreamed about.

As these images bounced across my brain, my focus trailed past the black words on the page in front of me. I looked at the pages like I always did, but none of the words got into my brain. Still, I kept my eyes trained down. I knew that if I glanced up, I would see a sad old man all alone in his bed on wheels, or a white lady with curls and a long dark skirt sitting in the next row, crying into her hands. Even when I had gotten up earlier to pace the blue line drawn on the ground, toward the nurses' desk and back, I kept my eyes on the floor until Ba Ba told me to sit down because I was moving too much, making him nervous.

I wondered about the old lady with the bear: Was she waiting for me to show up? Did seeing me every day mean as much to her as it did to me? I wondered what Mr. Kane was saying in class and whether I would be able to catch up. I had just read **Where the Red Fern Grows,** and every time I thought about the ending, my eyes throbbed with new tears. I had so much to say about the book, but now, when I got back to class, it would be too late. My thoughts would be irrelevant. I had missed my chance to speak up in class for once and finally prove to Mr. Kane that I was really smart enough to be the person who wrote my essays.

One by one, the hours crawled past us, and my butt grew sore from the chairs. At some point, Wu Ah Yi and Lin Ah Yi arrived. Ba Ba greeted them and smiled, but it was a smile formed by his mouth only. Ba Ba had not smiled, not really, for many days.

I looked toward the hallway to the right of the waiting room every now and then. Ma Ma had been wheeled in that direction in the morning, although it felt like years ago. The surgeon had talked to us then, just before his people took Ma Ma away. He had a face formed by sharp angles and blue eyes so light they were almost silver. His strides and gestures were quick and efficient. It was something that Ba Ba had noticed, too; I knew because he had told Ma Ma that she was in good hands, literally. Actually, he had said, "I can just picture his hands dancing while holding the knife."

At this memory, I squeezed my eyes to shut out the image of the angular doctor slicing Ma Ma's belly open with one of the X-Acto knives

Mr. Kane sometimes handed out for projects. In that vision, his dancing fingers were wearing ballet flats.

I was not looking when the doctor emerged again from the corner. I had failed. I had not checked the hallway for a while, in fact, because Lin Ah Yi was asking me about my book and I was trying my best to remember all that I had read in the past few hours.

It was not until Ba Ba stood up that I noticed the thin figure all clad in blue. Shaking off Lin Ah Yi's gentle touch on my wrist, intended to hold me back, I followed on Ba Ba's heels.

The doctor wore a blue cap, and a blue mask for his nose and mouth like the one Ma Ma had worn while biking in China. Under the mask, his nose and chin formed a mountain ridge that created an impenetrable divide between the east and west of his face. As he removed his mask with a swift wave of his hand, I noticed for the first time that he had thin, light-colored lips that were redder in some places than others. He sank his white teeth into them during surgery, I imagined, as his hands danced with the X-Acto blade.

"The surgery went well." He spoke like he moved: kindly, but at a clipped pace. I had just read that Charles Dickens was paid per installment. This had contributed to the flowery and belabored prose I had just started to love. This doctor, it occurred to me, would not have been able to feed himself as a Victorian writer.

"There was no cancer."

And for the first time that day, I was able to gather my thoughts. I spotted a new feeling in my stomach—relief? Joy? Yes, but also: hunger. Ba Ba and I had had no thought of food at any point in the day, but Lin Ah Yi had brought some homemade buns and I already felt myself wriggling toward the bag next to her.

"But we did have to remove the entire gallbladder and a large part of the liver, so she will have to be careful with greasy foods and alcohol—"

Ma Ma was allergic to alcohol. The slightest bit gave her hives. Didn't he know that? I wondered whether we should be worried that Ma Ma had been cut open and sewn up again by a doctor who didn't even know that. I looked to Ba Ba for signs of anger but found only relief.

"—you should be able to see her soon. We'll let you know when she's ready for you. Do you have any questions?"

I did not need to turn to Ba Ba to know that he would have no questions. He asked fewer and fewer questions in America. Somehow, by leaving China, Ba Ba had grown more Chinese, starting to adopt our government's silly ideas about how asking questions was bad and disrespectful. He took on the form of what America expected of us: docile, meek. He had even started teaching me the importance of keeping my head down, of not asking any questions or drawing any attention, seemingly forgetting that he had taught me the exact opposite in China.

The night before, I had watched Ba Ba pull the brown briefcase out from under our bed. Ye Ye had a similar briefcase, so even without Ba Ba's habit of pulling it out every night, I wouldn't have needed to look at it to know what it contained. The briefcase held our entire lives: our birth certificates; Ma Ma and Ba Ba's marriage license, with a picture of them at twenty-four, unrecognizable and young, faces bright with hope; our three passports, in covers that were still stiff because they had each been used only once; and finally, stacks of cash that Ba Ba spent nights counting and recounting and then strapping together with the rubber bands we got off scallion bunches.

The night before the surgery, Ba Ba had taken particular care to tally the bills, most of them in fives and tens, some twenties, before separating out a chunky stack and placing it in a wrinkled brown envelope from China.

Now, standing in front of the dancing-hands doctor with a mountain down the middle of his face, Ba Ba reached deep into his pants pocket and produced the envelope. Ba Ba had already told me that he and Ma Ma would give the doctor a whole five hundred dollars of our life savings.

"Is it really necessary?" I had asked.

"We have nothing else to give," he had responded.

Ba Ba handed the offering to the doctor with both hands and the slightest bow.

"Thank you, Doctor, for saving my wife. We don't have much—and without you—who knows—"

Ba Ba had never had trouble with words before. The doctor smiled.

"Really. It's nothing."

His ice-blue eyes beamed warmth. But then he grabbed the envelope casually with just one hand, as if it contained coins instead of our life savings, and strode down the hall.

Ba Ba and Ma Ma would see him again, but that was the last I remember of him. In the years to come, I would forget his name and the color of his hair, but I would never forget—could never forget—the saint who graced St. Vincent's; the surgeon who charged us a mere five hundred dollars for saving Ma Ma's life.

* * *

We returned to sitting on the metal chairs a while longer until an Asian nurse waved at us to follow her. Wu Ah Yi and Lin Ah Yi were not allowed in, but they had to go home anyway, so we said our goodbyes, me making sure to hang on to the bag of Lin Ah Yi's homemade buns.

Then we followed the nurse, who barely looked at us. Discontent was painted on her face. I thought nothing of it at the time, only that she was a fancy nurse and we were poor. Only later would I gather the life experience to wonder whether she had treated us that way because she had been assigned to us for no reason other than our shared race.

As we turned down the hall that the surgeon with the dancing hands had disappeared into, I saw that there was a set of doors, above which bold font spelled out INTENSIVE CARE UNIT. This seemed promising to me. Intensive care sounded better and more important than laid-back care, after all. And as we walked through those doors, which swung every which way on loose, squeaky hinges, I saw that the rooms were very different. The hallway was much narrower, and instead of windows looking out into the sky, the windows of the rooms looked onto the hallway, such that we could see into every room as we walked down the hall. And although there was just one bed in each, the rooms were not much smaller than the other room Ma Ma had stayed in. The rest of each room was filled with equipment: cords and machines, tubes and needles. Most of the rooms at the beginning of the hallway were empty, and I winced each time we passed a new room. I did not want to see a person in the beds, hooked up to all the machines and plugged with needles. Even less did I want to see Ma Ma like that.

I was relieved to see, though, that the figures in the occupied rooms were not Ma Ma but small, old, shriveled. But then I came upon the window overlooking the sixth occupied room and realized that it was just an optical illusion. For there was Ma Ma, also looking small, old, shriveled. As I had feared, she had many things plugged into her, tubes and screens, as if she were the power source for all of the dripping and beeping.

I held my breath as we pushed the door open, not knowing whether it was safe to breathe out, not knowing whether she was fully closed up yet. Were we supposed to change into the blue outfit the doctor had worn? I had seen people do that on TV. But surely the nurse, irritated though she was, would have told us.

Ma Ma was not awake yet. She would wake up, right?

Ba Ba exchanged English words with the nurse and approached the bed just as I was about to sit in the chair pushed up against the opposite wall. Were we to wake her? I ran to Ba Ba's side.

"Neng ting jian ma?"

Ma Ma's eyes remained shut and she moved only her lips. Her head tilted to one side of the pillow.

"Zhen tao yian. Hai bu kai shi. Deng duo chang shi jian le."

She thought the surgery had not yet begun, that she had been waiting all day for it.

Ba Ba was silent, but I figured one of us should assure her that the surgery had already taken place, that it was successful.

"Ma Ma! Shi wo, Wang Qian."

"Wang Qian?" At my name, Ma Ma shifted her head toward the center of the pillow.

"Ma Ma, shou shu yi jing wan le. Mei shi le!"

Ma Ma did not respond. She had fallen asleep again.

We turned to the nonplussed nurse.

"She's still under anesthesia. She will be drowsy for the next few hours, but she will come out of it."

I had no idea what "anesthesia" meant. By the looks of Ba Ba, he wasn't sure, either. But the words had jumped so curtly out of the nurse's mouth, one after another, that we did not dare ask.

Keep your head down and don't ask any questions. I guess the new rule applied with other Asians, too.

Out of the corner of my eyes, I caught sight of two bulging bags of liquid hanging low from Ma Ma's bed. One was dark yellow and the other was deep red. My mouth opened and I was powerless to stop the words from running out.

"Is that—her blood?"

Ba Ba stayed silent, but his eyes darted to Ma Ma's body. It took a few seconds before they fell upon the bags.

"We have a catheter for urine and bodily fluids. It's normal. She's on her period."

I had no idea what "catheter" meant, either, but found myself comforted by the matter-of-fact way the nurse delivered the news. She would not have talked about something dangerous just like that, no matter how poor we were. Then the nurse sauntered out of the room, and it was just Ba Ba and me alone with Ma Ma, hooked up in her socket of a bed.

Ma Ma moved only a few times. We thought she would awaken each time she did, but every time it turned out that she was just shifting to get more comfortable. There would be a shuffle and then the room would again fall into silence, punctured only by the beeping and dripping Ma Ma powered.

Ba Ba and I remained seated, helpless in the cacophony of a certain, indeterminate fate.

Chapter 25
GIFTED

....

The week Ma Ma was to finally come home from the hospital—after nearly a week of monitoring, several days out of the ICU—PS 124 had an overnight trip to some castle just north of the city. It was a special event, just for those of us who were due to graduate soon. My classmates were all abuzz with excitement over their first official sleepover trip, but I refused to go. I would have no fun, I knew, and I would do more good at home, where I could take care of Ma Ma.

Not so, said Ba Ba. It would be easier to get Ma Ma acclimated back at home without me around. I was just something else he had to take care of. He didn't come out and say that, not really, but I knew that was the truth. He had said it enough in days past, especially when Marilyn had returned to our door and Ba Ba had caught me feeding her rice and meat that I had siphoned out of my dinner plate and into my greasy pockets.

How could you take on this burden, especially now? Don't you think I have enough to worry about?

This was not exactly what Ba Ba said, but he had said versions of these things, in softer notes, and over time, his voice had gotten trapped in my head, feeding on my brain cells and growing larger and meaner. It was an ever-present roar now, among the loudest of the ones I carried inside myself. It spoke to me even when Ba Ba was absent, when I was all alone.

So when Ba Ba said no, I should go on the field trip, I heard the rest of what he meant without his actually saying any of it. I acquiesced, praying only that what I had shared with Marilyn would be enough to carry her until my return.

* * *

The bus ride was long, forgettable. Every time I left the city—and it had happened only one or two times—I was shocked that the rest of the country was not just like Manhattan and Brooklyn, draped in cement and steel. I had assumed that everything in America was the same as all that was around us, but as I stared out the window at the budding greenery, I realized that there was a lot of America I had yet to see.

By this time, my friends had gotten used to my vacillating between silence and bullying.

It made for excitement, I suppose: they never knew if they would meet with quiet assent or sharp retort. I never dwelled on the verbal abuse and lies I unleashed on them; my focus was on Ma Ma. I would be rid of them in a few weeks, anyway. I was going to attend a special public school next year, called the NYC Lab Middle School for Collaborative Studies. It was in a different part of Manhattan, Chelsea, an area that was closer to St. Vincent's and had few Chinese people. Back then, the school labeled itself as one for gifted children, and I had passed a written test and an interview to get in.

The entire process had been dramatic. Ba Ba insisted that I keep my head down and draw no attention to myself:

Why not just attend the school that we are zoned for in Brooklyn?

You don't need to commute to Manhattan now that you speak English, Qian Qian. Now you can really claim that you were born here!

You don't need to prove that you're special. Plus, do you really think you can compete with those rich white kids in Manhattan? Their parents have fancy jobs; they pay for all sorts of things we don't even know about. Too much pressure.

How sad will you be when you get rejected? How embarrassing. So much face lost!

Ma Ma would have been the tiebreaker, but she was out of commission, and where I went to school next year was not important enough to bring into her hospital room.

Instead, I made the decision on my own. I figured that if what Ba Ba said was right, then I wouldn't get in anyway, and there was no harm in trying without his knowing. Chances were that nothing would change. I didn't understand what he meant about feeling embarrassed and disappointed. I had never understood it, the big deal about saving face. I figured being rejected was just the same as not trying—worse probably, because I would always wonder. Perhaps that was Ma Ma's voice within me, telling me that I could do everything she hadn't done but wished that she had, promising me that whatever I saw out there, whatever I envied, could be mine as long as I chose to make it so.

I took the subway to Lab on my own and attended the interview without Ba Ba knowing about any of it. Like the very first school I had seen in America, Lab had security guards and metal detectors. But it also had kids of all colors. I was directed down one hallway and then another, and as I marched my way down each, I pretended not to let on how very startled I was by the size of the other kids, how brown and empty the walls were, and how different they looked without bright, childish drawings of stick figures and birds with beaks and wings just a little too big. When I was at last in the right office, I found a dark-haired man who was so short that his torso came up only partway in his large office chair. The man had brown beady eyes that studied me so closely that I would have switched cars had I seen him on the subway. But there was little I could do during the interview other than remain seated under his eyes, feeling small and scared and thinking that I had made the wrong decision by not telling Ba Ba where I was. What if this man had me deported? What if he abducted me? Ba Ba had enough problems without my adding to them.

But the beady-eyed man did nothing more than ask me mundane questions about what subjects I liked (English) and what subjects I didn't (science—I had decided that the year before, when I had gotten sick of being the one kid who did not have a least favorite subject). He also asked me what book I was reading. It seemed like he was expecting only one answer, even though I was in the middle of five different books at the time—one for the subway, two for home, and two of course for the bathroom, depending on my mood. So I told him the name of the subway book I had with me: **Alice in Rapture, Sort Of.** For years later, I would reflect how fortuitous it was that the title happened to have a fancy word in it, one that I had looked up just a few days before, when I had come upon the cover in the library.

The beady man looked impressed when I mentioned the title, as if he knew the book and that it was of great renown, but that could not have possibly been the case: the entire Alice series was about a girl growing up with her father and her brother. Alice's mom had died from leukemia when Alice was very little. Male teachers, I had learned by then, were rarely impressed with stories about girls. Mr. Kane was always telling me to read something more worthwhile, like **Hatchet.** But I didn't understand why a boy's stories about growing up were more worthwhile than a girl's. Even so, immediately after my tongue tripped over the **Alice in Rapture** title, I wished that I had said **Hatchet** instead.

From there, the interview proceeded uneventfully. I startled only once, when the beady-eyed man asked what my parents did for a living. I said that Ba Ba worked as a translator (which was technically part of his job) and that Ma Ma was not working at the time (also technically true). He seemed content with that as he jotted down some notes, and soon I was set free again to roam the halls. Lab was the first place where I saw kids of different races hanging out together, as if it were no big deal. Down the hallways, there were groups of Chinese kids laughing with white kids and Black kids and Latino kids, just like on **The Puzzle Place**.

PS 124 was mostly Chinese—the few white kids in the gifted program kept to themselves and their colorful, reusable lunch bags full of home-cooked meals—and there weren't that many other types of kids for us to hang out with, even if we were interested, even if we didn't see ourselves as inferior and lesser, by virtue of being Chinese. And outside school, in Chinatown and Brooklyn, I had never seen many casual gatherings across races. Most interactions were tense and distant, and I was on guard at all times. I found myself wanting to linger within the walls of Lab, if only to continue watching these kids who did not seem to care about skin color. But my stomach reminded me that I was getting too close to missing lunch period.

A few weeks later, when I received my acceptance to Lab, Mr. Kane and Ba Ba expressed shock. Mr. Kane called me up to his desk again, and this time tried to talk me out of attending. He had his protective voice on, and said something about how the classes might be too hard for me, that being hardworking would only get me so far, but I stopped listening as soon as I confirmed that he was not accusing me of copying my recent assignment. At home, Ba Ba was dismayed that I had been sneaky enough to apply without telling him, but he quickly lost interest in fighting me. The hours on the subway traveling to and from the hospital had depleted him.

After the acceptance, I passed more time in my head, jumping from thoughts about the past to reveries about the future. The present was scary, depressing: Ma Ma was sick and we didn't know if she would get fully better and whether the hospital would come after us. But somehow, I had gotten into a school that Ba Ba had said was meant for the white kids who were born here and who were so rich that they lived in Manhattan and probably had parents who worked in tall buildings. If that had happened, what else was possible? Maybe Ma Ma had been right: maybe I could create everything I wanted for myself, for the three of us. And this was the first step.

It was in this egotistical, deluded fantasy that I spent the bus ride up to the castle. When we pulled up in front of a giant gray brick building with a circular driveway, Mr. Kane stood up and launched into his standard comedy routine.

"Okay, everyone, we're finally here at Mickey D's!" He paused, awaiting laughter that would never arrive. It was in those pockets of silence—as the realization emerged on his face that he had disappointed his audience yet again—that I found him to be most like me. He covered it up well, though: he used his pointer finger to push his glasses up by the bridge and gave an awkward chuckle.

"I'm just kidding, guys. We're here! Let's line up to get off the bus, single file. And if you were supposed to be on the bus but aren't, let me know, would ya?" Pause. Chuckle. "I'm just kidding, guys."

When I got off the bus, I saw that there were trees all around. For all I knew, they could have just taken us to the middle of Central Park. The castle wasn't really a castle, just a big gray building with sparse furniture and no heating. It was still only May, warmer, but chilly once the sun was gone.

We wandered around the building as a group. There were some paintings and animal heads stuck to the walls. There was no explanation of the history or meaning behind any of it, but it was better than the classes where Mr. Kane had us sit in front of the TV on wheels and rewatch the same episode of **Tom and Jerry** that we had watched for the preceding three years.

After dinner—some stew and bread at a long table so roughly carved that I fancied we were knights in the Middle Ages—Mr. Kane and the other teachers had us sit in the main lobby by a fireplace. A white man with tan overalls and a tan bucket hat stood at the front of the room. He had a yellow, thick, fleshy thing resting on his neck and shoulders. When I first entered the room, I thought it was some sort of scarf, but as I approached, even my eyesight was not so bad as to miss that the scarf was actually a scaly python. The thing was so long that its tail draped all the way down the man's right arm. I suppressed an instant urge to vomit—I couldn't ruin Christine's shoes again; she'd never stop talking about it—and shuffled toward the back of the room.

As the tan man blathered on, we were forced to touch the snake, one by one, as it opened its mouth at us and showed us its vacant gums. I managed to get by with touching it using just the tip of my index finger while looking in the opposite direction. This sufficed for Mr. Kane. I had learned much earlier in the school year that we had two choices: do what he said or make him laugh.

We got hot cocoa after the excitement of the snake—though my stomach was too unsettled for me to swallow any of it—and then we were shown to our rooms. My room was among the smaller ones: just two bunk beds for four girls. Christine and I shared a bunk, of course, but the two other girls have since fallen away from my memory.

Lights out was at nine p.m., and for once, I was excited to go to bed early. The earlier I went to bed, the sooner I would see Ma Ma. I was sick of being around so many people all day, removed from the cocoon of my family's little room. We were assigned to a hall just for girls, and I was new to the teacher who was our floor's chaperone, though I had seen her around school. She was among the few non-Chinese teachers, and she was shaped like a grapefruit. As her footsteps clacked down the stairs, fading from our hall, I heard room doors creak open all down the floor. Emerging from those creaks were the excited whispers of girls already giggling from breaking the rules.

My roommates joined in on the giggling and shuffles.

I groaned. "Do we have to?"

"It's freezing in here anyway. Come on!" And with that, the two faceless girls disappeared through the door. Christine stayed in the dark with me. She had many faults, but loyalty ran deep in her bones.

We lay in silence together, one stacked on top of the other like cinder blocks. We listened to our breaths and the hushed laughter and chittering just beyond the door. I pulled the thin blanket all the way up, snug across my shoulders and neck, but soon found myself in shivers, my teeth clacking against each other. I had gone to bed fully clothed and still I was shaking. Christine started snoring. How had she managed to fall asleep in such cold?

For the next few minutes, I debated grabbing the blankets from the two other beds, but even in my mind's eye, I could not orchestrate the task without my current blanket slipping off of me, exposing me to frostbite. I didn't quite know what frostbite was, but the final scenes of "To Build a Fire" had stalked me since my first reading, and I figured that I was not about to risk my limbs for two blankets so loosely woven that they would have let cold air flow in anyway.

It was the first time I had been cold enough for my teeth to clack. I thought back to the itchy sweaters that Lao Lao had mailed to us, neatly lined up against our drafty windows; to the strong little radiator in our main room that hissed and spat whenever it woke up. It was then that I realized I could be homesick for a place even though I no longer knew where home was.

I took my mind to the only place that brought peace. I pictured Ma Ma and Ba Ba laughing together at home, on the couch where they shared their rare happy moments. In the alley outside our window, Marilyn was licking her paws, her belly stuffed with food, her body purring with warmth. And then I stepped through the threshold of sleep.

* * *

Ma Ma's return did not go well. She stayed in bed and was in constant pain. I wondered why we had gone through the trouble of the surgery and the hospital if nothing was going to change. Ba Ba did all of the cooking now, and we soon pushed up against the limits of his culinary knowledge. Ma Ma had refused to teach me to cook. Cooking well was a curse for women, she said, because it meant you would have to do it every day for the rest of your life.

A few times, when Ma Ma was asleep or in too much pain to have me around, I went to the store with Ba Ba. I spent most of that time standing by the deli section, where a glass case displayed shiny brown chicken bodies rotating on a silver stick. Just outside of the case were plastic bags with holes poked through them, each a coffin for those who completed their spinning dance. That display case was a delight for every sense: an ever-changing performance under bright lights; wafts of yummy oil and grease; the hot air rosying my cheeks and sending heat through my body. If I closed my eyes and indulged in the smells, I could almost taste the savory chicken between my teeth, on my tongue, sliding down my throat.

* * *

One day, I happened to be reading **White Fang** in the sunroom (spring was sliding into early summer and it was just bearable in there) when I saw Marilyn through the window. She was climbing up the outdoor steps with something brown, white, and bulbous in her mouth. Ba Ba was busy preparing our dinner, and Ma Ma was passed out, as she always seemed to be now. I slipped out of our room and through the double front doors, where Marilyn sat waiting for me on the landing. Just in front of her was a brown feathered thing with a large white belly. Pride beamed from Marilyn as I bent over to examine the item. I then stared back at her as paragraphs from the many cat books I read came back to me—notes about cats who presented to their humans gifts of dead birds and mice.

"Marilyn!" I stepped past the bird, my fourth gift in America, to scoop her up, grateful for the surprise reunion. "You saved the sparrow for me, even though you must be hungry." She purred and I walked the two of us past the front doors and into our room. In the bedroom area, Ma Ma was still asleep, lying on her side with her hands wrapped at her waist, her body curled like a shrimp. I placed Marilyn on the bed and she spun around three times before settling into a ball against the crook of Ma Ma's arms, her face purring into her tail.

Reluctant to leave Marilyn, I retrieved **White Fang** from the sunroom before returning to the sleeping area, where I climbed onto my bed with the book. I must have fallen asleep because the next thing I knew, Ba Ba's anger filled the room.

"What is this filthy **thing** doing in bed with Ma Ma?"

I opened my eyes to Ba Ba towering over me, holding Marilyn with just one hand as she hissed, writhing and squirming in search of freedom.

"I—I let her in—" I jumped up to grab her, but Ba Ba walked out of our room and toward the kitchen. I gave chase, catching out of the corner of my eyes a view of Ma Ma, who was now sitting up in bed, still clutching her mid-section.

By the time I entered the kitchen, Ba Ba was already dropping Marilyn out of the open window.

"No!"

Time slowed and my speech slurred, but I got to the window just in time to see Marilyn land on her feet and scamper off. Ba Ba pushed the window shut so quickly that I had to pull my hands back to avoid having my fingers smashed.

He used the calm, low voice that scared me most. "That cat is bad luck, ni ting dong le ma?" I willed myself to nod but wasn't quite sure that I was actually doing it.

"We have enough bad luck without you bringing in more. Now, set the table for dinner."

We ate in quiet unease. The late-descending sun of June kept the sky lit, the rays of dusk filtering in and setting our dinner portrait in sepia tones. With each tasteless gulp of food, I swallowed the realization that going to a better school would do nothing to change our family's bad luck.

Chapter 26

GRADUATION

....

Ma Ma was back at St. Vincent's the next week. It happened while I was at school: Ma Ma felt sharp pains, and she called the doctor, who told her to come back immediately. Ba Ba met her somewhere: an in-between subway station in Manhattan, or perhaps just the hospital. I was in class—maybe math or English, attention fixed on dumb daydreams while Ma Ma got hooked up to needles again.

I was sad but not shocked that Ma Ma was sick again. Ba Ba had warned me and I had not listened. I saw Marilyn several times after the incident. Instead of feeding her, though, I ignored her and pretended she was just like any other cat on the street. One morning, she followed me three blocks to the subway station, and when it was clear that she was not giving up, I grabbed a long, broken-off tree branch from the ground and waved it at her.

"You're bad luck. Go away!"

I had not seen her since.

But it didn't matter; it was too late. The bad luck I carried in had infected Ma Ma again.

Ma Ma's body, it turned out, had not adjusted to being without its gallbladder and half its liver. And the food that we had been eating had not been clean or healthy enough, so Ma Ma now had something called pancreatitis. I had no idea that something like the pancreas even existed, and now it was ruining my life.

It turned out that pancreatitis was a common disease for alcoholics, so the rotating set of nurses and young doctors always asked that about Ma Ma. I took it upon myself to inform all of them that Ma Ma was very, very allergic to alcohol.

The doctors had Ma Ma stop eating entirely. Instead, they hooked her up to bags of clear liquid. "Each bag," Ma Ma said as she pointed at the liquid that dripped from the suspended plastic sacs, "costs four hundred dollars. If I go through three of these every day—that's twelve hundred dollars!"

After three days on the bags of the expensive water, Ma Ma's cheeks grew rosy and she lost the swollen, waterlogged look that we had both developed during our years in the Beautiful Country.

"You need to eat less sodium," one Korean doctor said with a shiny smile and a white coat.

"Less grease. Eat natural, healthy," directed another doctor, who was white but not the surgeon with the dancing hands and clipped words.

"No more canned goods," admonished a third with brown skin and hazel eyes.

By the time Ma Ma collected a full plate of advice that we could ill afford, she had been in the hospital for nearly a week, and was pumping—by her own meticulous calculations—over six thousand dollars in liquid nutrition. The veins on her arms and hands grew so poked-through that they again had to resort to those on her feet.

That was also the week before graduation, five days filled with useless but pricey trips to museums, movie theaters, and restaurants, all so our teachers would no longer have to go through the motions of teaching us. I skipped all of it, attending school only when we were scheduled to practice for the graduation ceremony, and then taking the subway to the hospital.

For the ceremony, girls were to wear white dresses and boys were to wear white tops and black bottoms. It seemed odd to me that we had to dress like we were getting married just to sing random songs. And it created a problem for me because I did not have a single piece of white clothing. I eschewed dresses, embracing the tomboy look because it was cheaper for us to buy separates that I could grow into over the course of the year. And we almost never bought white; it was much too likely to dirty and yellow. But I had no choice: wear any other color and I would be a gob of mud among my classmates' purity.

One of Ma Ma's friends took me shopping for the dress. I can't remember who it was, but I'd like to think it was Lin Ah Yi, even though we never got to go when I stayed with her. Whoever it was, she took me to Macy's, which Ma Ma and I had only dared to window-shop. She led me to the floor of fancy dresses for girls and told me to choose whatever I liked. The racks upon racks of frills and bows were terrifying. I had never had the luxury nor burden of such choice in America. Most of the dresses were tiny—perhaps for girls who ate non-greasy, low-sodium, and all-natural diets, and whose mothers never had to be rushed to the hospital to be pumped full of nutrition—but I managed to find one that fit and did not make me look like a tiered cake with legs. At the cashier, I uttered a few feeble protests as Ah Yi reached out to pay. We both knew it was an act, that Ma Ma and Ba Ba had no money for this frivolous little bridal gown.

* * *

Ma Ma was released again from the hospital just before my graduation. Still, I held my breath—by then I had learned that bad luck did not just go away, even though Marilyn had.

On graduation day, I found my place early in the playground, where we were to line up in alphabetical order before filing into the cafetorium, which had its divider walls removed so all of our parents could enjoy our off-key performances. I was muttering the newly learned lyrics to myself when Mr. Kane came upon me, his glasses tinted under the sun's rays. He had the fancy ones that turned into sunglasses, but when the shade only partially came into effect—like under the courtyard's semi-light now or when our classroom's bulbs had just been replaced and were still a little too bright—he looked like he was blind.

"Qian! There you are! I've been looking for you all week."

I responded with a meek smile. One of the things I was most looking forward to was getting away from Mr. Kane. My first experiences with a male teacher—and a white man—had me worried about how I would do in the world, where, according to Ba Ba, they controlled everything. Mr. Kane had a knack for bringing out only two modes in me: uncomfortable or sad. He never did anything overtly bad, so it was hard to explain. But he was, as Ba Ba mentioned after a parent-teacher conference, a "liu mang." The word has no real linguistic equivalent in English, though America had many human equivalents. Roughly translated, the word meant something between a rogue, a pervert, and a creep. That gray space was a good fit for Mr. Kane, but even so, I was loath to use the term for him, because there were so many moments when he seemed to be no more than a lonely child, just like me.

When I offered no response, Mr. Kane released the sigh that always preceded his protective scolding.

"You did not go to at least half of the Graduation Week activities, Qian. I know because I checked. You have to participate. I don't want to tell you this, but I am only offering this for your own good: if you don't participate, if you skip out at every chance, you will get nowhere in life. You hear me? Let those be my parting words to you."

I didn't know why, because I had lasted all year with Mr. Kane, but it was at this point that I felt my throat hitch and develop a lump. All the scents and smells from the previous week came back to me—the needles and jars and packs of medicine, the dripping bags of fancy water, Ma Ma tiny, so many tubes coming out of her. I blinked fast and avoided eye contact. Then I croaked out a clumsy "thank you" before walking out of the courtyard and into the bathroom, where I slid into a stall and drenched the top of my wedding gown with tears.

* * *

The ceremony was long and balmy. The school had no air-conditioning and limited ventilation. The cafetorium had few windows—certainly not enough to cool the polyester-covered bodies of my entire fifth-grade class and all of our family members—and I started dripping sweat within just a few minutes of sitting down. We students were in the auditorium half of the room, with the teachers on the stage in front of us, and our parents behind us on the cafeteria benches. The teachers gave many speeches about how wonderful and special we were, a message belied by the dullness in their eyes. They gave the same speeches year after year—this truth hung in the viscous air. I didn't know why they needed to pretend, especially because many of the parents and children in the room, like Elaine's family, had already attended identical ceremonies for older siblings, who had also been declared special and wonderful in the exact same ways.

The ceremony plodded toward its end with the songs we had rehearsed in pain (for our throats and ears alike). At the principal's command, we all rose in unison like the sweatshop workers at lunchtime and turned to the back of the room to face our families, who were cocooned in their own sweat. We then launched into our three songs, one after another, as the speakers blasted renditions sung by the original performers. Our contributions were juvenile and unnecessary, like drawing penciled, school-desk etchings on top of subway graffiti art.

And then there was the most confusing part of all: to this day, I do not understand what two of the three songs had to do with graduation. They were old, adult songs, nothing like what we listened to. First there was "Every Breath You Take," which Mr. Kane said was popular for weddings, but after I read the lyrics, I didn't understand why married people would threaten each other, or why we had to threaten our parents at our graduation. Then there was "True Colors," which seemed to be about one person asking another person to reveal his true self. I didn't understand why we were asking that of our parents. Ma Ma and Ba Ba were always their true selves with me and sometimes it was scary. If they were hiding more, I didn't want to see it.

The last song, though, made perfect sense to me. As the music shifted and swelled, I continued looking around the room for Ma Ma. But there were too many faces and eyes, and we were all standing at the same level. I leaned this way and that, searching the audience, before a teacher came and put a firm hand on my shoulder. Because we had turned around, alphabetical order had, for the first time in my life, placed me in the very front row.

When Bette Midler's crooning began, I gave up on finding Ma Ma. I contented myself with looking up instead, at the ceiling, and singing with my full, tone-deaf voice. I did not last very long, though. At the end of the second verse, as we hit upon "A beautiful smile to hide the pain," I came undone. But there was already so much sweat on my face that no one could tell I was crying.

For the first time since stepping into that school, there, in that cafetorium with my classmates, each of us soaked through in our now-translucent whites, I let myself cry in abundance. We limped toward the song's closing, sputtering, "Thank God for you, the wind beneath my wings." For the entire song, I kept my blurred vision fixed on the ceiling, by turns thanking God for Ma Ma and begging him not to take her away from me, as he had done with everything else I loved.

Chapter 27
TAMAGOTCHI

....

I stepped into the summer with caution. Without school, it was my sole job to monitor Ma Ma and get her back to the hospital as soon as necessary. I had failed her twice. I could not do it again.

That summer, Ma Ma managed to graduate with her degree, too, having stacked the little swiveling table by her hospital bed full of books with big titles like **Algorithms,** a word I remembered and pronounced as "Al Gore Rhythms." We attended the graduation on a sweltering day. Ma Ma had lost so much weight that the black robe swallowed her up, and from where Ba Ba and I sat in the audience, she was a tiny face drowning in a black sea.

The graduation didn't seem to make much of a difference, though: she had a computer science degree now, but she still couldn't get a real job. Ma Ma looked, but each time they asked her for paperwork, she came home stomping, mumbling about how we had to figure out a way to become legal or we would have to leave. In the meantime, she was back to spitting in tea mugs for Henry Yee, who had hired and then fired two women in Ma Ma's absence.

Ma Ma insisted that she was all better, but I noticed all the ways in which she was frail: She ate with care now, and she moved slower, no longer rising as soon as she was done with her plate. She stopped frying chicken. She drank more water. But most of all, she stopped talking to me so much about everything that was worrying her. Written on her smaller, deflated face was everything she was not telling me and carrying on her own. She spent more time out, too; she had made a new friend who lived on Long Island and she often went to visit her.

"Ma Ma, zen me le?" Sometimes, I managed to coax her stresses out of her. Other times, she remained distant, brows furrowed. I wondered if she had decided not to tell me anything anymore because I had failed her twice.

Ma Ma pointed out that bad luck hit our family every five years: the entire past year, with the sickness and surgery, and five years before that, with Ba Ba leaving China. We needed to change things, she said, before the next wave hit.

I took note of what she had left unspoken: that five years before Ba Ba left China, I had been born. I thought back on what Ma Ma had told me long before—that they had me because Ma Ma had already gotten pregnant twice and was afraid to get another abortion. The previous pregnancies were boys, Ma Ma had said, but then she ended up with me, a girl.

For weeks thereafter I pictured my two older brothers with me everywhere I went. How much fun it would be to have them in real life! How much safer I would feel. I mentioned that once to Ma Ma, but she only chuckled. "Silly Qian Qian. We were only allowed to have one child in China. So if I had one of them, you wouldn't be here."

That was less fun to imagine, so I started imagining that I had a twin sister who was with me everywhere I went. Being a twin meant that I could be born but still have a sibling. But of course, all of that was before Ma Ma got sick, when I was not preoccupied with the task of watching her and making sure I was ready to call 911 at a moment's notice.

The other change in Ma Ma was a fun one. She had always saved a dollar or two from our grocery budget to buy a lottery ticket. It was important, she said, to have hope. But after the surgery, she started putting even more money into the lottery. She had spoken to a lawyer, she told me, and as it turned out, there were business visas we could pay for if we had enough money. I had asked her how much we needed, because maybe I could go back to working at the sweatshop, but Ma Ma had responded that it was a number bigger than what I could even imagine.

On Ma Ma's way home from work every day, she bought two or three lottery tickets that together cost a total of five dollars. She always bought a boring one—the one with many black numbers printed on a small white sheet. Whenever I complained that it was no fun, Ma Ma reminded me that it had the largest jackpot—millions of dollars, maybe close to the big number that we needed for a visa.

The other two were much more fun. They were always in shiny color foil—some pink, some red, some blue, with a numerical chart down the right side that said BINGO on top. On the left were balls with hidden numbers under them. The goal was to scratch the foil off the balls to reveal numbers, one by one, and then scratch off the same numbers where they appeared in the grids on the right. Winning meant having five scratched off in a row, across, down, or diagonally.

Ma Ma always saved the Bingo sheets for me. With a fresh sheet in hand, I'd give a good-luck blow to my quarter and set about the game, relishing each scratch. The game could take me up to thirty minutes, especially when I doled it out in small bits, scratching off a number, placing it on the charts, blowing off the gilded dust, and then reclining on the couch to watch a few minutes of **Family Matters.** I dragged out the game as long as I could. So long as I had not yet finished scratching off the numbers, there was still a chance I could win.

Ma Ma had told me early on that there was a special spot on the Bingo pages where you could scratch to see if you had won without needing to play the actual game. But it felt like cheating to me, and in any event, I didn't understand why anyone would want to skip the game and cut short the window of hope where it was possible to be hundreds of dollars richer. I always made sure to scratch that spot at the end of the game, though, just to make sure I never missed a win.

The most Ma Ma and I ever won was five dollars. When we realized what we had won, we celebrated for a few minutes by talking about how we might actually get to the number we needed to buy visas. Then we walked back to the bodega to invest our winnings in new shining tickets of hope.

* * *

The summer of 1998 marked the most acquisitive time of my American childhood. At graduation, my dream had come true: I had won an award from the local Lions Club that came with a fifty-dollar gift certificate to Barnes & Noble, a store I revered so much I rarely dared to enter its doors. After the ceremony, I had walked to the East Broadway subway station between Ma Ma and Ba Ba in a daze, pinching the gift certificate between clammy fingers, rings of wetness developing on the paper. Even so, I couldn't bring myself to stow it away in a folder in my backpack, as Ba Ba had urged. If I stopped holding it, I would cease to believe it was real, for I had never dreamed that I would one day have so much to spend at an actual bookstore.

The following Sunday, Ba Ba took me to Barnes & Noble. The green awnings and gold letters stood on the chest of the multilevel store that beamed with pride over the trees of Union Square. For the next two hours, we made our way through the store, I poring over the titles on the shelves as Ba Ba looked on through sleepy eyes. At the end of each floor, we took the escalator up to the next level, my arms loading up with far more prospective purchases than I could afford.

We settled down in the kids' section and sur-veyed my choices. The decision weighed on me, drooping my shoulders. On the one hand (quite literally), I had several Baby-Sitters Club books that I had for years longed to own for myself. Their covers were shiny and smooth; their pages still rested tightly together, unmarked by the intrusion of strangers' fingers. On the other hand, I had books of duty that Ba Ba commended to me: a textbook with a tree on the cover, overlaid with the words **What Your 6th Grader Needs to Know,** and a hardcover Merriam-Webster dictionary that I had only ever seen on a special wooden stand at the library. The dictionary was so large that my arm had started to shake under its weight.

"Qian Qian"—at the tone of Ba Ba's voice, I knew his mind was made up—"you know you can come here and read those babysitter books anytime."

"I can?"

"Yes. This is just like the library, except you can't take the books home for free."

I looked around and took in for the first time the little white boys and girls, sitting on stools, on the floor, and on their parents' laps, flipping through pages with all the time in the world.

"I didn't know. I thought they would kick me out. But I have fifty dollars—shouldn't I use it?"

"Of course. But use it on something you can't read here. Something you need to have at home." He pointed to the books of duty.

I hesitated. The covers did not excite me. They did not comfort me. They made me sleepy.

"You can learn big words, so they'll never know that you're an immigrant. Look"—he grabbed the dictionary with indentations along the side for each letter of the alphabet, and flipped to a section just before the C indentation—"you can look up a word like **bird**, and here's a section showing you what it means."

"But I already know what **bird** means."

"Oh, but think of everything you don't know! They're all here, Qian Qian. The whole world is here, between these covers."

I liked the sound of that. Most of all, I liked that I could help Ba Ba believe that one day, no one would think we were immigrants, that we really and truly belonged here.

Wo zai zhe li sheng de. Wo yi zhi jiu zai Mei Guo. I was born here. I've always lived in America.

"And, you see?" He knocked his fist against the cover. "It's great quality. It will last you until college."

I thought back to what Ma Ma had said before she got sick, that there were certain colleges that didn't ask too many questions, if I was good enough to get in. I could not spare a single effort. That solved the dilemma: I bought the dictionary and spent the remaining amount on the textbook, vowing to work through each of them every day. I left the Baby-Sitters Club books in a neat pile by our chairs. Perhaps I could come back to visit them. Or they might bring joy to someone else.

I walked away from the cashier hand in hand with Ba Ba, proud to give him hope. I would study five words a day every day, I told him, and within a year I would know all the words in the world.

He smiled and it was all I could do to reflect his joy.

But as I carried my purchases out, I noted that the bulging green bags brought me no happiness. Instead, I felt heavy. Somber. At least, I reminded myself, I was fifty dollars closer to attending college.

I never did touch those books again. For the rest of our days in America, they sat by my bed, a reminder of Ba Ba's waning dreams for me.

* * *

My second big acquisition came later in the summer, when the Brooklyn heat had us passing time on the front steps after dinner, enjoying the breeze that fanned the setting sun. Ba Ba came home through that heat one evening in a soaked-through white shirt and pride on his face. Before changing out of his clothes, he presented me with a box in a stiff, translucent plastic bag.

Hope dashed through my chest over what it might be. For the entire school year, I had lusted after my classmates' Tamagotchis, little egg-shaped electronic toys in varying colors, each housing a digital chick that needed to be fed and played with, like Marilyn. Over the fourth-grade summer and into the start of fifth grade, all of my friends got one. I had showed up to class one morning to find that I was the only one who did not have a beeping, needy pet in her palm. Some of my classmates even had three, each in a different color. I would spend most of my classes looking over my friends' shoulders at their pet chicks—a constellation of black pixels, really—and all that they demanded. They needed to be fed, cleaned, played with, and disciplined, all within hours. If they were ignored, they died, something that once happened to Hanna Lee twice in one day. The whole idea seemed stressful and not particularly fun, but everyone had one, so of course I wanted one. I had spent most of my fifth-grade year walking around with my eyes fixed on the ground, convinced that I would find one dropped by a careless kid. I pictured myself picking the egg out from between a grate, dusting it off, and giving the chick a clean, loving home full of games and food and discipline. Whenever a friend let me hold her Tamagotchi, I imagined running off with the chick and living together in happiness until I raised him into a full-grown rooster, with a pixelated comb and all.

Now, time slowed as I retrieved the box from the bag Ba Ba handed me, and quickened again as soon as I saw what it was. The box was rectangular, white on the sides. The front was clear, and in its center was a flattened, oval white egg with a keychain attached. The white shell was cracked in the center, exposing a screen edged in blue. At the bottom, three blue buttons protruded. I looked up at Ba Ba.

"Did I get the right one? I asked for the egg with a chicken in it."

A few months before, Ba Ba had scolded me for not checking both ways while crossing the street. I had been too busy searching the ground for a homeless Tamagotchi in need of adoption. I told Ba Ba what I was looking for, going into lengthy detail as to what the game looked like and how it worked. Ba Ba responded only, "Look where you're going, Xi Mou Hou. You're not going to get your chicken that way."

I forgot the conversation as soon as it was over, returning to scouring the streets with my eyes. It never occurred to me that we might be able to somehow afford a brand-new Tamagotchi, and even then, it wouldn't have felt right to buy a baby chick instead of more healthy food for

Ma Ma. Plus, I had had many other similar, unrequited obsessions in America: the full-size Barbie doll, the Furby, and the G-Shock Baby-G watch. None of them ever came to fruition, and they all petered off into a whispered longing.

But with the Tamagotchi, it was different. I finally had one. I wrapped Ba Ba in a great big hug, he bending down in his sweaty shirt, I reaching up on the tips of my toes. Then I ripped open the box and yanked the plastic tag out of the egg, hurling myself onto the couch as my chick beeped into life, leaving Ba Ba free to unburden himself of his sodden clothes.

* * *

It was, in fact, an acquisitive summer for all of us. After the Tamagotchi, and just before I was to start at Lab, Ba Ba came home with yet another surprise.

Ma Ma had come home first that day, and she was already in the kitchen steaming the vegetables we had ferried from Chinatown earlier that week: onions, carrots, and cabbage. We took care to go toward the end of the day, when vendors were eager to dispose of what had baked for long hours in the mixture of summer sun and car exhaust. Sometimes, when we went late enough, we even got sweet potatoes on steep discount.

Meanwhile, I was splayed out on our new forest-green couch, playing with my little chick. The couch was a new find from a recent shopping day. It was stiff and uncomfortable but looked much cleaner than our old one. Earlier that week, as we dragged that old couch out through the doors and onto the front steps, I looked at the embracing cushions, slouchy and soft from the years of sitting we shared, and asked Ma Ma why we had to get rid of a reliable, comfortable couch for an unknown hard one. Ma Ma explained that the look of things sometimes meant more than how they felt. The green couch looked newer, cleaner, more expensive. It would inspire us to work harder. It might even bring us good luck and prosperity. The toughness of the polyester bumps under me flowed in and out of my mind as I got my chick up to full health. I had developed a habit of doing that whenever I could, because I never knew what was to come the next day, and how long it might be before I could get back to my chick. It was better to load her up early. Like with Marilyn.

Then Ba Ba burst into the room, startling me into a seated position. "Come, come! Hurry!" By the time I left my chick and walked out of the room, he had already run down the hall to the kitchen, from which he was leading Ma

Ma out by the hand. I could not remember the last time I had seen Ba Ba holding Ma Ma's hand, so I figured that the news must be big, important. Ba Ba had left the front doors open, which he never did, and he waved all three of us through. He pointed at a car parked just outside our door. It was a four-door sedan that reminded me of a long, flat shoe, and it had the same shimmery gold color of the scratched-off shavings from the Bingo cards.

"There's always a car parked here, Ba Ba." I was eager to return to my chick; I was so close to getting her health to perfect.

"The stove is on—I should get back." Ma Ma did not seem impressed, either.

"No, no," and with this, Ba Ba ran down the steps and opened a door of the car. "This car is ours."

I started to laugh at first, so impossible was the idea of us owning a car. Money aside, Ma Ma didn't even have a driver's license. Ba Ba had been learning with Lao Jim and had only recently gotten his. I still could not believe that Ba Ba had been willing to walk into a government office. Wasn't he worried that they would arrest and deport him? Lao Bai had told him that he was able to get his license with no trouble, but how did Ba Ba know for sure that it would be safe? Wasn't he worried that it was a trick?

In the end, he said, he just wanted a taste of what it was like to be a real American.

Ma Ma and I remained silent for so long that Ba Ba launched into a series of explanations: there had been a really good deal, a once-in-a-lifetime offer; he had to accept it in the moment or else; we still had some money left in that brown suitcase—we just had to save a little more later this year to get our savings back; there had been no time to check with Ma Ma before he made the decision; with the car, we could get to places, buy food for less, and maybe even move to another state where everything was cheaper and there would be more opportunities for Ma Ma and her degree. I bobbed my head from Ba Ba to Ma Ma and back as Ba Ba engaged in his plea. But it was too late: there was a storm on Ma Ma's face.

"I have to check on the stove."

As Ma Ma walked back into the house, I watched Ba Ba stare at his feet. He looked up again and offered me a smile. "What do you say, Xi Mou Hou—want to go for a drive?"

I didn't understand what had happened, but I did know that Ba Ba had done something bad. I very much wanted to know what it was like to own a car. I wondered whether the ceiling also drooped. And I wondered whether, like Lao Jim's car, it smelled like old man and garlic, whether it also shuddered before coming to a stop. Most of all, I wondered what it would be like to drive down any street we liked—not just the streets that led to McDonald's. What was it like to slow down or speed up at our will? What was it like to have the cool air roll through the lowered windows and kiss my cheeks as Ba Ba and I navigated through our neighborhood, just the two of us—me in the front seat for once!—chitchatting about starting middle school like I was any other normal American kid?

But instead of finding out, I shook my head. Ma Ma was mad at Ba Ba about the car, so I would be mad at Ba Ba about the car.

"I don't want to miss dinner," I said.

Just as I turned to walk back toward my little chick, I caught the sight of Ba Ba standing alone by his new car, face dark with the sadness of a boy who had no one to play with.

* * *

We ate dinner in the simmer of contempt that night. Although we sat in the same spots around the same table as we always did, Ma Ma and Ba Ba were now farther away from each other. I wished for them to scold me and yell at me, about my lack of discipline, my teeth, my sloppiness, my anything. But they exchanged no looks or words, staring only at the plates of steamed onions, carrots, cabbage, and bland, boiled chicken. The meal concluded when Ba Ba got up. He placed his plate and chopsticks in the sink before cleaning the large bowl that Ma Ma had used to rinse the cabbage. He then filled it with water and grabbed our dish towel before walking out of the kitchen and down the hallway. Ma Ma and I sat staring at the table as we heard him open the front door and then slam it shut. He stayed out for almost an hour, and I knew only from looking through the sunroom windows later that he was washing the car by hand, with tender care that I forgot he possessed.

After Ba Ba stepped out, Ma Ma got up and began placing the leftovers into the fridge, gathering in the sink the dirty plates and bowls. I walked over to the sink and began my nightly dishwashing. To our roommates, it must have looked like just another night.

Chapter 28
COMMUNITY

....

On my first day of middle school, I arrived in Chelsea early and walked across West Seventeenth Street until I saw the building. I had half an hour before they would start serving the free breakfast, so I dodged eye contact with the kids standing just outside the door, some of them smoking. Instead of walking toward them, I continued on to Ninth Avenue, which then led me up to West Eighteenth Street. Halfway down that street, I came upon another school. There were also kids smoking outside that school. They looked similar but taller, and one of the girls carried extra weight only around her belly. I stood and watched for a while, comforted by the fact that these were not the kids I would be going to school with; they were just regular kids whose behavior I could consult for reference. I no longer knew how to act now that I was not attending a Chinatown school, full of Chinatown kids whose parents were just like mine. I studied them for ten minutes or so, until it became more appropriate to show up to school, at which point I walked back toward Lab while practicing the hand gestures and facial expressions that seemed to suggest cool nonchalance in this new world.

Back at the door to Lab, I pushed past the smoking kids, among them posh girls with eyes encircled by dark makeup. A security guard in uniform greeted me, and I was thankful that I had already been through the process for my interview. The secretary in the vice principal's office at PS 124 had assured Ba Ba that Lab was like PS 124, and had the same rule of not asking about citizenship, but Ba Ba's voice played on in my head, telling me that we could never really be sure. I unshouldered my JanSport backpack and placed it on the black conveyor belt. The bag was the same red one from elementary school on which I had drawn the cool letter S in white-out—every girl at PS 124 had one such S on her backpack—along with flowers and cats. I had added the other drawings later, when Ba Ba had noticed the S and asked me if I was in some sort of gang, and of course he knew I wasn't, but wasn't I worried that people might think that it was some sort of gang insignia? And then they might look into us and see that we were here illegally. I laughed but added the cats and flowers anyway—innocent little-girl things. Ba Ba had enough to worry about.

The guard waved me through the detectors and I held my breath as I walked past. I wasn't sure what they were testing for; I prayed only that I didn't have it. I let my breath go only after I was all the way through. The machine stayed quiet as I retrieved my backpack from the other end of the conveyor belt. The bag's white-out drawings, which had once seemed so adult, now looked glaringly childish under the lights of the middle school. I shoved the thought out of my mind as I followed the trail of kids into the cafeteria. All of the sixth graders had been told to show up early, and it struck me that unlike my first day at PS 124, I was not the only one who didn't know anybody. Best of all, I now spoke the language and understood the rules. There would be no walking into the boys' bathroom here.

On our way from security to the cafeteria, I had caught others giving one another shy, furtive smiles, each of us praying against being the last to make a friend. For me, that hope was overshadowed by my empty stomach. I grabbed a tray at the front of the cafeteria and entered the small separate area where the smell of breakfast beckoned. The week before, I had received by mail two booklets of vouchers for free meals, orange for breakfast and red for lunch. I took an orange one out now and handed it to a stoic white lady with a hairnet, who then placed two scoops on my plate: one of hash browns, still steaming, and another of omelet, bright yellow with cheese. My mouth watered at the sight. The food here was better than anything I had seen at PS 124. But then again, that was why I had gotten the vouchers. Ba Ba explained to me that I was going from a school where almost everyone got free lunches to a school where I might be the only one. It might be hard, he'd warned, but I shook it off.

As I watched a white girl behind me hand five dollars to the stoic lady, though, shame crept up my ankles, past my legs and belly, and onto my face. I kept my face down at my tray and noted with gratitude that at least the flushing had dissipated quickly. Back out in the seating area of the cafeteria, I saw that, indeed, it had been a bad idea to give in to my hunger. Some of the other students had already made friends, sitting together, talking and laughing cautiously. But others were still trailing in, with uncertain looks on their faces. It's not too late, I told myself. Plus, maybe those other kids already knew each other from elementary school.

Rather than barge in on an established group—I was much too shy for that—I sat down on my own, facing the door, willing myself to eat in the most friendly, welcoming way possible. As I sat, I noticed that even the table bench was sturdier, fancier, than anything

I had ever touched at PS 124. Even so, I hoped that I wouldn't start middle school as the girl who sat on it alone.

Just as I stuffed a fork full of hash browns in my mouth, a clump of three girls trailed into the cafeteria, one after another. They did not seem to know each other, and wore on their faces the terror I had felt on spotting the tables where kids were becoming fast friends. I gave each of the three my warmest, friendliest smile, realizing only afterward that I had hash browns and eggs in my teeth.

The girls didn't seem to mind. They walked over, one by one. First there was Gloria, a petite Cantonese girl who reminded me of my friends from PS 124. Then there was Elena, a willowy Romanian girl who slouched, her upper body curving ever so slightly in on itself, reflecting back at me the diffidence I felt about my own towering height. And last was Mia, a Latina with a smile bright enough to light the sweat-shop room. As it turned out, all of us were in the same class, and all of us were from immigrant families. And for the rest of the year, we were unbreakable.

Mia was the outspoken one. She made herself heard, but only on things that mattered. She was our moral spine, and her decisive loyalty and friendship formed a model for me for years to come. Elena was the de facto leader. She had an easy smile and a certain charisma that the rest of us lacked. Plus, she was the only one of us who had a brother, so she knew how to talk to boys. Only we fellow immigrants saw through her poised veneer and recognized her self-deprecating jokes about being a "Romanian Gypsy." And Gloria was the peacemaker, the studious, quiet one who spoke up only when it became important to give way and make amends. She annoyed me and reminded me of Ba Ba's repeated admonitions about how Asians needed to act in America. It would take me much longer to see her artistic spirit, which showed itself in the Beatles songs she hummed and her ability to soak up the otherwise invisible pain of all those around her.

At the time, I never thought about who I was in the group. Looking back, it is clear that I served many roles: the brain, the bully, the tomboy.

With the three of them, exploring the new world full of not just Asian classmates but also white and Black and Latino ones, was no longer so scary.

* * *

At Lab, for the first time, I was not bored in school. Classes were different. Instead of only teaching us how to conjugate verbs or having us translate from English to Spanish or vice versa, Señora Torres, a tiny stick of pep, planned a lunch trip to a nearby Spanish restaurant and gave us a list of words we needed to order off the menu. We could order only in Spanish, she warned, so we'd better know how to order what we wanted, because we would have to eat whatever arrived on our plates.

Our humanities teacher reminded me of Miss Pong. Ms. Rothstein was a small white woman with short brown hair and eyes that stayed bright with attention even as students talked. She had us read all sorts of books and focused our discussions on not just what happened in them but why they happened, and what those things were supposed to mean. And instead of just having us watch in silence the movie version of whatever book we were assigned, Ms. Rothstein actually had us ask questions—of her, of each other, of ourselves.

Just as Miss Pong brought **Charlotte's Web** into my life, Ms. Rothstein gave me **The Giver,** a dystopian novel in which society was without pain or strife. The protagonist was a twelve-year-old boy, Jonas, who carried the unique gift and burden of the memories from older, more painful, more emotional times. Jonas was another piece of my new life that made me feel less alone. Reading Jonas's reflections on remembering and seeing too much gave voice to my own feelings. I stopped at many of the paragraphs and sentences, reading them, rereading them, and repeating them to myself. So many words from that book were talismanic refrains that, for the the first time, brought to life for me the very depths of my hurts, my joys, my loneliness.

* * *

Things at home had gotten worse. Ma Ma and Ba Ba rarely talked. We lived in two extremes: silence and screams. The only good thing that came of this was that the uncomfortable human sounds no longer emanated from their bed in the middle of the night, so I didn't have to worry about falling asleep while covering my ears. Ma Ma still refused to tell me as much as she had before the surgery. Every now and then, she missed dinner or a full weekend day to visit that new friend on Long Island, the friend I had yet to meet. I didn't know how to win back her trust after all my failures, and the quiet of the room once filled with words suffocated me.

I remained sneaky, though, and gleaned two things from what was said and what was not said: Ma Ma was mad that Ba Ba had gotten the car without telling her, and now she wanted him to agree to something she wanted. She was convinced that she had found a way to get us out of our situation, but Ba Ba demurred. "It's the only way she'll be able to go to college," Ma Ma yelled, sometimes in the kitchen when I was in our room, and sometimes over my head at Ba Ba at the dinner table, as our roommates scampered out.

Usually Ba Ba said nothing, but once he mentioned that sometimes the white people in government used immigrants to win elections, and in the past they had handed out green cards to people like us. I had no way of finding out more, but the idea clung to the membranes of my brain.

The second thing was that, because Ma Ma was mad that Ba Ba had bought the car, she had decided to use it to learn to drive. Ba Ba did not like this. What if she crashed it, he yelled. The car was his baby, more than I felt myself to be. He spent most of the nights after dinner out on the street, wiping the entire thing down with a wet towel and then a dry one. This was a great sacrifice: we did not have that many towels.

Twice, the car was damaged overnight. The first time, a thief took the radio and some other parts that I did not even know existed. Ba Ba brought it to the nearest shop immediately, as if it were a child with a swollen wrist who needed to be rushed to a hospital, and within the week, it was good as new. Ba Ba then bought a stick to lock the steering wheel so no one could drive the car without unlocking the stick first because it would hit the window. The stick was off-brand, the cheapest and smallest available, and never sat snugly against the wheel.

Even so, the expenses made Ma Ma angrier, and all the more determined to drive it. "You place this—this **thing** above us—" she'd say, "above our safety and our future? I am your wife, and this is your child."

In those moments, I spotted a familiar look in Ba Ba's eyes before they hardened and shadows took over. It took me some time to trace it, but upon observing it a few times, I knew: it was the same look he wore when he talked about his home being ransacked when he was a child, about Nai Nai being dragged out and beaten before the entire village. It was not a look of pure sadness or fear, but instead something that I imagined the brown and white bird might have felt when it caught sight of Marilyn just before she pounced.

The second time, the car was gone completely. Ba Ba was sick. The realization of what happened seemed to suck all strength from his body and he crawled back into the bed even though it was morning and he was due at work and I was due at school. His face reminded me of the boulder in my heart that first day without

Marilyn. He refused to call the police, so later, when I had returned from school and he had regained the ability to walk, we wandered from street to street, hoping to come upon it. This worked: just two blocks from where we lived, in the direction opposite of where we had started our search, there was our car, parked in a no-parking spot. The car's doors had been stripped and the windshield shattered—**this was the way to take two left turns even with the small stick,** Ba Ba pieced together, **ta ma de, I knew I should have bought the expensive one**—and many things, among them the new radio, gutted. Still, the exposed dashboard was papered with parking tickets. Justice, I learned then, was blind.

Undeterred, Ba Ba once again restored the car to its previous condition, and after this, Ma Ma had Lao Jim give her lessons in the car after McDonald's outings. I learned to retreat to the bathroom each time Ma Ma returned from those lessons. Sometimes, though, I could hear the shouting even from there. When that happened, I did what I could to overpower it. Where I otherwise would have sat on top of the toilet lid with both hands clasped together, silently beseeching Marilyn, God, or whoever possessed the power to help Ma Ma and Ba Ba, I stood and launched into prayer at full volume.

Please please please, I repeated until my words linked together in a secure chain, **please please please make them happy again. I will do anything. Whatever you want.**

* * *

As sixth grade wore on, I grew uneasy with the sense that Gloria and I were on the bottom rung of our friend group. More and more, Elena and Mia hung out with the other non-Asian girls in our class, the ones who were cool by virtue of the fact that they hung out with boys, the ones who wore bras with bright straps that showed through their shirts. Elena and Mia invited us to join, of course, but there was a social barrier that felt impossible for me and Gloria to pierce, perhaps because we were Chinese, perhaps because we could not afford bright bras we did not yet need.

Gloria was one of the few others in our class who also got the meal vouchers. She was also the only one who also liked to go to the free library that the school had, full of more volumes than were ever available at my local public branch. She liked everything that I liked, and she could not afford the same things I could not afford. She was my best friend. But she was also so easygoing and self-effacing that she made it impossible for me not to punch down at her, in hopes of lifting myself into the upper social echelon.

On a day I'll never forget, the four of us spent lunch with the cool kids—among them, boys. I had been careful to tuck away my voucher booklet. Still, Gloria and I had little to contribute to the conversation at the table until it veered toward popular music and Usher. I had already begun studying the culture of cool music, doing what I could without cassettes or a Walkman. Ba Ba had a handheld radio with an antenna, and before Ma Ma and Ba Ba returned home to fill the air with anger and tension, I did my homework to the sounds of 103.5 KTU, a radio station that Kailey—one of the cool girls, with blond hair, blue eyes, tight spaghetti-strapped tops, and long legs—had once mentioned. The studying had equipped me with a general sense of what was going on in the debate, and who Usher was, though not enough for me to contribute anything meaningful. When the chatter among the cool kids broke for a second, though, Gloria intruded on them with a question:

"What's R&B?"

I felt my face flush as it had on the first day, when I'd noticed that white girl paying for the breakfast I had gotten for free. I hated Gloria for asking the question. I hated myself for not knowing the answer.

"God, Gloria, you don't even know what R and B is? How much of a loser are you?" The cruelty came out before I recognized my own voice.

Everyone turned to stare at us, including the two cute boys at the other end of the table. Gloria's natural blush deepened. Mia was the first to speak.

"Qian, why do you have to be so mean? Do **you** even know what R&B is?"

"Of course I do," I squeaked, convincing no one.

"What is it?"

"Rock and blues."

"Wrong."

I sat immobile, steeped in mortification. After a long while, the silence gave way to tittering, and I passed the rest of the day muted, humbled.

* * *

My prayers were useless at home. Ma Ma started spending a few nights at her friend's home on Long Island. When she returned, Ba Ba and Ma Ma began throwing at each other words that I had never heard them use before. I began to tune out their dinnertime fights, mouth chewing and throat swallowing but mind shut off, body numb. I had stomachaches after those meals, maybe because I ate too fast, maybe because I ate too slowly, maybe because I barely ate at all. I could not pinpoint a reason because the mind that remembered too much suddenly decided not to remember at all.

One such meal, however, called my brain back into place. Ba Ba had said something in a sharp tone, to which Ma Ma responded in an even sharper, defiant tone. This gave Ba Ba the look again—a scared little bird trapped inside a thirty-six-year-old man—but it lasted for just a moment before it was replaced by hardened steel. And then Ba Ba stood up and did the thing that snapped me awake:

He reached across the table, hand moving past me, and slapped Ma Ma.

The sound bounced from one wall of the kitchen to the other, like a homemade kite in choppy winds, catching on this corner and that until it was all around us.

Then Ba Ba charged out, stomping into our room, presumably to get his jacket and the car keys, before slamming the two external doors, one after another.

"Ma Ma—Ma Ma, are you okay?" I so wished that she would talk to me again like she used to.

"Mei shi, mei shi." She kept her face down but forced a smile. "He just didn't like the meal."

Ma Ma continued putting food in her mouth and chewing but I could tell she was not tasting any of it. Her head stayed down toward her bowl, her left hand covering her left cheek. All I could see was the top of her head, her hair parted in a straight line a little off to the side. Among the black strands were a few hairs that had morphed into shocking, bright white.

When Ma Ma looked up again, I knew that she thought she looked normal. She thought that she looked okay, that she was playing the part of a protective mother to her shaking daughter. She would not have looked up otherwise. Believing that she looked no different than usual, Ma Ma opened her mouth to say something to me, something assuring and soothing, no doubt, but something I don't remember. I never heard it because when she lifted her head and removed her hand, all that filled my world were the thick red lines across her cheek, the bright imprint of my father's fingers on her face.

Chapter 29
GONE

....

It happened quickly. The weekend after the incident, Ma Ma set about cleaning the room. It was time to put away our winter clothes and take out our summer ones, she said, so she had us both pack and unpack our clothes, placing in one pile the items with too many holes and the items I had long outgrown, while neatly folding for a second pile those that were salvageable. Then, Ma Ma said, we needed to go to the local Brooklyn library to return all the books I had checked out. When I asked why, Ma Ma said that it was not nice to keep from others the books I had already finished reading, and anyway, she felt like taking a walk. I gathered the volumes—the usual Baby-Sitters Club and Sweet Valley installments, along with some more Alice books and **Harriet the Spy**—and arranged them into a tall stack that Ma Ma stuffed into my JanSport, swinging it onto her back.

"What about this one?" Her eyes fell on another book still on the couch.

I ran to pick it up. It was almost as if I believed that the faster I grabbed it, the more likely I would be able to keep it. The book was **Julie of the Wolves,** and it had caught my attention because it had on the cover a girl who looked kind of like me, with a name that I had chosen for myself but was still afraid to wear. Julie, like the main character in the Alice books, had lost her mother young, and had to live with her father. But then her father disappeared, too, and her life became very, very hard. I was almost done with Julie's story, and I was eager to see her arrive at a happy ending. I told Ma Ma this, promising to return the book as soon as I finished it, so other kids could meet Julie and spend time with her and wolves. Besides, the librarian who had checked out the book for me had shown me another book with the same girl on the cover. That book was titled **Julie.**

"This is the book that comes after the one you're borrowing," she said with a crinkle at the corners of her eyes. "When you're done with it, come get this one. It is great."

"Thank you," I said. "That's my name, too." The words tumbled out before I realized that it was not the name on the library card she was holding. Luckily, she didn't notice.

"It's a very pretty name."

"Thank you," I said again, hungry to claim something not quite mine.

I told Ma Ma about this exchange, if only to assure her that I meant what I said about returning the book as quickly as possible. She took it the wrong way, though, because she looked sad.

"I can return it today if you'd like, Ma Ma."

Ma Ma turned to me, the sad look slipping off her face. "Hao, guai. Mei shi." So we left the book on the couch and walked to the library together, hand in hand.

Ba Ba was around for all of the packing and cleaning up, but he stayed out of our way, watching TV and then going out for a drive. Neither Ma Ma nor I had spoken to him since the incident. Had I known what was to come, I would have said a lot to him over the weekend. But by the time I knew, it was too late.

* * *

Monday begun as usual. I awoke and gathered myself for school. Ba Ba had already left for work, but Ma Ma was home, fumbling with the suitcases we had brought from China, the ones into which we had placed our wearable sweaters for summer storage the night before.

Before leaving, I kissed Ma Ma on the cheek and promised that I would return **Julie of the Wolves** after school. I had finished it late the night before and was breathless for the next installation. Ma Ma nodded absently, and I thought it was odd that she no longer seemed to care about something that had mattered so much to her just a day before.

The commute to school was different because for once I did not have a book to read, having returned all my volumes without borrowing any new ones. I was left only to people-watch and stare at the signs of the stations that had become the fixtures of my life.

The rest of the day passed without significance. It was not the sort of day one remembered, with special events or notable details. Had I known better, I would have taken the time to capture the moments and people and things, as I had when we left China. Had I known better, I would have been nicer to my friends, and committed to memory the jokes we shared that day. I would have thanked Ms. Rothstein and Señora Torres for inspiring me, for getting me to pay attention in class again, instead of passing each day in deafening boredom. But instead, the hours ticked by in complacency, and when the last class was over, I peeled off from Gloria, Elena, and Mia to head to the school library. I could not bear another subway ride without a book, and I was eager to grab several—and maybe even **Julie!**—before catching the A train.

After greeting the librarian and receiving with disappointment her news that she did not have

Julie, I dove into my routine. I had a habit of perusing each shelf systematically, savoring every spine, cover, and blurb. By the time I had settled on two books to tide me over on the commute home—**A Ring of Endless Light** and **From the Mixed-Up Files of Mrs. Basil E. Frankweiler**—thirty-some minutes had passed. I walked out the school doors with my face already glued to the early pages of **From the Mixed-Up Files** and did not look up until a sequence of blaring honks snatched my attention. When my eyes left the dog-eared pages, I realized that our shimmering gold shoe was parked along the sidewalk.

The window at the driver's seat was open, and protruding from it was Ma Ma's furrowed face.

"Qian Qian! I was so worried I had missed you."

"Ma Ma? What's going on?"

"Get in, get in. I'll tell you on the way."

It was not until I stepped into the front seat that I noticed our two bulging suitcases piled in the back.

"Ma Ma? What's going on?"

"We are going to Canada."

"What? Why? Right now?"

"No. Right now, we are going to a place on Long Island. Called . . . Neck. Something Neck." She pulled out a map and a sheet of paper. "Dui, Great Neck.

"Here, take this map. I studied the route already but I need your help, Qian Qian. See this path that I marked? Keep your eyes on that and make sure we're going the right way, okay?"

There were too many words. So many words that I could not understand any of it. But staring at the map was concrete enough, easy enough. I was Ma Ma's little doctor, and it came back to me all at once: all that mattered was that I helped Ma Ma do what she wanted to do. With some effort and several wrong turns, we found what was called the I-495, a big and wide road with many lanes.

Over the course of the next hour and a half, we made many more wrong turns, incurring honks and screams. It was also during that hour and a half that Ma Ma explained everything to me— how she had learned from her new friend who lived on Long Island that Canada was looking for educated immigrants; how that friend had introduced her to a lawyer, and how Ma Ma had worked with that lawyer for many months to get us permission to move to Canada; how we would not just have visas but full green cards once we got there, except it was not called a green card, but a "maple leaf card"; how I would be able to go to any college I wanted and she could work at a real job; how there was free healthcare; and how Ba Ba had refused to leave, how he was scared, how he loved America too much, maybe more than he loved us. It was a lot and I didn't understand it all, not all at once. All I took from it was that Ma Ma had been working on this for a while, without telling me. She had assumed that Ba Ba would agree eventually, but he never did. And then there was the incident. And that was that.

We were headed to Ma Ma's friend's home on Long Island first. It was going to take us many hours to get to Toronto, where Ma Ma had a friend from China, and she did not feel confident driving all the way there herself. What if we got stopped before we reached freedom? No, this way was better, safer, she said; this way she and Ah Yi could take turns driving.

Plus, Ah Yi lived in a big old house with her son and her white husband in a white neighborhood. Wouldn't I like to see how Americans—true Americans—really lived before we left for good?

At this thought, our Brooklyn life played out before my eyes. The tests and essays, empty and unwritten, that I would never get to complete at Lab. My thin, long bed next to Ma Ma and Ba Ba's bigger, fatter bed, and how I made those beds in the morning immediately upon waking, tucking in each edge until the comforter was sandwiched between the secondhand mattresses and their matching boxes. My friends, their faces around a long cafeteria table, talking with their mouths full of home-cooked lunches, except for Gloria, who poked at her tray of school food. The alley our room's windows looked onto, and through which I still looked for Marilyn, even though I saw her less and less after I had decided that she was bad luck that needed to be threatened away with a stick.

And then there was Ba Ba, his smile when he handed me my Tamagotchi; his mouth as he sang and danced to **Xi Mou Hou;** his eyes when he looked over at me over the course of that last, wordless weekend.

It is odd, the images that come to your mind once you know you'll never see any of it again.

* * *

When we came upon the large brick house, I had trouble believing that we had arrived at the right place. It was huge, like the one I pictured Sweet Valley twins Jessica and Elizabeth Wakefield living in. But it made sense for the Wakefields because their father was a lawyer. I didn't know much about Ah Yi, but I assumed that Ma Ma would have told me if she was rich. Then again, Ma Ma never talked about her with me or Ba Ba. I knew only that Ah Yi had been divorced and then had remarried, a fact that Ba Ba did not like. "Divorce, it's contagious," Ba Ba had said once. "Better to stay away."

It was better this way, Ma Ma said, because even if Ba Ba wanted to look for us, he wouldn't know where to look.

Ah Yi came out the door as Ma Ma pulled the car into the driveway. She was older, with very long hair and a similarly long face. Her face was dark and had more wrinkles than Ma Ma's. She reminded me of a handsome horse, stern from too many rides.

Ah Yi ushered us into her house, which had numerous rooms and hardwood everywhere—on the furniture and on the walls. Her husband was an old man with an amiable face, pink skin, and stark-white hair. He smiled often. Ah Yi's son must have been from her previous marriage because he was all Chinese, just like us. He was older than I and had the same disinterested look of the kids I had studied on my first day at Lab. He was tall and thick and looked like he played basketball. I don't remember him doing anything other than eating.

Ah Yi was the kind of adult who was always talking and giving commands. She herded us here and there, showing us the library—yes, a room at home just for books!—the sunroom, and the basement gym full of equipment I didn't recognize. Finally, she showed us to a bedroom on the top floor that she said was ours, with a private bathroom. I walked through the room and its connecting bathroom in awe. We had never had our own American bathroom before. Back in the bedroom, I set down my backpack, which I had carried throughout the tour even though it was full of school items that were now useless, irrelevant. There was no need to bring in more stuff from the car, Ma Ma had said. We were staying only for the night and we would be leaving at sunrise.

Ah Yi gave us a few precious minutes in our room. I used them up checking on my Tamagotchi. Then we were herded again, this time to a dinner table full of unappetizing American food—it was white and brown everywhere I looked, full of cheeses and meats and eggs. I should have been starving, but the idea of eating anything off the gooey piles elicited only a gag from my throat. I picked up a piece of bread from the nearby basket and chewed as I watched Ah Yi pile clump upon clump of brown and white foods onto my plate.

"Eat, eat. You must eat. Then, we go to the movies. The boys, they will see **The Mummy**. We girls will see **Notting Hill**."

I had heard about **The Mummy** at school. It was sad that the one time I got to go to the movies with Ma Ma, we could not watch the movie I wanted to watch. Ba Ba would have liked **The Mummy**, too, but he was not here anyway.

Ah Yi continued with her commands through

the meal, the men in her family in full submission, eating and nodding along. Ma Ma picked politely at the plate Ah Yi filled for her, looking for a garnish or two to chew on. I was glad that Ma Ma was not eating the cheeses and meats. It would not have been good for her, and we were too far away from St. Vincent's now for her to be rushed there.

After dinner, we left the dirty plates in the sink and filed out to two of the family's several cars, boys in one, girls in the other. The drive to the movie theater was full of trees and grass; more trees and grass than I had ever seen in all my life. The theater itself was on an island of pavement, where cars pulled into spots marked by straight white lines. Ah Yi drove ours into one such spot and then we rushed into the theater, where the movie had already started.

I remember little of the movie from that viewing. I tried to pay attention to the walleyed man with the British accent, but it was hard to hold on to my thoughts. My brain was a melting ice cube, impossible to clutch, slipping this way and that.

On the way out of the theater, I noticed a poster for **The Mummy** on the wall, with a face forming from something that looked like both the sky and mountains. I resented the silent, big, feeding boy who got to see the movie while

I had to sit through a bunch of mushing about feelings.

* * *

The face from **The Mummy** poster came to me in my dreams that night. It was all around me and Ma Ma, the mouth moving as if it were going to chew us up. We ran and ran, but it was no use because the face was everywhere. I moved my legs as fast as possible, my hand in Ma Ma's, but as we ran, all I could think of was the opening of **From the Mixed-Up Files**: it was better to run toward something than to run away from something.

I was rescued by Ma Ma's hands, shaking me around my shoulders. I opened my eyes and thought I was staring into the sun, but no, it was just the orange orb of the light bulb at the center of the ceiling. Through the windows, I saw that there was just a sliver of light, the sky still orange-brown.

Ma Ma, zen me le?

Gai zou le, Qian Qian. Zhong yu gai zou le.

It's time to leave. It's finally time to leave.

Chapter 30

HOME

....

We drive for years that day. I age with each stretch of the road. Since leaving China, I have not seen the horizon except in my dreams, but on this drive, the horizon is all I see. Between us, the skies, and the trees, there is nothing. We are in a rush, stopping only a few times. Ma Ma speaks little, as if conserving her energy for something ahead.

Ah Yi prattles in the front, alternating between the driver's and passenger's seats. Between her and carsickness, I choose the latter, sitting in the back, eyes fixed on my Tamagotchi.

Tell her to stop playing with that thing. It's bad for her.

If Ma Ma hears Ah Yi's command, she chooses to ignore it. So I continue doing as I do.

I have no means of writing Ba Ba, no way to yell at him and tell him how mad I am, of saying how dare he. I have no way of finding Marilyn, either, of making sure she is okay, of telling her I love her, of saying goodbye.

I have only the Tamagotchi, who I by turns take doting care of, and by turns neglect and watch waste away in hunger. And each time a new little chick hatches, I cannot decide what I want for it: a full, joyous life or a quick, empty death.

The scenery changes as the sun descends. There are more trees all around us, and soon, some bridges over dancing currents. I roll down my window and breathe in the flowing air. It tells me about grass and bugs, and about rivers and birds and many more living things.

As darkness begins to unfurl across the sky, I make out at the end of our road a series of little booths and barriers. To the side is a house that looks like a ski lodge I have once seen on TV.

Near the lodge, Ma Ma pulls the car aside. There are men and women all around, in uniforms. Above them, a red and white flag with a maple leaf billows in the gentle wind.

Ma Ma, should we hide?

She does not answer.

Ma Ma, is it safe?

Nothing.

Ma Ma, they are everywhere.

Finally, Ma Ma rouses.

Don't worry, Qian Qian—she speaks slowly, emerging from a deep sleep—**it's safe.**

We get out of the car and walk toward the

uniformed men. We go into the lodge, which turns out not to be for skiing. It has many little booths with more uniformed men.

Will we be locked up?

Don't worry, Qian Qian.

But what do I have but worry, after all this time?

Ma Ma goes up to a booth with Ah Yi. The familiar hesitation awakens in my body, but I follow.

The guard, a white man in uniform, looks at Ma Ma through the glass. Then he looks at me. Next, he does an unthinkable thing: he smiles.

"Go sit down now, little girl. Your mother will take care of this."

I look at Ma Ma, who nods. Having no choice, I find a cold seat across the room, on the row of hard, plastic chairs all linked together, hand in hand. I take out my Tamagotchi and stare at it.

My Tamagotchi is hungry, but I just keep staring.

I strain to hear what is happening across the room, but give up when I feel my ears all but bleed.

I keep the screen of my Tamagotchi on, pressing it to attention when it dims. My chick's health is dwindling from full to mediocre to dire. Soon, her eyes will turn into x's and her little body will be replaced by a tombstone. But I do not care. All I can think about is whether

Ma Ma is okay, how she will understand what they are saying without me by her side.

After some shuffling of the papers, Ma Ma gestures for me to join them.

"Lai ba, Qian Qian."

I sprint over, and we, all three of us and the guard, walk out of the lodge. The guard does the unthinkable thing again, smiling at me as he puts on a red and white hat with ear covers that flap down from the top. He reminds me of one of those happy polar bears from the Coca-Cola Christmas commercials.

We walk to the car and watch as the polar bear circles it, examining the trunk and then the interior.

"All set." He smiles at all three of us. Never before have I seen so many smiles from a uniformed man.

And then I realize that for the first time since our ascent, Ma Ma seems to know what is going on more than I do.

She opens the door and steps into the driver's seat. Ah Yi does the same on the passenger side, still prattling on. The polar bear opens my door, gesturing for me to enter before doing another unthinkable thing:

"Welcome home," he says.

Ma Ma thanks him and smiles. I almost do not recognize her face in the mirror, so full it is of delight and peace.

And then we start driving again. There is more horizon, more trees. Ma Ma stays silent, but the car feels different; lighter, bigger. Ah Yi nods off to sleep and serenity falls upon us.

The sun has set, the sky a fabric of dark blue beaming with little rhinestones.

Ahead of us, there is still more horizon, but in the darkness it is hard to tell where land ends and sky begins. I turn back to my Tamagotchi and press the buttons. It awakens, the little window on the egg the only source of light in our vehicle.

HOW IT BEGINS

....

My story continues decades after we cross over.

Ba Ba follows us to Canada weeks later, after Lab sends a social worker to our apartment to investigate my absence. The knock on the door propels Ba Ba into the belief that at long last, his deportation has arrived. But no, it is just someone with the Administration for Children's Services, a woman who surveys the room with furrowed brow and then comforts Ba Ba as he drops his weathered face into his hands, his defenses retreating for once.

By the time Ba Ba arrives in Canada, Ma Ma and I are already visiting China for the summer, our new papers a safety net that allows us to travel—and return—for the first time. There, I set free the parts of myself that I had locked up with my bike. I find that where in English I am logical, distant, hardened, in Chinese I am excitable, warm, still tender. I am surprised to discover that I am still the child whose steps direct themselves toward the light of Ye Ye's face.

After a detour through Canada on the papers Ma Ma had prepared for him, Ba Ba surprises us at Lao Lao's doorway, which is still adorned with red paper cuttings from Lunar New Year celebrations five months past. The sight brings me back to the other side of my childhood, and it is as if I am seeing him for the first time again at JFK Airport. The long years—he wears them on his face.

A month later, the three of us board a Toronto-bound plane, headed for the first time to a North America we are permitted to call home. We don't know then that, legal or not, home no longer exists.

In the peace and quiet of Canada, there is too much room for the voices and fears in Ba Ba's head. The sunlight shines too brightly onto the fault lines the preceding five years had carved into our little family. Possibilities open anew before us, but we cannot see past the razor edges we had grown for protection in that beautiful country.

We do not know what to do with stability.

Ma Ma and Ba Ba admonish me never to speak the truth of our time in America, so I adopt Julie as my name and begin to hide that tired little girl, the one who had waded through the fish-processing plant under a flowing blue cape; the one who had snipped at threads with scissors much too heavy for her hands. When I make it to a dentist, he asks if anything extraordinary happened to leave my teeth in such condition. I can muster no lie other than that I never bother to brush my teeth, that my favorite bedtime snack is soda with candy. He lectures me for many minutes as I remain reclined in that fancy execution chair, and then he lets me go, but only after denying me the lollipop I later see in the proud hands of a white girl my age.

For the years we are in Canada, my attempts to conceal the little girl are noncommittal. She is behind the curtains and under the bed, always visible in part: a dirty sneaker here; a bruised, swollen hand there. I ignore the signs of her presence by focusing on everything else. I look at my coworkers during my many part-time jobs throughout high school, where I pretend as if I am just like everyone else, as if my first job were not at a sweatshop, as if I do not still feel the hot breath of poverty and hunger on my neck. I look at Ma Ma, who gets sick and then better again, and Ba Ba, in and out of rage, fear, and paranoia, the scenes of his childhood playing out over and over in his far-away eyes. And most of all, I look at the corpse of their marriage, decaying in the mortuary we three built.

* * *

I do not start burying that scared little girl, do not begin to wrap her up and cast dirt onto her curled-up body, until I resolve to return to America—legally this time—for college and law school. After all, to live out the happy ending of **Beijinger in New York,** I must first return to New York.

I find a shovel at Swarthmore College, where my adviser, a professor with a graying beard, laughs when I declare my intent to attend a top law school. It is the first week of freshman year, and he declares that because he has never heard of my high school, I am no superstar. On that lush campus, I learn for the first time just how little I have grown up with, how much everyone else has had, deprivations stacking on my shoulders, one after another, so many years after the fact.

I rush to scoop loose earth onto the little girl in law school, where I realize one beat too late that I might forever be surrounded by those who do not carry my deep wounds, those who grew up within the padding of privilege.

At this discovery, I shovel faster, pelting her head and unwashed hair with loose pebbles and rocks. I inquire after my classmates' origin stories and mimic them. "I grew up in Manhattan, too," I venture. "My dad is also a lawyer." They are half lies. Part lies. But lies all the same because they omit the pivotal truth. As I did as a child, I put these lies on and live inside them. But they refuse to fit.

The stack on my shoulders grows.

As I walk onto the stage with a mortarboard and tassel, I see movement beneath the little pile of soil I have created. I look away. I move far across the country, where my past cannot follow, where judicial clerkships would at long last declare my belonging, my worth.

But that sneaky little girl, she follows me anyway. Months into my second clerkship, on opening the file of yet another immigration appeal, my body carries me into the judge's office. She sits at her mahogany desk, reading glasses perched on her narrow, regal nose. There, in a seat opposite hers, I let the little girl climb out. I don't know why I do it. It comes to my mind that only weeks before, the judge gently inquired why I go by "Julie," and whether I had ever used my real first name.

I sit across from the judge, watching as the little girl works her way loose, atrophied limbs and all. It takes a while but finally she is all here, her naked, malnourished body shining under the incandescent chambers lamps.

Words roll out of my mouth, one after another, and I do not dare to interrupt them with a breath. They are new words, foreign words, but

familiar all the same because they have been sitting at my throat for over two decades, waiting
their turn.

The judge, she does not speak for a while. She
wants to make sure I am done. It is an expanse
of space I've never before occupied. It feels like
years and thoughts pile on top of each other.
**I am fired. I am deported. Illegal again. This
whole time, Ma Ma and Ba Ba were right. Is it
too late? Can I say it now, take it all back? I was
born here, I have always lived in America! But
no, it must be too late. This, here at last, is the
end of me.**

The judge removes her reading glasses and
looks at me in a way that no da ren ever has
before. When she speaks, her voice is thick with
understanding, slow with certainty. She says
many things. They are things I have waited a
lifetime to hear; things I have imagined and
whispered to myself in the darkness of that little
room, my bed too close to Ma Ma's and Ba Ba's;
things that I cannot believe are finally before
me, mine for the taking. I cannot trust that they
are real, and yet I do not question their truth.
I simmer in the words, baking in each syllable
as it seasons my spirit. I wrap myself up in the
letters, tuck them in all around me.

But there is one sentence that stands apart,
that puzzles me, that cradles my brain as I lie

awake at night. It is what she opens with. She says, as though she knows just how heavy and exhausting it has all been, as sure as if she has lived it all herself—the hiding and the running and the lying and the protecting:

"Secrets. They have so much power, don't they?"

* * *

From then on, the little girl makes her home in my shadows, even as I make the move back to New York City to work in a top law firm. I know she is there, watching as I play my assigned role in my gilded American Dream, living my empty Manhattan life full of all the food and clothes and things I could ever want. You cannot know that some things are not enough until you have them.

At first, I act like she doesn't exist. I try to kick dirt over her in my mind again. But it is too late: she has been unearthed.

It comes to me clearest in the first seconds of every morning. Upon opening my eyes, I forget who I am and how I've come to chase this life. And then I see her in the corner of my bedroom, still scared, still starving. I look past her and out the window, my mind roaming beyond the Hudson River and into Jersey City, through the door of the condominium unit where Ma

Ma and Ba Ba now live, apparently free and safe, but really behind bars wrought from trauma. And then I slide forward in time and see myself many decades older, hair gray and skin loose, behind those same bars myself, the little girl still cowering next to me.

I repeat the judge's words. It has become a daily morning practice, but this time, after almost a year, I feel the lies slip away through the weave of my mantra. My muscles lose a tightness I did not know they have been carrying, and against the backdrop of my truths I am at long last free to admit: I am tired. I am so very tired of running and hiding, but I have done it for so long, I don't know how to stop. I don't know how to do anything else. It is all I am: defining myself against illegality while stitching it into my veins.

The judge's words are my blanket nest, and in its snug embrace I rediscover a safety I knew once, long, long ago.

I turn back to the window and see for the first time the little girl cast aglow against the light of the waking sun. And then I try something new. I look that wise little girl in the eyes and reach my hand out for hers.

ACKNOWLEDGMENTS

....

It takes a certain level of foolishness to build your first book around your deepest childhood traumas. It also requires luck and support. I have the good fortune of possessing all three.

First and foremost, thank you to the members of the undocumented community, and in particular, the Dreamers and DACA recipients. To those whose stories I know and those whose stories I've yet to hear: your courage and resilience are my inspiration, and I look forward to continuing to learn from you. I am now privileged beyond belief, but I will stand with you for as long as you will have me.

I am forever indebted to my one true home, New York City and my beloved Chinatown. Had we arrived anywhere else in America, I don't know that I would have received anything approaching the access to public resources that the city afforded me. I owe so much to the New York Public Library, where I first discovered the books that shaped my dreams. And I am grateful for the subway system, which exposed me to so many sides of the city· I otherwise never would have seen. I am thankful even for the train delays, as they created the conditions that enabled me to write the first draft of this book on my daily commute.

Thank you also to the great people of Canada and of Toronto, Ontario, who took us in and gave us refuge when we had nowhere else to turn. Your generosity was our lifeline, and I am proud to call myself Canadian as well as American and Chinese.

I have been blessed with incredible teachers. To Ms. Poon, Ms. Rothman, Mr. Berenstein, Gregory Frost, and most of all, Betsy Bolton: it may have been many years since we last spoke, but I carry your indelible influence with me every day I dare to call myself a writer. Thank you also to Michele Filgate, in whose workshop I wrote the first words of this book, and whose early encouragement emboldened me to keep going. And I am forever grateful to the inimitable Hillary Frey, for understanding this book when I barely knew what it was, and for holding my hands as I took my first shaky steps into the publishing world.

Thank you also to fellow authors Stephanie Scott and Roseann Lake, each of whom generously shared her guidance on publishing a debut. I promise to pay it forward.

Without Ryan Muir's photography brilliance (and Cecilia Galliani's assistance), I would look like a nervous frog in all of my author photos.

To my agent Andrianna Yeatts, who took a chance on a manuscript from a nobody, who always seems to know exactly what I mean and how to make it sound better, and who has read this book more times in more iterations than anyone else: I could not have entrusted my life dream to a more gifted, dedicated, or capable partner, and I am so incredibly lucky to be on this ride with you. And thank you to Karolina Sutton and Josie Freedman, the titans of industry I'm also lucky to call my agents, as well as to Sophie Baker for representing this project in foreign markets. My deep gratitude also goes to John De Laney, a lawyer of the first order, for his wise counsel and zealous advocacy.

To my editors, Margo Shickmanter and Mary Mount, who saw my vision and believed in it so very deeply: I will never get over how fortunate I have been to bring my first book into the world under your astute guidance. A very special thank-you goes to Doubleday publisher, Bill Thomas, for showing so much faith in this project from the very beginning; talented publicists and marketers Todd Doughty, Elena Hershey, Lauren Weber, Lindsay Mandel, Jane Gentle, and Rose Poole, for tirelessly championing this book in what feels like every corner of the Earth; and gifted artist Linda Huang for designing a better jacket than I ever could have fathomed. Thank you also to everyone who gave me a literary home at Doubleday (in particular, Michael Goldsmith, Ana Espinoza, Erin Merlo, Daniela Ayuso, Amy Edelman, Peggy Samedi, Pei Koay, Yuki Hirose, and Dan Novack) and Viking UK (especially Karishma Jobanputra, Julia Connolly, Leah Boulton, Samantha Fanaken, Guy Lloyd, Kyla Dean, Tineke Mollemans, and Ruth Johnstone). You have magicked my pipe dream into reality, and I will forever be pinching myself.

To everyone in the publishing industry committed to amplifying the voices of authors from marginalized backgrounds—and particularly Margo Shickmanter, Bill Thomas, Todd Doughty, Elena Hershey, and everyone at Doubleday: thank you. Progress would be impossible without heroes like you.

To my therapists (yes, it takes more than one!), Julia Werman Zwerin and Thomas Neuschul: thank you for helping me process and understand my childhood, work through the anxiety that came with sharing it with the world, and most of all, reclaim my life from its jaws.

I am grateful to Judy Zhou Yi, Bonnie Doyle, Toby Xinghua Wu, and Sarry Zheng, for their ad hoc Chinese consultations. Thank you also to my former writing group (Isa Chandra Moskowitz, Kathryn Jergovich, Jessica Slattery, Taryn Rothstein, Anita Anburajan, and most of all, Edwin Poché) for the priceless support that got me past the impossible stage of starting a first book. Deepest gratitude to the early readers of my full manuscript—Laurie and Eric Camiel, June Lee, Sonja Belau, Yana Mazin, Amy Seife, and Melanie Spaulding—for their feedback, and to dear Rebecca Weintraub and Jeremy Edelman for cheering me on at every step. To Emma Thomasch and Christopher Donahue-Wait: I would not have made it through this process sane without each of you and your professional insight and generous friendship. Thank you.

I first began to think about this project during the difficult year during and after the divorce of my first marriage. That time, and the act of embarking on this project, was made all the easier with the love and support of my friend and sister in spirit, Emma Grunberg.

It seems odd to leave out my rescue dogs, Salty and Peppers, even though they cannot read, because they have supplied so much emotional support throughout the time it took to write this book. Salty and Peppers were each rescued just hours away from being euthanized, and they have taught me as much about life as any human being. So in their honor, I thank all the animal rescue and shelter workers, and in particular Debbie Rhone of Peninsula Unwanted Pets. Thank you for all that you do, and for teaching me that it's never too late for a second chance at life.

Judge Morgan Christen: it is among the most distinct privileges of my life to call you my mentor and dear friend. Thank you for affirming my faith in justice; for helping me see the power in my truth; for giving me the security to tell it; and for keeping me from deleting it all as soon as I had it down on paper.

Thank you to Barbara and Jay Gottlieb, my rocks of stability, my font of enthusiasm. I don't know how you manage to read every draft and show up to every event, but I struck the in-laws lottery with you.

I would not be who I am without Lao Lao and Lao Ye; my late Ye Ye, Nai Nai, and Da Da; as well as all of my aunts, uncles, and cousins. They have taught me the true meaning of courage and family, and their love kept me afloat throughout so many years of loneliness.

To Marc (who has read every word of every portion of this book except, much to his chagrin, this paragraph), my number one reader, editor, cheerleader; my personal stand-up comedian; my partner in law and life—by your side, I am in hiding no more. My decisions are not always the easiest to support, yet you somehow manage to do it time and again. Even after a newlywed year in a global pandemic, my heart still dances at the sight of you, and every day is still a slumber party with my very best friend. I am the luckiest person in the world to be spending my life growing, laughing, lawyering, crying, and yes, even arguing, with you.

And finally, to Ba Ba, my model of resilience and determination, with whom I share my gross sense of humor and my tenacious love for this beautiful country, and to Ma Ma, who loves me so fiercely and who gave me the tools so early to create any life I dared to dream for myself: When you had nothing, you somehow managed to give me everything. For that alchemy, no thank-you can ever be enough.

ABOUT THE AUTHOR

Qian Julie Wang is a graduate of Yale Law School and Swarthmore College. Formerly a commercial litigator, she is now managing partner of Gottlieb & Wang LLP, a firm dedicated to advocating for education and civil rights. Her writing has appeared in major publications such as **The New York Times** and **The Washington Post**. She lives in Brooklyn with her husband and their two rescue dogs, Salty and Peppers.